"Evangelical politics are a bit of a mess, and seem to be guided by impulse rather than by thought. Covington, McGraw, and Watson have given us much to think about in their reflections on natural law. They recognize that God speaks to us through both Scripture and creation. God's creation has laws that govern it, and the authors of *Hopeful Realism* help us to think through how those laws help us to think through the most crucial political issues that we face today. This book is a must-read for evangelicals in the present political season (and beyond)."
Tremper Longman III, distinguished scholar and professor emeritus of biblical studies at Westmont College and author of *How to Read the Psalms*

"*Hopeful Realism* is a welcome conversation partner in the current renaissance of Protestant natural law theory. What stands out in this volume is the careful drawing of important categories that allow for principled distinctions to be drawn in how a society reasons morally. While not every one of their policy considerations are options I would personally adopt, what the authors have done is to help bring sobriety, restraint, and realism to the realm of Protestant political thought. This book is measured, clear, and thoughtful."
Andrew T. Walker, associate professor of Christian ethics and public theology at Southern Baptist Theological Seminary and fellow at the Ethics and Public Policy Center

"Evangelicalism has suffered badly from a thin political theology that leaves its members flailing in public life. I have long been convinced that the most fruitful but underappreciated resource for us is the natural law tradition. *Hopeful Realism* lays out this approach in a particularly biblical way, grounded in the Protestant tradition. Not satisfied to merely present their theory and defend it, the authors boldly and thoughtfully explain the 'hopeful realist' position on some of our most contentious political questions. This book isn't just abstract theorizing for fellow scholars; it's a serious resource for the evangelical church that could ground our political conversations in the unchanging wisdom of the Christian natural law tradition. It's desperately needed in one of American evangelicalism's most fraught moments."
Rachel Ferguson, director of the Free Enterprise Center at Concordia University Chicago and author of *Black Liberation Through the Marketplace: Hope, Heartbreak, and the Promise of America*

"This sober, energizing work is a testament to the value of putting politics in its proper place for its own sake, and for the health of the church. Jesse, Micah, and Bryan have long been stalwarts for robust Christian political engagement and beacons of Christian faithfulness in academia and in our public life. Their intellect and the witness of their lives have been a blessing to a generation of students. Now, we all get to sit in their classroom, learn from these thoughtful men, and then go out into communities and our politics to pursue faithfulness there ourselves."
Michael Wear, president and CEO of the Center for Christianity and Public Life and author of *The Spirit of Our Politics: Spiritual Formation and the Renovation of Public Life*

JESSE COVINGTON, BRYAN T. McGRAW,
AND MICAH WATSON

HOPEFUL REALISM

EVANGELICAL NATURAL LAW
AND DEMOCRATIC POLITICS

An imprint of InterVarsity Press
Downers Grove, Illinois

InterVarsity Press
P.O. Box 1400 | Downers Grove, IL 60515-1426
ivpress.com | email@ivpress.com

©2025 by Jesse David Covington, Bryan Travis McGraw, and Micah Joel Watson

All rights reserved. No part of this book may be reproduced in any form without written permission from InterVarsity Press.

InterVarsity Press® is the publishing division of InterVarsity Christian Fellowship/USA®. For more information, visit intervarsity.org.

All Scripture quotations, unless otherwise indicated, are taken from The Holy Bible, New International Version®, NIV®. Copyright © 1973, 1978, 1984, 2011 by Biblica, Inc.™ Used by permission of Zondervan. All rights reserved worldwide. www.zondervan.com. The "NIV" and "New International Version" are trademarks registered in the United States Patent and Trademark Office by Biblica, Inc.™

The publisher cannot verify the accuracy or functionality of website URLs used in this book beyond the date of publication.

Cover design: David Fassett
Interior design: Daniel van Loon
Images: © xxmmxx / E+ / Getty Images, © Mint Images / Mint Images RF / Getty Images, © Amanda Impens

ISBN 978-1-5140-0770-9 (print) | ISBN 978-1-5140-0771-6 (digital)

Printed in the United States of America ∞

Library of Congress Cataloging-in-Publication Data
Names: Covington, Jesse David, author. | McGraw, Bryan T., author. | Watson, Micah Joel, 1973- author.
Title: Hopeful realism : evangelical natural law and democratic politics / Jesse Covington, Bryan T. McGraw, Micah Watson.
Description: Downers Grove : InterVarsity Press, 2024. | Includes bibliographical references and index.
Identifiers: LCCN 2024028302 (print) | LCCN 2024028303 (ebook) | ISBN 9781514007709 (paperback) | ISBN 9781514007716 (ebook)
Subjects: LCSH: Natural law. | Natural law–Religious aspects–Evangelicalism. | Religion and law–United States. | BISAC: PHILOSOPHY / Political | POLITICAL SCIENCE / Religion, Politics & State
Classification: LCC K460 .C68 2024 (print) | LCC K460 (ebook) | DDC 340/.112–dc23/eng/20240624
LC record available at https://lccn.loc.gov/2024028302
LC ebook record available at https://lccn.loc.gov/2024028303

For the City of God on its earthly pilgrimage

CONTENTS

Acknowledgments ix

Introduction 1

Part I—Foundations

1 The Bible and Politics 29

2 Hopeful Realism: An Evangelical Theory of the Natural Law ... 47

3 Hopeful Realism's Political Principles 68

4 Making Hopeful Realism Practical 90

Part II—Application

5 Economics 123

6 Marriage, Sex, and the Family 145

7 Coercion, Violence, and War 180

8 Religious Liberty 198

Conclusion 219

Bibliography 231

General Index 241

Scripture Index 249

ACKNOWLEDGMENTS

IN THE ACKNOWLEDGMENTS SECTIONS of single-authored books, writers sometimes describe how the solitary practice of writing nevertheless was supported by a host of friends, critics, colleagues, and loved ones without whom the project would have been quite different or would not have emerged at all. We can't claim that our writing process has been lonely, but we too have a host of debts that we have accrued over the last several years as we have presented at conferences, foisted sample chapters on colleagues, adjusted this or that part of an argument to account for a brilliant insight from friends, and enjoyed the capacity to work together given the encouragement and support of families, friends, and more formal institutions.

The word *institutions* doesn't normally bring to mind (or heart!) warm feelings of gratitude, but consider it a vocational hazard for political theorists who reside in political science departments to highlight how thankful we are for the institutions that shape our lives.

We are grateful for the church universal and our brothers and sisters in Christ across the globe, and we are especially grateful for the particular churches in which we worship, learn, labor, and love on a regular basis: Christ Presbyterian Church in Santa Barbara, California; the Church of the Resurrection in Wheaton, Illinois; and LaGrave Reformed Church in Grand Rapids, Michigan. In an important respect we wrote this book for the church: we hope it may be received as a token of our gratitude.

We are also grateful for the academic institutions that actually pay us to read books, talk about important things with earnest and bright young people, and sometimes even write a book. We're blessed to work with great colleagues at Westmont College, Wheaton College, and Calvin University. We deeply appreciate the relationships and practical institutional support—including professional development funding, research funding, and sabbatical leave—that have facilitated progress in this work.

Thanks are certainly due to the institution of InterVarsity Press, and especially Jon Boyd, who thought this book worth pursuing, and Colton Bernasol, whose sharp eye, gentle but incisive editing, and generous comments made this a better book.

It may sound rather odd to think of our families as institutions, but they are, and we are grateful for God's blessing of family as an institution, and his particular grace to each of us in the families he has given us. Our calling to this work is always shared with our spouses, so we affectionately thank Holly Covington, Martha McGraw, and Julie Watson for their innumerable contributions—both direct and indirect—in partnership with each of us. We are truly in your debt for these reasons and many more.

Several friends and colleagues also offered specific contributions that made this book a better one than it would otherwise be. We beg the pardon of anyone we inadvertently miss here, and we acknowledge that some of these dear friends will think we didn't take their criticism to heart quite enough. Nevertheless, we thank them heartily for reading all or part of the manuscript, talking with us about much that made it into the book and some things that did not, and for other contributions over the last decade and more: our anonymous peer reviewer, Jim Auker, J. Budziszewski, Sharon Covington, Chris Dinh, Kristen Deede Johnson, Robert George, Peter Jonker, Roger Phelps, James K. A. Smith, Bree Snow, Ed Song, Matt Woodley, and Dan Young.

Other institutions have offered important space for conference presentations and helpful feedback through the years, so we also thank the American Political Science Association, Christians in Political Science, the American Enterprise Institute, and the Henry Institute at Calvin

University for such opportunities. We are grateful for the chance to develop earlier forms of these ideas in several publications over the years, including *Public Justice Review* and *Public Discourse*.

Finally, we give thanks to God for the rich gifts of intellectual fellowship and friendship realized in the unique experience of coauthorship.

SDG

INTRODUCTION

Then we will no longer be infants, tossed back and forth by the waves, and blown here and there by every wind of teaching and by the cunning and craftiness of people in their deceitful scheming. (Ephesians 4:14)

SAINT PAUL

WHAT HAS HAPPENED TO AMERICAN EVANGELICALS? Members of every religious tradition change their minds about important issues on occasion, but American evangelicals seem especially prone to being tossed back and forth by the waves of the broader society, particularly when those waves are driven by political winds. In the mid-1800s, millions of White evangelicals defended slavery.[1] In 1973, prominent evangelical leaders welcomed the *Roe v. Wade* decision striking down abortion restrictions in all fifty states. From the 1990s to until right before the 2016 election, an overwhelming majority of evangelicals believed that individual moral character was a prerequisite for serving in public office. White evangelicals today count slavery as a wickedly sinful institution and are especially prominent in the campaign against modern-day slavery and sex trafficking. By the late 1970s, evangelicals joined Roman Catholics in creating and sustaining the pro-life movement. And in 2016, White evangelicals comprised the

---

[1] Here we are using *evangelicals* to describe a group or subset of evangelicalism within society. As our argument proceeds, however, we will use *evangelical* more theologically than sociologically—in terms we will specifically define.

demographic *least* likely to agree that moral character was a necessary component for good political leadership. A closer look at each specific example contributes to understanding the wider pattern.

In December of 2018 Al Mohler, president of the Southern Baptist Theological Seminary (SBTS), penned an introduction to a seventy-two-page report that detailed the historical origins of SBTS and the founders' defense and practice of slavery. The seminary, founded in 1859, still serves as the flagship educational institute for the Southern Baptist Convention, itself formed in 1845 in Augusta as a result of a controversy over whether slave owners could be commissioned as missionaries. After slave-holding Baptists from Georgia and Alabama were rejected as missionaries, southern Baptists followed their fellow southern Methodists in breaking off and forming their own denomination as Southern Baptists (and southern Presbyterians soon followed). It is not surprising, then, that SBTS leaders and other Christians at the time would be deeply complicit in American slavery. Following the Civil War, they would promote segregation, encourage the subjugation of Black Americans as second-class citizens, and embrace the "Lost Cause" mythos of the Civil War.[2] "How could our founders," Mohler asks, "serve as such defenders of biblical truth, the gospel of Jesus Christ, and the confessional convictions of this Seminary, and at the same time own human beings as slaves—based on an ideology of race—and defend American slavery as an institution?"[3]

How could they indeed? We look back at churches splitting over slavery and the racist legacies of seminaries and colleges as not just wicked but bewildering. And yet many Christians not only found slavery and racism permitted by their faith, but actually supported by it. It seems easy, perhaps too easy, to alienate ourselves from such errors. We might conclude that "those" Christians in fact just let their faith get outweighed by a dehumanizing and demonic but profitable social institution. We, of

---

[2]For a good discussion of the "Lost Cause" mythology that helped sustain southern segregation after the Civil War, see Gaines M. Foster, *Ghosts of the Confederacy: Defeat, the Lost Cause, and the Emergence of the New South, 1865–1913* (New York: Oxford University Press, 1987).
[3]For the full report, see: www.sbts.edu/southern-project/.

course, would never make mistakes of such magnitude—except that we have, and continue to do so.

Consider evangelicals' early ambivalence about abortion—a reality surprising to many contemporary evangelicals. Every January the Southern Baptists' denominational calendar includes a Sanctity of Life Sunday coinciding with January 22, the anniversary of *Roe v. Wade* (filed first by a lawyer who was herself a Southern Baptist). Today, it is difficult to think of a more firmly held moral conviction among Southern Baptists and conservative Protestants generally than the pro-life position.[4] Yet the SBC's initial response to *Roe v. Wade* was measured approval. The *Baptist Press* subsequently published an editorial praising the ruling as having "advanced the cause of religious liberty, human equality and justice."[5] This was not surprising given a resolution passed two years earlier by the Christian Life Commission (now the Ethics & Religious Liberty Commission, or ERLC) and confirmed by the convention acknowledging the sanctity of life but calling for abortion to remain legal in cases of rape, incest, fetal deformity, and the "emotional, mental, and physical health of the mother."[6] The same editorial following the decision considered the question of whether there is a Southern Baptist position on abortion and concluded, "There is no official Southern Baptist position on abortion, or any other such question. Among 12 million Southern Baptists, there are probably 12 million different opinions."[7] Southern Baptists were hardly alone in their

---

[4] About two-thirds of self-described evangelicals say that abortion should be mostly illegal. See a good collection of survey data at www.pewresearch.org/religion/religious-landscape-study/religious-tradition/evangelical-protestant/views-about-abortion/. The numbers may vary, and there's daylight between denominational stances and poll data, but the basic point is unassailable and attested to by both those who affirm and those who decry it.

[5] See Ethics and Religious Liberty Commission, "5 Facts about the history of the SBC and the pro-life cause," January 17, 2020, https://erlc.com/resource-library/articles/5-facts-about-the-history-of-the-sbc-and-the-pro-life-cause/.

[6] Note that the companion case to *Roe v. Wade* largely eviscerated any real possibility for restrictions left open by Roe, precisely on the grounds of women's health. See *Doe v. Bolton*, 410 U.S. 179 (1973). The notion that a "pro-life" position could expect the rulings to offer meaningful limits on the abortion license is strikingly naive. See Justin Taylor, "An Interview with Robert P. George on Roe v. Wade," *First Things*, January 22, 2010, www.firstthings.com/blogs/firstthoughts/2010/01/an-interview-with-robert-p-george-on-roe-v-wade.

[7] See Trevin Wax, "Baptist Press Initial Reporting on Roe v. Wade," *The Gospel Coalition*, May 6, 2010, www.thegospelcoalition.org/blogs/trevin-wax/baptist-press-initial-reporting-on-roe-v-wade/.

ambivalent response.[8] Unlike with slavery, leading Southern Baptists went quickly from being effectively pro-choice to being some of the most prominent voices in the pro-life movement. Most evangelicals (the present authors included) think this particular change is all to the good, but it raises the question, why did so many conservative Protestants in the late 1960s and early 1970s have such an ad hoc and apparently unprincipled approach to abortion? Why could they not see it clearly as an injustice?

The evidence suggests that this continues in our own day. For example, why have evangelicals flipped so dramatically on the expectation that our political leaders should meet some standard of moral virtue? Democracies certainly do not require that their leaders be saints, but the idea that some degree of virtue is necessary is deeply embedded in our political traditions.[9] Shortly before Donald Trump's election in 2016, Sarah Pulliam Bailey noted a shift that had taken place among White evangelicals on the question of moral character in candidates for political office.[10] In 2011 only 30 percent of evangelicals responded that yes, someone who commits an immoral act can behave ethically in public office. That rose to 72 percent in 2016 as White evangelicals faced the prospects of choosing between Hillary Clinton and Donald Trump. Particularly interesting is that the poll that Bailey relied on shows that the 2011 30-percent figure for White evangelicals was the lowest among all groups polled. That is, at that time evangelicals were the *least* likely group to think that an immoral person could act ethically in public office. By 2016 they were the *most* likely group.

The simplest explanation for this sort of switch might be to say that the prospect of power just makes principles take a back seat—and

---

[8]See Daniel K. Williams, *Defenders of the Unborn: The Pro-Life Movement before Roe v. Wade* (New York: Oxford University Press, 2016).
[9]Consider the hotly contested presidential election of 1800, where the proxy journalism wars between Adams and Jefferson were focused mostly on their personal character—or lack thereof. See Edward J. Larson, *A Magnificent Catastrophe: The Tumultuous Election of 1800, America's First Presidential Campaign* (New York: Simon and Schuster, 2007).
[10]Sarah Pulliam Bailey, "The Trump effect? A stunning number of evangelicals will now accept politicians' 'immoral' acts," *Washington Post*, October 9, 2016, www.washingtonpost.com/news/acts-of-faith/wp/2016/10/19/the-trump-effect-evangelicals-have-become-much-more-accepting-of-politicians-immoral-acts/.

certainly that is part of the story. We are all more affected by considerations of interest—power, money, prestige, and so on—than anyone would like to admit. But we are convinced that is only part of the story, in large part because of the witness of those who *did* see things clearly and testified to truth and goodness as they perceived it, sometimes at great personal cost. Which raises a broader question. What sort of moral tradition or institutions or education might have helped Protestants do better in these sorts of cases: recognize just how evil slavery and its progeny were, understand *Roe* and *its* progeny at the outset, and stick to their convictions about the place of moral virtue in politics?

What do evangelical Christians need so that we are *not* tossed back and forth according to the political or cultural winds of the day and that we get better at making and acting on good political judgments? This book is meant to help with just these sorts of questions.

Our Current Moment

These three examples, as different as they are in content and historical context, illustrate something of the conventional wisdom about contemporary evangelical politics in the United States. Evangelicals' moral and political witness sits at a nadir.[11] Churches have become politicized, riven by partisan and ideological disputes that are at times more central than theological or biblical claims.[12] On the right, many White evangelicals' embrace of Donald Trump—and, in some cases, their uncritical acceptance of his vulgarity, sexism, nationalism, and thinly veiled racism—have significantly undercut their public moral standing, to the point where even their religious liberty advocacy has become politically

---

[11] Attitudes toward evangelicals in the United States are rather negative, even more so than attitudes toward atheists and Muslims. See www.pewresearch.org/religion/2023/03/15/americans-feel-more-positive-than-negative-about-jews-mainline-protestants-catholics/. See also Peter Wehner, "The Deepening Crisis in Evangelical Christianity," *The Atlantic*, July 5, 2019, www.theatlantic.com/ideas/archive/2019/07/evangelical-christians-face-deepening-crisis/593353/.

[12] See Michele F. Margolis, *From Politics to the Pews: How Partisanship and the Political Environment Shape Religious Identity* (Chicago: University of Chicago Press, 2018). The Southern Baptist's Lifeway Research shows similar patterns: https://research.lifeway.com/2022/11/01/churchgoers-increasingly-prefer-a-congregation-that-shares-their-politics/.

controversial.[13] On the left, progressive evangelicals' agendas are often indistinguishable from those of their secular counterparts, leaving them open to similar accusations of uncritical party capture and moral relativism.[14] Selective, inconsistent, and divisive policy stances leave evangelicals open to critiques of incoherence, hypocrisy, and pursuing status and power over moral convictions, let alone biblical and theological ones. The upshot is that *our public witness has been seriously compromised by moral inconsistency and incoherence, and by this we have contributed significantly to the polarization and conflict currently roiling American politics.*

As grim as things may seem, more significant problems may be in the offing. It is not just that evangelicals don't have a coherent moral framework for politics. It's also that what is emerging from some parts of our political culture (Christian and non-Christian alike) explicitly sets itself against any reasonable sense of what makes for a liberal democracy. (To be clear, as political theorists, we use the term *liberal democracy* to refer to limited, liberty-respecting governments characterized by democratic accountability—using *liberal* to describe those commitments that US founders might have called those of a "republic"—rather than its contemporary popular meaning in contrast to *conservative*.) Whether these emerging challenges are Christian arguments for "post-liberal" confessional states or progressive ones in favor of setting aside central liberal protections in the name of equity, liberal democracy's critics are clearly having a moment.[15] While this might have been unthinkable fifty

---

[13]Some of this, of course, reflects the conflicts between religious liberty and LGBT issues. But it is also the case that at times, religious liberty advocacy has been about Christians' specific interests more than religious liberty for all.

[14]To just take one example, *Sojourners* magazine has long been at the center of progressive evangelicalism. It straightforwardly opposed the *Dobbs* decision, which overturned *Roe v. Wade*: https://sojo.net/about-us/news/sojourners-opposes-supreme-courts-ruling-ending-constitutional-right-abortion.

[15]For the argument in favor of an ethnically based confessional state, see Stephen M. Wolfe, *The Case for Christian Nationalism* (Moscow, ID: Canon Press, 2022). For the Catholic version of this, see Adrian Vermeule, "Integration from Within," *American Affairs Journal* II, no. 1 (Spring 2018): 202–13, *American Affairs Journal* (blog), February 20, 2018, https://americanaffairsjournal.org/2018/02/integration-from-within/. From the more progressive perspective offering a critique of liberalism

years ago given the political and social norms of the time, a commitment to liberal democracy is no longer as widely shared.

None of these arguments are new, exactly, but they have a kind of salience for evangelicals (and others) that requires our attention. In particular, we are increasingly faced with a culture that suggests we can *either* be faithful Christians *or* we can endorse a liberal democratic political order with its constitutionalism, limited government, and respect for individual liberties. As messy as contemporary American politics can be, the extent to which evangelicals see their faith commitments as supportive of or even compatible with liberal democratic politics will be critical to the path of both evangelicals and the American political order in the years to come. These are questions that obviously matter far beyond our own religious community: can a coherent, religiously informed moral framework be reconciled with liberal democracy in a pluralistic society? Or are they ultimately incompatible? Here we find a second layer to the first problem of compromised moral witness: *it is far from clear to many whether evangelical moral commitments have a place in a liberal democratic order.*

This book argues the two can in fact be reconciled and that the Christian natural law tradition, in the context of evangelical theological distinctives, offers something important both for evangelicals and the broader political community. It offers on the one hand moral and theological principles that can speak to the issues of the day, neglecting neither deep moral truths nor the realities of sin and human finitude, all in ways that can *strengthen* liberal democracy, not undermine it. It also on the other hand offers evangelicals a framework within which we—in all our variety and disagreement—can think through what a good political community might look like, and act accordingly. The Christian natural law tradition offers meaningful and coherent moral guidance apart from merely instrumental calculations of political power and success. What this book has on offer here will certainly not fix all that

---

from within critical theory, for an overview see Richard Delgado and Jean Stefancic, *Critical Race Theory: An Introduction*, 4th ed. (New York: New York University Press, 2023), 26-30.

ails evangelicalism, American politics, or democratic politics more broadly, but we are convinced that it could go some distance toward easing the two particular challenges identified here—namely, ad hoc moral judgments and tension with liberal democracy.

This is, caveats aside, more than a bit ambitious. For some, trying to think theologically and philosophically about evangelical politics is at best a fruitless task and at worst a cover for evangelicalism's less savory impulses. After all, evangelicals are notoriously difficult to define, either theologically or sociologically, and even then, evangelicalism's well-known tendencies toward anti-intellectualism complicate connecting the dots between the definitional "who" and the politically salient "what." The best of arguments won't do much good if they are directed at the wrong people who aren't likely to pay attention anyway. Some might also worry that, in attempting to do theological and philosophical work, we will end up ignoring what some identify as the "real" wellsprings of evangelical politics: the stew of racial resentment, sexism, and economic dysfunction that many recent authors argue have motivated most of post-WWII evangelicalism.[16] Maybe the reason it has been so difficult to articulate a tradition of evangelical political thought is that there isn't really any "there" there—or, at least, not anything to encourage. Thus framed, this project may seem doomed from the start.

We believe that it is instead a rather auspicious time to think about the future of evangelical politics. Mainstream evangelicalism's political influence—for good and ill—is in significant decline, and there is little reason to suspect that those fortunes will be soon reversed (recent Supreme Court decisions notwithstanding).[17] Perhaps more to the point, it seems that the broad sweep of evangelicals' political agenda has largely been a failure.[18] The prospect of a sojourn in the political and cultural

---

[16] For just two examples, see Kristin Kobes DuMez, *Jesus and John Wayne: How White Evangelicals Corrupted a Faith and Fractured a Nation* (New York: Liveright, 2021) and Randall Balmer, *Bad Faith: Race and the Rise of the Religious Right* (Grand Rapids, MI: Eerdmans, 2021).
[17] We have in mind cases like *Dobbs v. Jackson* (which overturned *Roe v. Wade*) and *Masterpiece Cakeshop v. Colorado Civil Rights Commission*.
[18] It is true that evangelicals played a key role in the overturning of *Roe v. Wade*, which has long been a central element in their political agenda. But on a whole host of other issues, it has been

wilderness offers us a chance to reconsider who God has called us to be as citizens in our political communities, without the temptation of thinking of this calling as a pathway to power and influence. We can explore the question of political faithfulness anew, from a posture of humility that recognizes both the successes and the failures of evangelicals' moral witness.[19] To be absolutely clear, the goal of such soul-searching and careful intellectual work is not to find better strategies for successfully gaining political power. We care about making progress in the public square on behalf of the common good and justice for our neighbors, to be sure. But our priority here is quite simply to grow in faithfulness regardless of the political outcome.

Such a reimagining of evangelical politics is both possible and desirable for three reasons. First, *there is indeed such a thing as evangelicalism*, despite its definitional challenges. There remain many millions of Protestants whose theological commitments (as opposed to sociological, political, or identitarian conceptions of evangelicalism) include a deep sense of human sin; the centrality of Christ's redemption through the cross for justification and sanctification; a transformed heart and life through a personal relationship with Jesus; and the authoritative role of God's special revelation in Scripture.[20] Evangelical Christians will continue to exist and be involved in politics in ways more or less consistently motivated by our theological convictions (our hope, per this book, is more rather than less!). Second, *evangelicals already have access to a faithful and vibrant tradition of Christian thinking about politics in the biblical natural law tradition*. Although this tradition has been neglected for more than a century, it deserves reconsideration. Third, *evangelical engagement with this tradition can provide a framework for a convictional Christian political witness that can engage fruitfully within a pluralistic and liberal democratic political order*. As we noted above, an evangelical

---

failure after failure. And even with abortion, it is quite far from obvious how things will turn out.

[19]To be clear, it is not our aim to restore evangelicals' political power. We are interested in political faithfulness.

[20]We explore the definition of *evangelical* further below.

natural law tradition can help reconcile meaningful moral guidance with the norms and processes of a liberal democratic order that takes divergent ultimate commitments seriously and serves the common good, not a sectarian good. In short, we believe the way forward requires looking back.

We call our approach Hopeful Realism as a way of signaling our commitment to two crucial convictions. First, our arguments can be aptly described as a sort of *realism* because we hold to the traditional Christian teaching about the pervasiveness of original sin and the reality of the Fall. On this side of the eschaton (end times), we do not expect any human endeavors to be free from the taint of the Fall, and that most definitely includes the political realm. Thus while we pray with the church universal that God's will be done on earth as it is in heaven, we recognize that only in God's timing will that prayer be fully answered. Our attempts at Christian witness in the political realm will never achieve the Kingdom of God and will be marked by human frailty, finitude, and sin.

Yet, and second, while we reject utopianism of all stripes, we do not fall into cynicism nor despair, for realism has another, deeper sense. Our realism is also *hopeful* because we can indeed know things, including moral things, and claim them as public knowledge, if not always common sense.[21] More importantly, the object of our ultimate hope, God the Father, Son, and Holy Spirit, calls us to steward his good creation, love our neighbors, pray for those in authority, champion justice, protect the weak, feed the hungry, visit the prisoner, and promote the well-being of the city. We think political engagement is one legitimate and important way (though by no means the only way) to answer this call. If God has called us to follow him into the realm of politics, then we have reason to hope that good things may come out of it. Our recognition of the stubbornness of sin—individual, corporate, and structural—tempers our expectations of what we will achieve, but, as the saying goes, we are in sales and God is in management. The brokenness of the world is not the

---

[21]See Dallas Willard, *The Disappearance of Moral Knowledge*, ed. and completed by Steven L. Porter, Aaron Preston, and Gregg A. Ten Elshof (New York: Routledge, 2018).

final word. The goodness of the created order is not obliterated by the Fall. Hope is a theological virtue to be cultivated as we follow our God who is in the business of setting right what is broken.

In the rest of this introduction, we address some preliminary questions and assumptions necessary for making the case for Hopeful Realism as an expression of an evangelical natural law tradition. We start by mapping out some concepts: describing who we mean by "evangelicals," how we understand an intellectual "tradition," and providing an introductory gloss on what the natural law is. We then offer a brief road map to the rest of the book and close with some caveats about the scope of our project and more particularly what we are *not* trying to do. As we explore these important framing and contextual features, we do so with our central thesis in view: *a Hopeful Realism approach to the natural law tradition can provide much-needed guidance for evangelical political engagement and can contribute to the flourishing of a liberal democratic order.*

Evangelicals and Tradition

What does it mean to be an evangelical? And what distinguishes evangelical Christianity from other parts of the Christian tradition? This is a question that warrants (and has received) extensive attention. While we cannot fully engage this body of work here, a working understanding of evangelicalism is vital for distinguishing our use of the term from that of others. Our use, which is primarily theological, differs from other common usages, including sociological, historical, political, and identity-marking conceptions. That is, we treat *evangelical* as describing a certain type of Christian orthodoxy marked by particular theological commitments.[22] A theological account of evangelicalism is quite different from, say, an exit poll asking someone if he or she identifies as an evangelical Christian, regardless of worship attendance, theological commitments, and so on. This theological approach is important because our work, while drawing on descriptive accounts of society's religious and

---

[22] Often, these commitments are shared across Christian traditions but receive different emphases in different traditions.

political context, is ultimately a normative project. That is to say, we aspire to encourage and equip evangelicals to not only understand what is the case (descriptive) but what we should do about it given our theological convictions (normative). Like the "hopeful" aspect of our theory of natural law, our conception of evangelicalism is itself aspirational.

Evangelical Protestants share most basic commitments with other Christians, affirming with them core beliefs such as those summarized in the Apostles' Creed. Still, as we have explored elsewhere, evangelical Protestants emphasize distinctive themes within the big tent of Christianity.[23] David Bebbington's famous "quadrilateral" describes these "priorities" as *biblicism* (a singular emphasis on the authority of Scripture), *crucicentrism* (emphasis on Christ's atoning work on the cross), *conversionism* (a conversion experience), and *activism* (a transformed life following one's turning to God).[24] Another historian of evangelicalism, George Marsden, characterizes evangelicalism according to five doctrinal distinctives: "(1) the Reformation doctrine of the final authority of the Bible, (2) the real historical character of God's saving work in Scripture, (3) salvation to eternal life based on the redemptive work of Christ, (4) the importance of evangelism and missions, and (5) the importance of a spiritually transformed life."[25] James Davison Hunter limits evangelical doctrinal commitments to three: "the unique authority of the Bible; the divinity of Jesus; and the relevance of his life, death, and resurrection to the salvation of the soul."[26] Without parsing all of the details between these (or other) summaries of evangelical distinctives, for present purposes we are content to begin by describing evangelicals as we have elsewhere: "Protestant Christians who emphasize the unique

---

[23] Jesse Covington, Bryan T. McGraw, and Micah Joel Watson, "Introduction" in *Natural Law and Evangelical Political Thought*, ed. Jesse Covington, Bryan T. McGraw, and Micah Joel Watson (Lanham, MD: Lexington Books, 2013), ix-x.

[24] David W. Bebbington, *Evangelicalism in Modern Britain: A History from the 1730s to the 1980s* (New York: Routledge, 2003), 2-3.

[25] George Marsden, *Understanding Fundamentalism and Evangelicalism* (Grand Rapids, MI: Eerdmans, 1991), 4-5.

[26] James Davison Hunter, *American Evangelicalism: Conservative Religion and the Quandary of Modernity* (New Brunswick, NJ: Rutgers University Press, 1983), 7.

Introduction

authority of the Bible, the centrality of Christ to salvation, and the active response of the believer," including evidence of obedient holiness.[27]

If what we've just described briefly spells out what we mean by *who* evangelicals are (or the commitments that we take to define this group), *what* exactly do we mean by a "tradition"? The etymological root of *tradition* is to "pass down" or "deliver."[28] We pass down to the next generation the beliefs and practices that make us who we are. We follow Catholic philosopher Alasdair MacIntyre's description of a tradition as an argument conducted internally and externally such that any tradition can be described in terms of its beliefs and practices by three levels or tiers.[29] The first and foundational tier is composed of those beliefs and practices that are not debated, what MacIntyre calls "fundamental agreements." They are constitutive of the tradition itself. They are the core of what it means to belong to the tradition, and while people may struggle with this or that belief or how to apply it, to reject a component at this level is to effectively leave the tradition. And for a living tradition to shift on a belief or practice at this level is to transform into something different entirely. The second tier is identified by internal arguments among those who agree on the fundamentals but differ on important but second-tier matters. And the third tier is made up of external debates between those who hold to the fundamentals, even if differing on secondary matters, and those outside the tradition altogether.

A sports analogy can help clarify MacIntyre's schema. One of us is fortunate enough to be a fan of the greatest basketball team in the NBA—the Los Angeles Lakers—and is bound by a few dogmas and practices that are nonnegotiable. One's first and only basketball loyalty belongs to

---

[27] Covington, McGraw, and Watson, "Introduction," x. Italics added.
[28] See Oxford English Dictionary, "Tradition," accessed February 20, 2024, www.oed.com/dictionary/tradition_n?tab=etymology#17870898.
[29] "A tradition is an argument extended through time in which certain fundamental agreements are defined and redefined in terms of two kinds of conflict: those with critics and enemies external to the tradition who reject all or at least key parts of those fundamental agreements, and those internal, interpretative debates through which the meaning and rationale of the fundamental agreements come to be expressed and by whose progress a tradition is constituted." Alasdair MacIntyre, *Whose Justice? Which Rationality?* (Notre Dame, IN: University of Notre Dame Press, 1988), 12.

the Lakers alone; the five championships won in Minnesota count toward the total for the franchise; and the Boston Celtics are loathsome, uncouth, and vile. While all bona fide Laker fans should agree with this, there is room for good-natured debate on the second tier. Who is the greatest Laker of all time? Jerry West or Magic? Kareem or Kobe? Would the 80s Lakers have defeated the Kobe-Shaq Lakers? And so on. One can take part in these debates while still being entirely within the "Laker tradition." And finally there are those external debates between Laker fans and partisans of lesser teams. While genuine Laker fans don't really see these debates as entirely fair, one could engage in debates about which franchise could provide the greatest starting five of all time, or which team is the greatest of all time.

We think this three-tiered schema is a helpful diagnostic with which to identify traditions of all sorts and not just in the athletic world: political traditions, philosophical traditions, religious traditions, and others. While clarifying, it does not solve all the descriptive challenges, as some of the thorniest debates can occur when adherents to a tradition disagree themselves over to which tier a contested issue belongs.

The three tiers also apply to evangelicalism, and thus can play a key role in how evangelicals think about an evangelical natural law tradition, or what we're calling Hopeful Realism. We understand the first tier as those foundational beliefs that define who evangelicals are. As described above, for evangelicals this foundational tier will include biblical authority, the centrality of Christ for salvation, and the believer's active response. To the extent that a Christian demurs from any of those commitments she will be moving away from what it means to be an evangelical. As we will demonstrate, the commitment to Scripture will be particularly salient in thinking about natural law and politics. The second tier comprises those issues that are important but debatable, such as the particular mode of baptism, gender roles, or the role liturgy should play in worship.[30] The third tier consists of those arguments or perhaps

---

[30]These differences here raise the need for an important clarification. It matters whether we are speaking of the Christian tradition broadly, an evangelical Protestant tradition more particularly,

interactions evangelicals have with those outside the Christian tradition altogether. It is the burden of this book to establish what we mean then by an evangelical natural law tradition, and so it is to the natural law that we now turn.

The "Nature" of Natural Law by a Roundabout Way

There has been a widespread resurgence of natural law thinking across the landscape of Protestant Christian higher education. While Roman Catholic colleges and universities have long incorporated natural law theory into their curriculum and practice, given its pride of place in Catholic social thought and the ongoing influence of Thomas Aquinas, Protestant and evangelical colleges and universities in the Council for Christian Colleges and Universities (CCCU) and beyond have only recently become a veritable hotbed of one particular type of natural law activity—though from an unexpected direction.[31] The CCCU as an umbrella organization has made grants to several colleges to promote these initiatives, and scores of schools now include classes, clubs, lectures, conferences, and off-campus trips that indicate a commitment, conscious or not, to natural law thinking by way of creation care or environmental studies. Westmont College has a new minor in environmental studies and hosted "Faith. Climate. Action." advocacy workshops in the summer; Houghton College sponsored "Caring for God's Creation" Life Together groups and a major in environmental studies; Wheaton College has a science center partly dedicated to sustainability concerns and hosts competitions to promote environmental concerns while advancing them

---

or one individual denomination more particularly still. For while all three traditions will include the doctrines expressed in the Apostles' and Nicene creeds, how different beliefs fit in other tiers depends on how specific the tradition is. Thus the Christian Reformed Church to which Calvin University belongs would put some specifically Reformed beliefs into the first foundational tier, and the first tier of the Southern Baptist tradition of the SBTS would look rather different. These same beliefs that are first tier for Calvin or SBTS might be, in the larger tradition of evangelical Protestantism, better placed in the second tier of debated beliefs. One can be an evangelical Protestant without holding to the Belgic Confession, but not an elder in good standing of the Christian Reformed Church. And one can also be an evangelical Protestant without holding to believer's baptism, but not a member in good standing in most Southern Baptist churches.

[31]The CCCU was founded in 1976 and has 185 member institutions. See www.cccu.org/about/#heading-our-work-and-mission-0.

on campus, in Chicago, and around the world; and Calvin University lists environmental sustainability as one of the four essential components of the core curriculum and boasts no less than fifteen creation-care initiatives.[32] Visiting the websites of others among the other CCCU members shows similar offerings.

Whether they know it or not, tens of thousands of students, staff, faculty, and alumni have been relying on the core precepts of natural law thinking and practice as they have sought to be faithful stewards of God's creation. All things considered, we think this is a very good thing. But what does creation care have to do with natural law?

The answer is that creation care *proceeds from the belief that the created order is good, we understand it can be ordered in better and worse ways, and that our actions should align with a right ordering of creation—we can and should seek its flourishing.* Consider the college student who arrives on campus and finds herself inspired by a powerful lecture from a gifted professor in an environmental sustainability class. Persuaded that Scripture gives us sound reasons for investing our time and energy into preserving and protecting the environment, she sees this as one way to love God and her neighbor. She changes her major to environmental science and joins a campus club that hosts speakers and events and partners with other groups in the community—some Christian, many not—to clean up a local polluted creek. She becomes more interested in state and national legislation regarding climate change and the environment and writes letters to her representatives about various proposals and legislation. She recognizes that not everyone agrees with her convictions and the policies that flow from them, and so she winsomely advocates for her beliefs, both with her fellow believers and those outside the church. Our student, whether she knows it or not, is acting like a Christian natural lawyer.

---

[32]See, variously, www.westmont.edu/caring-gods-creation; www.westmont.edu/westmont-news/workshop-inspires-christians-climate-action; www.wheaton.edu/academics/departments/envsci/; https://calvin.edu/about/sustainability/; https://calvin.edu/academics/core/; www.houghton.edu/campus-life/sustainability/houghton-college-adds-new-major-in-environmental-studies/.

While chapter two will expand on this, natural law at its most basic involves two propositions that apply to the creation-care description above. The first is that human beings have a normative nature that is directional: some behaviors accord with and promote the fulfillment of that nature, and others hinder and corrupt it.[33] Second, people have the capacity to reason and thus understand to some extent what helps or hinders this nature. In Christian terms, (1) God created our natures, and (2) he gave us reason, through which we can understand some of this nature even without special revelation. And the conclusions of reason about our nature entail obligations about what humans ought to do. God made us a certain way, and all people, Christian or not, can know something about this.[34]

To be clear, a Christian approach to natural law does not cordon off the witness of Scripture or special revelation, even as we must take care to distinguish between them and the purposes to which they are put. As we will argue, Scripture itself points to God's authorship of the natural law. The Christian advocate of natural law believes that God reveals his purposes for his creation, including human beings, through Scripture. While Scripture does not address every moral issue or ethical dilemma, where it does speak, it is authoritative and obligatory. Scripture informs us of the sort of creatures we are and the kind of world we live in, sometimes describing the people we are to be as well as the things we should do, and not do. "He has shown you, O mortal, what is good. / And what does the LORD requires of you?" proclaims the prophet Micah (Micah 6:8). We can know that we are to care for the poor, honor our parents, pay taxes, defend the weak, and act as good stewards of God's creation.

Yet Scripture does not offer us everything we might want or need to know regarding exactly how we are to take care of the creation, how we are to responsibly exercise that stewardship. Even where God has

---

[33] While perhaps most obvious when it comes to goods like nutrition and exercise, we extend such goods well beyond the physical.
[34] How much they can know, and how effectively they can act on that knowledge, are matters of debate. We should also clarify here that we do not think this knowledge of and acting for the good is in any way salvific.

revealed truths about worthy *ends* to pursue in the world through his word, he mostly seems to have left it to us to use our reason to figure out the best *means* available to achieve those ends. For example, Scripture clearly teaches that physical healing is good, but it doesn't provide guidance for training surgeons. Likewise, we can know from Genesis that we ought to care for creation but look beyond Scripture for the particulars of resource stewardship in our particular context. Our reason contributes to how we discern what is good for us as human beings and what is good for our world and the other creatures in it.

The Christian natural law advocate thus believes that God has given us general revelation in addition to the special revelation of his word. One can believe that theft and domestic abuse are wrong without deriving those norms from sacred writ, offering good reasons for these positions. One can know that we should honor our mother and father without even knowing about the Ten Commandments. God has given human beings *reason*, just as human beings irrespective of religious identity, and with that reason we can know certain things about our nature, and nature generally, and what is and is not good for both. Just as God has given human beings who are Christians the capacity to reason, with which we can determine the best means to accomplish various ends, so God has given human beings as such the same human capacity to know not only means but also ends. God speaks through his word (2 Timothy 3:16-17), and God speaks through his world (Psalm 19, Romans 1), and he has given us the faculty of reason with which we can, albeit imperfectly, understand and act on both.

It is worth emphasizing the critical balancing act we aim to achieve here. We posit some measure of confidence in our capacity to know things about ourselves and God's world with the undeniable reality that our knowledge is partial, incomplete, and not only impaired by creaturely finitude but also tainted by sin and self-interest. Throughout the history of the church, Christians have, in true Goldilocks fashion, often veered too far toward one of this divide, usually out of understandable concern about the dangers of the other side. We aim to say yes to both

Introduction

sides but insist the two insights hold together in an uncollapsible tension on this side of the eschaton. As the apostle Paul teaches, we see through a glass darkly. Thus, we should be cautious about overconfident claims to have ascended from the dark shadows into the bright daylight, but we must also recognize that we still can "see" to some extent. And this is true in an important sense not only for Christians but non-Christians as well. If non-Christians were in complete darkness with regard to the creational goods, it would be hard to make sense of Jesus' teaching in the Sermon on the Mount:

> You are the light of the world. A town built on a hill cannot be hidden. Neither do people light a lamp and put it under a bowl. Instead they put it on a stand, and it gives light to everyone in the house. In the same way, let your light shine before others, that they may see your good deeds and glorify your Father in heaven. (Matthew 5:14-16)

What would it mean for nonbelievers, the "others" in that last verse, to recognize good deeds if they had no capacity to understand what is praiseworthy and good for human beings?[35]

This is why our student committed to stewarding God's creation is not puzzled that many non-Christians share her convictions about what is good for the environment and what harms it, and that it is good for human beings to protect the environment, and bad for us to harm it. It is true that the Christian will tell a different story than the secular citizen—a truer story—about why creation matters and who is behind it. The Christian will also have the resources to better resist an idolatrous posture toward the creation, whether from fellow believers or unbelievers, because she knows that God has commanded us not to have any gods before him. We want to be clear in affirming that God's special revelation gives us a more complete story than we would have from observing the creation on our own—and it transforms our interpretation of general revelation. And yet we maintain there is

---

[35]Of course, there are Scriptures like Romans 1:20 that suggest that this knowledge may operate to render the unbelieving "without excuse."

something very important about our shared humanity that makes common cause and action with nonbelievers possible given our shared creational context.

Finally, this common cause and action can at times be political in nature. Creational goods are also often public goods, and even in a society characterized by a plurality of ultimate commitments, we can and should engage our neighbors about the public goods we share as citizens and how best to employ the unique capacities of the state to protect and promote these goods. It is true that the Christian environmentalist is motivated by her faith, but that is no reason for embarrassment in the public square because her positions can be shared by others with different motivations and grounding principles. We'll say more about this later.

We begin in this roundabout way with environmental stewardship to get to the heart of natural law thinking while trying to sidestep some of the concerns that the mention of "natural law" may elicit. If you believe that God has so ordered the world that there are goods genuinely constituent of healthy and flourishing human beings (and our environment); that Christians and non-Christians alike can know about these goods and to some extent act to promote them; and that some goods are so paramount and some evils so wicked that governments can and should act to protect the former and prevent and punish the latter, then you may be an unwitting natural lawyer. Indeed, our tongues are only slightly in our cheeks in claiming that "we may not all be natural law theorists, but we are all natural lawyers."

Road Map

We go about making our case by dividing the book into two parts. In the four chapters of part one, we describe what we mean by Hopeful Realism as an evangelical natural law theory, and in part two we apply it to four important and controversial policy areas. In the next chapter we start in the beginning, literally, as we consider what a biblical approach to politics should look like by drawing some core lessons from the opening of

Genesis. We then turn to a confrontation between Jesus and the Pharisees in the Gospel of Matthew, and finally we conclude with the famous thirteenth chapter of Paul's epistle to the Romans.

The second chapter moves from a biblical account of politics to a biblical account of the natural law, with Saint Augustine serving as a particularly helpful guide for navigating theological distinctives of particular concern to evangelicals. We draw here not only from Scripture itself, but from the venerable tradition of scriptural commentary from figures like Augustine, Luther, Calvin, and others. These first two chapters together describe the biblical ground for politics after the Fall and before the eschaton and demonstrate how that same biblical authority witnesses to the reality and contours of the natural law. Our aim here is to persuade readers that Hopeful Realism is grounded in scriptural truths, faithful to evangelical distinctives, and consistent with the broad Christian tradition.

In chapter three we turn to a rather different concern: whether Hopeful Realism is compatible with a liberal democratic order. While we do not think that an evangelical natural law theory leads to liberal democracy as a matter of necessity, we show how Hopeful Realism can support liberal democracy. Here we describe four political principles drawn from our natural law account that contribute to a healthier and more stable liberal democratic order: *the common good and civic friendship*; *confessional pluralism and religious liberty*; *democracy and decentralization*; and *restraint and liberty*. That is, on the one hand we think Christian politics and a liberal democracy can be compatible insofar as principles drawn from the former can inform and invigorate the latter; and on the other hand, faithful Christian politics resists the totalizing temptations for Christians either to take over society with reins of power or withdraw entirely in a quietistic retreat.

If we have succeeded in explaining our biblical approach to politics, connected that approach to the natural law (with help from Augustine), and demonstrated at least the compatibility of Hopeful Realism and liberal democracy, it remains to lay out how we make political and moral judgments consistent with the natural law but also attentive to the social and political realities of the world around us. In chapter four, we describe the four different types of goods (*physical, rational, volitional,* and *relational*) that we think are central to a Christian understanding of human flourishing, and we map out a framework for thinking through how those goods might best be realized in particular political contexts. This framework offers Christians a means for applying their deepest moral commitments to practical judgments about everyday political questions. We think that this is among the more pressing needs for evangelical politics today, as it provides tools that we can actually use in bringing moral clarity to political judgments.

The four chapters of the first part of the book are necessarily more theoretical and abstract. In the second part of the book, we illustrate how the ideas and principles described in part one might apply to tangible and at times controversial contemporary issues. In chapter five we look at the organization of economic life; chapter six tackles marriage and sex; chapter seven considers war and the coercive power of the state; and chapter eight looks at the good of religious liberty. We mean these treatments to be illustrative rather than exhaustive, examples of how Hopeful Realism could apply politically rather than comprehensive arguments meant to settle those issues in some definitive way.[36]

What We're Not Doing

As we wrap up this introduction, we think it will be helpful to do our best to ward off potential misunderstandings from the start. We're reminded of the advice C. S. Lewis gave in an interview about sound writing:

> The reader, we must remember, does not start by knowing what we mean. If our words are ambiguous, our meaning will escape him. I sometimes think that writing is like driving sheep down a road. If there is any gate open to the left or the right the reader will most certainly go into it.[37]

---

[36]Though we do, of course, think the conclusions we've come to on these matters are correct!
[37]C. S. Lewis, "Cross Examination," in *God in the Dock: Essays on Theology and Ethics* (Grand Rapids, MI: Eerdmans, 1994), 263.

So we don't expect to avoid misunderstandings altogether but rather aim at being as clear as we can. To that end, we offer up the following four thoughts about what we are *not* trying to do in this book.

First, we are not engaged in an apologetic for some version of Christian nationalism, understood as an argument for a coercive confessional state. As already mentioned, we are persuaded that faithful Christian presence is compatible with liberal democratic institutions and norms. (See chapter three for our more complete argument.) Even more than this, we think—all things considered—that there are good reasons for Christians to prefer and advocate for liberal democracy, even if there is not a straight deductive line from Christian natural law reasoning to liberal democratic politics. As with anything else, liberal democracy cannot live up to the outsized expectations that some have burdened it with. And when it fails to deliver on those expectations, it is perhaps not surprising that many Christians and others might look to more authoritarian or explicitly religio-political alternatives. Nevertheless, we find in Hopeful Realism powerful theological reasons for unequivocally rejecting Christian nationalism.

Second, while we are academics writing with some degree of scholarly detail, our primary audience in this effort is the church—our fellow believers and colaborers in Christ. This is to say we know well that we are not responding to all scholarly concerns or perspectives in the present work—even if this volume may prove to be of some benefit to our fellow academics. Moreover, a corollary of this is that we aim primarily to *equip* our fellow believers more than *persuade* those who disagree with us. Our hope is that this is just a first step and that others will join us in developing what we offer here.

Third, we are not writing about what we take to be an entirely original or new approach to faithful Christian political thought and action. We are borrowing, and unashamedly so, from a long, rich, and diverse tradition—indeed, so diverse that we should probably refer to it as "traditions" in the plural. Christian political theology, theory, and philosophy have been alive and well for some time and remain so today. However, even when its insights are sound and could help meet the needs of the church in context, theory and practice do not always come together. And this is particularly pressing as regards the focus of this book regarding political morality. But more than reinventing the wheel, we seek to build on an already existing theological chassis, and where it has come loose, help to re-attach or reestablish the place of the natural law tradition as part of the vehicle of evangelical politics—though recognizing that this provides a unique "take" on the natural law tradition.

Fourth, and finally, we are not writing about natural law as if it is a magical algorithm that acts as an infallible political guide. There are limits to natural law reasoning, and there are limits to what even an entire book can do. Consistent with our earlier illustration with our eager creation-care student, natural law describes the *means* by which persons can fulfill their purpose given that they have an essential nature. Some things contribute to flourishing, and others impede it, and we can know (to some extent) about these things. Natural law is law insofar as it is authored by a lawgiver and is meant to regulate behavior. Natural law *theory* is the attempt to describe the various components of natural law: where it comes from; what it says about the purpose of things; its precepts and goods and how we know them; its application; and its ramifications for political life. The irony is that this tradition of thinking, which posits the ability of human beings to successfully reason about human goods, is so often badly misunderstood.

Natural law does not wax or wane. This or that natural law theory's influence may increase or decrease in a culture, just as recognition of the truths of faith may increase or decrease.[38] Thus one could argue that natural law doesn't exist or it gets things wrong about the realities of human nature or the world, but it won't do to say that natural law is out

---

[38] For example, legal realism was quite in vogue prior to the Second World War, and natural law was found only in the confines of some Catholic institutions. After Nuremberg, however, natural law theory became more fashionable, as we see in the sixth edition of renowned legal realist jurist Jerome Frank, *Law and the Modern Mind* (1930; repr. New Brunswick, NJ: Transaction Publishers, 2009). There, Frank professes to be a natural law advocate in the mold of Thomas Aquinas.

of date. The natural lawyer believes that moral precepts do not go moldy with time, even if the prudential application of them may vary depending on changing cultural realities. If rape is wrong, the natural lawyer insists, then it is always wrong.

Natural law is also not a magical reasoning bullet. The modest epistemic claim of natural lawyers is that human beings *can* apprehend some measure of truth about themselves and the goods and practices and rules that will contribute to human flourishing (and the evils, vices, and atrocities that will frustrate the same). The claim is not and never has been that all people *will* see these truths or what follows from them. Some skeptics of natural law present evidence that people happen to reject this or that claim of natural law as if such data refute the claim itself. Such an argument would only work if natural lawyers claimed that natural law positions, even if universally binding, *will* find universal or unanimous acceptance. No natural lawyer has been so daft as to make this claim, even as they vary as to the different reasons people may reject various teachings of the natural law.

Indeed, there is no reason that a natural lawyer would disagree with Alasdair MacIntyre, who opened the second chapter of his *After Virtue* by describing three intractable arguments in our culture that stem from incommensurable premises. Natural law reasoning claims to shed some light on our understanding of first principles and what follows from them. But there is no guarantee that such an articulation will win over those committed to rival principles and rival conceptions of human nature. If people start from fundamentally different premises, you cannot argue to a common conclusion unless someone has something of a conversion with regard to those premises. This is not a weakness particular to natural law reasoning. There simply is no philosophical (or religious) tradition that would meet the standard required by the unanimity objection. This is why the criticism expressed by some well-meaning Christian natural law skeptics falls short. If natural law was valid, the reasoning runs, then we would not see the radical shift in mores witnessed in Western culture over the last few decades. Not only does this argument prove too much (as much explicit Christian teaching would be invalid as well), but it suggests the opposite conclusion.[39] Moreover, if natural law reasoning is correct, the ability to deny it *consistently* may prove limited, as this would require transcending one's creational context.

Even if we should have modest expectations for how persuasive natural law reasoning (about marriage, the economy, war, etc.) will be to those who begin from a different starting point, such conversations can still be fruitful in that we can better understand another's approach; we can clarify premises and raise questions about the implications, as we see them, implicit in the chain of reasoning behind a rival approach. It goes without saying we should be open to the same process with our own thinking.

As we begin, it is worth restating the core contention of this book: a Hopeful Realism approach to the natural law tradition provides guidance for evangelical political engagement that is desperately needed today. This is compatible with a liberal democratic order and can contribute in important ways to the flourishing of such an order. If we are correct, then Hopeful Realism can help evangelicals like us be more faithful to God and more loving to those around us.

---

[39] If the rejection of sexual complementarity as intrinsic to marriage by one or two generations in one part of the world counts as evidence against natural law, then the millennia of acceptance of the same by peoples all over the world weighs more heavily on the other side of the scale.

PART I

FOUNDATIONS

1

THE BIBLE AND POLITICS

"It must be nice, it must be nice to have Washington on your side." So goes the lyric sung by the actors portraying Thomas Jefferson and Aaron Burr in Lin-Manuel Miranda's phenomenon and hit musical *Hamilton*.[1] Jefferson and Burr are needling Alexander Hamilton for how much he relies on George Washington's prestige to win an argument. It's much easier to carry the day if you have an American icon backing you up.

Given how important Scripture is for evangelicals on any contested subject, including politics, it must be nice to have the Bible on your side. The dangers of such a sentiment are that we Christians can rely on the thin reed of proof-texting or we can be tempted to find in Scripture support for what we already want to be true. Abraham Lincoln was reportedly once asked if God was on his side. The story goes that his response was that he hoped that he was on God's side, because God is always right. There's something similar to be said about Scripture. We should want to be informed and directed by what God has revealed in his Word; we should be wary of shaping God's Word to serve our political ends. There are important connections between authoritative biblical teaching and our political witness, but drawing these connections well is as important as it is challenging.

So how should the Bible inform a Christian's approach to politics? Given two thousand years of disagreement about the uses and misuses

---

[1]Lin-Manuel Miranda, "Washington on Your Side," *Hamilton: An American Musical*. Atlantic Records, 2015, MP3.

of Scripture as applied to politics, we recognize this is fraught territory. We first describe our positive view of Scripture's place overall and then briefly offer four guidelines for how Scripture relates to politics. Because such matters are so easily misunderstood, before moving to the treatment of our chosen passages we draw some crucial distinctions and try to state clearly what we are *not* trying to do with Scripture.[2]

Scripture's Place and Three Critical Passages

We start with the conviction that Scripture is the highest authority God has given us to govern our conduct and belief.[3] We think of this commitment to a high view of Scripture as a cluster of claims. First, God speaks intelligibly through the Bible such that Christians individually and corporately can draw moral and political conclusions (among other things) from Scripture. Second, where Scripture speaks clearly it is the highest epistemic authority—though we recognize that the Bible does not address every political question nor provide unambiguous answers to every issue. As a result, and third, any approach to politics (or any other subject) that occludes the witness of Scripture, arbitrarily cordons off biblical truths from the public square, or undermines scriptural teaching contradicts Christian convictions. The positive corollary of this claim is that Scripture is the "norming norm," the standard to judge all other standards. While we recognize the human and cultural influences that went into the inspiration of Scripture (and which impact its interpretation), Scripture itself provides the measure by which the church, guided by the Holy Spirit, measures everything else.

Moving from Scripture's place generally to its application to the political realm, we rely on four ideas to inform our understanding of Scripture's role for political thinking.

---

[2]The subject of how to appropriately read and apply Scripture is in itself a project worthy of a book or several books. We proceed nevertheless because we think some of our underlying methodology will reveal itself through our applying it, and because of human finitude.
[3]See the Belgic Confession, Articles 5 and 7, and the Lausanne Covenant, Article 2.

The Bible and Politics

1. First, drawing from the Protestant Reformers and their antecedents, who themselves drew from Scripture, all Christians are capable and indeed encouraged to learn the Scriptures for themselves. (A corollary of the perspicuity and authority of Scripture is the use of Scripture to interpret itself, including using the New Testament to interpret the Old.[4])

2. Second, the teachings of the church fathers and mothers, and tradition generally, complement our understanding of the Scriptures as an important and invaluable supplement, even as they are not ultimately authoritative.[5]

3. Third, we commend Augustine's teaching about how to approach and prioritize grappling with Scripture: with humility; with the clearer teachings prioritized first and the obscure passages later; with a hermeneutic of love guiding the interpreter; and also with a recognition that pagan wisdom can be put to Christian use to understand things.[6]

4. Fourth and finally, we acknowledge that Scripture does not address every topic, and this is particularly true about politics. While we think that the legitimacy of taxes follows from Scripture's teaching,

---

[4]This leads us to a Christocentric reading of the Old Testament, following Luke 24:27, where the risen Christ teaches the disciples on the road to Emmaus: "And beginning with Moses and all the Prophets, he explained to them what was said in all the Scriptures concerning himself."

[5]We admire John Calvin's treatment of this balance in his introductory letter to King Francis I of France, in which he responds to the charge that he and his followers oppose the church fathers:

> Still, in studying their writings, we have endeavored to remember (1 Cor. 3:21-23; see also Augustin Ep. 28), that all things are ours, to serve, not lord it over us, but that we are Christ's only, and must obey him in all things without exception. He who does not draw this distinction will not have any fixed principles in religion; for these holy men were ignorant of many things, are often opposed to each other, and are sometimes at variance with themselves.

John Calvin, *Institutes of the Christian Religion*, trans. Beveridge (Grand Rapids, MI: Eerdmans, 1993), Prefatory Letter, 10.

[6]Augustine describes a hermeneutic of love thus: "So anyone who thinks that he has understood the divine scriptures or any part of them, but cannot by his understanding build up this double love of God and neighbour, has not yet succeeded in understanding them." Augustine, *On Christian Teaching*, trans. R. P. H. Green (New York: Oxford University Press, 1999), 27. See also p. 80. Likewise, Augustine describes the value of pagan learning with the analogy of Israelites plundering Egyptians' gold when embarking on the Exodus—it should be "claimed for our own use" (64-67). See also Augustine, *Confessions*, trans. O. Chadwick (New York: Oxford University Press, 1991), 121-23.

we don't think Scripture teaches what the tax rate should be, nor whether a graduated income tax is an efficient or fair means of raising revenue.

Given what we've written above it's clear we disagree with those who claim that the Bible either does not speak to our political realities or that Christians cannot draw any conclusions from Scripture about human goods. But we also disagree with the position that the Bible, or the institutional church, offers a comprehensive blueprint or an instruction manual for grounding and exercising political authority. That sort of approach lends itself to a mild or strong version of church establishment or even theocracy, which we judge unsupported by Scripture and historically disastrous on both theological and political criteria.

We also distinguish between scriptural teaching for the people of God as the church proper, and what Scripture teaches about *creational* goods that can be pursued, promoted, and protected in the public square for all people. While we think natural law is a part of the latter category, teasing these matters out is no simple affair, which helps explain why Christians of goodwill have disagreed so often in years past and will no doubt continue to do so. For example, you can clearly derive from Scripture the norm against stealing while simultaneously believing that (1) you can know stealing is wrong *without* deriving that from Scripture, and (2) the norm applies to Christians and non-Christians alike. Contrast stealing with the moral duty to honor the Sabbath by attending worship. You can make a strong case for this norm from Scripture, but unlike stealing, it is a much harder case to make that worshipful Sabbath-observance is discernible via unaided reason. Thus, non-Christians should not be held accountable, morally or legally, for failing to keep the Sabbath by attending worship. Throughout this book we will refer to Christian-specific goods and norms as "redemptive" and use "creational" to refer to common human goods and norms (like property or education).[7] There is much more to be said

---

[7]Significantly, this language could confuse some, particularly those in the Reformed or neo-Kuyperian parts of evangelicalism, as here the restoration of creational goods (what we're calling creational) is sometimes called *redemptive*. While the restoration of creation is certainly part of

about these distinctions, and it is worth noting that we take a minimalist approach—focusing on a limited set of passages—in order to draw essentials to the foreground rather than answer every question. Hopefully these introductory remarks clear enough ground for us to proceed for now with the following passages in Genesis, Matthew, and Romans.

Scriptural Grounds

Scripture is replete with examples that inform our thinking about the importance of both redemptive and creational goods. This section offers a reading of three key passages to ground an understanding of politics and human flourishing: Genesis 1–4, Matthew 22:15-22, and Romans 13:1-7. There are of course other important passages for Scripture, but these passages address foundational questions at the heart of an evangelical natural law rooted in Scripture. In Genesis, what do the creation accounts tell us about how God authored our human nature and how the Fall has changed things? In Matthew 22, what does a famous confrontation between Jesus and the Pharisees tell us about the claims of Caesar and the claims of God? And in Romans 13, how does this crucial political passage from the apostle Paul build on the insights of Genesis and Matthew to situate our earthly and heavenly citizenships today in pluralistic and democratic societies?

Genesis 1–4: "In the beginning God created the heavens and the earth . . ." We sometimes move too quickly past the first four words of the first verse to get at what God is doing, and by doing so we can miss a prior declaration about the simple fact that "In the beginning God . . ." The beginning of Christian thinking about any discourse or subject—including politics—begins with God, and who God is, and then moves to what God is doing. In these opening four words we learn something about God's standing. Before all things, before history begins, God *is*. He is foundational. It should not surprise us that later he reveals himself to Moses as "I am."

God's redemptive work, our use of the term *redemptive* here focuses on the particular norms that are unique to a saving covenantal relationship with God.

When the God-Who-Is *acts*, we quickly see why professors and scholars have an affinity for the opening chapters of Genesis and all the defining and categorizing that takes place there. The Hebrew Scriptures begin with a series of definitions and categorizations, separations and distinctions. This light is distinct from that light, this body of water from that, this land will go thus far and no farther, these plants bear this seed, and these animals are of this but not that type. This first account of creation is crowned with the creation of human beings made in God's image, male and female; they are tasked with oversight and stewardship of God's creation and told to be fruitful and multiply. This account closes with God's benediction, God's blessing of all of this as "very good."[8] It is telling, on this account, that both male and female together reflect or somehow are God's image, and that their first task is to "be fruitful" and in so doing creatively partner with God to bring into being other creatures made in God's image. It is also significant that God simultaneously creates a *particular* type of being who bears God's image and declares that the *entirety* of the creation is very good. The special status of the human is not, at least at this point, in tension with the goodness of the creation.

The second creation account beginning in Genesis 2 describes a different "first task" given to Adam.[9] Though much has rightly been made of the priestly role assigned to Adam through his taking care of the garden, here we focus on Adam's second task. In this creation account God charges Adam to name the animals. In chapter one the male and the female, like other creatures, are to be fruitful and multiply. In chapter two we see Adam following God's practice of categorization and labeling from Genesis 1. God brings before Adam the natural realities that God has created and tasks Adam with naming those realities through the power of the spoken word.

---

[8]And thus we should anticipate the redemption of more than just individuals made in God's image, but the cosmos (Romans 8:22).

[9]For the interpretation of this task in terms of Adam's (and Eve's) priestly role, see John H. Walton, *The Lost World of Adam and Eve: Genesis 2–3 and the Human Origins Debate* (Downers Grove, IL: InterVarsity Press, 2015), 104-15. We don't claim Walton would agree with how we understand God's negative pronouncement on Adam's aloneness.

Significantly, at creation, God assigns humans the task of filling the earth, subduing it, and ruling over it—what many have referred to as the creation mandate or the cultural mandate. God charges humans with the task of imitating God in developing and ordering creation—building culture. The construction of culture involves using human reason, creativity, and agency to unlock the latent potentialities of the created order. The story of redemption begins with a garden and culminates with a garden-city—the new Jerusalem—signaling the *development* rather than the repristinization of creation.[10] Faithful humanity will rightly rule— "exercising dominion"—over creation.

What follows is rather surprising. Before the verses that describe the Fall, God declares that something is "not good." The first problem in Scripture is not Adam and Eve's disobedience but Adam's aloneness. It is "not good for man to be alone." God, the author of human nature, tells us that human beings are meant to live in community. Humanity is created male and female in God's image in Genesis 1, and Adam's aloneness (though not yet alienation) is a problem in Genesis 2. We are made to live in community. God's immediate response to the problem of chapter two is the creation of the woman, who acts not only as the man's helper,[11] but with the man comes together to create one flesh. This pairing bears an analogical relation to the Trinity insofar as God's triune nature cannot be completely captured by the Father, Son, or Spirit alone, and humanity in turn needs more than just the man or just the woman alone.[12]

Chapter three moves us from Adam's aloneness and its solution to Adam and Eve's alienation, both from God and from each other. While we cannot look back from this side of the curse to understand exactly how a disordered decision could be made before our natures became

---

[10] See Albert M. Wolters, *Creation Regained: Biblical Basics for a Reformational Worldview* (Grand Rapids, MI: Eerdmans, 1985).

[11] The Hebrew for "helper," *ezer*, should not necessarily be understood here as subordinate, as the same word is used to refer to God helping Israel elsewhere in the OT (1 Samuel 7:12).

[12] We can't treat this suggestion with any depth here, but the juxtaposition of the one and the many seems at work in the very nature of God and those who bear (or are) his image. How many of our perennial political problems stem from post-Fall contested visions as to the tensions between the good of the individual and the community?

disordered, we surely recognize the blame-shifting excuses that immediately follow, and the shame felt by Adam and Eve in their first awareness of their nakedness. No longer will God walk with them in the cool of the day, and with the declaration of the curse and expulsion from the garden we are given only a hint of what that loss of relationship between God and humans must have been for those who knew untainted fellowship with God. Yet even in the description of difficult childbirth, painful toil, and dust returning to dust, we see the first proclamation of the gospel in the "protoevangelium" of Genesis 3:15. Yes, the serpent will strike the heel of the woman's offspring, the son of man, but that same son will someday crush the serpent's head.

If the expulsion underlines the reality of rupturing the "vertical" relationship between God and man, Cain's murder of Abel in chapter four shockingly drives home the "horizontal" consequences as well.[13] Abel's blood cries out from the ground, and Cain's subsequent conversation with God and founding of the first city tell us something important about creational moral norms.[14] God's redemptive plan is perhaps also foreshadowed here in that while the first murderer founds the first city, God's people will someday inhabit not a renewed garden but the new Jerusalem, a city founded on a different sort of blood than that shed by Cain.

At this point the reader may be forgiven for wondering what any of this might have to do with a Christian approach to politics. In Genesis we find foundational truths about the *world* and *human nature* that prove

---

[13]It is not coincidental that the greatest commandments directly correlate with the bidirectional nature of our alienation. Love the Lord your God with all your heart, soul, and strength (vertical), and love your neighbor as yourself (horizontal).

[14]It is interesting that Cain cries out to God that anywhere he goes his life will be in danger, which has been interpreted by several Christian luminaries as indicative of humanity's moral knowledge of the wrongness of murder. Consider Calvin in his commentary on the book of Genesis:

> Cain, however, in this place, not only considers himself as deprived of God's protection, but also supposes all creatures to be divinely armed to take vengeance of his impious murder. This is the reason why he so greatly fears for his life from any one who may meet him; for as man is a social animal, and all *naturally* desire mutual intercourse, this is certainly to be regarded as a portentous fact, that the meeting with any man was formidable to the murderer.

John Calvin, *Commentary on the Book of Genesis*, vol. 1, trans. John King (Grand Rapids, MI: Baker Books, 1948), 213. Emphasis added.

foundational for political theory. Human identity and worth are bound up with God and God's purposes. In the beginning, God was, and in God's image he created them, male and female. While all of creation has value, there is something special about human beings. Christians thus have good reason to affirm human dignity. Moreover, God has created human beings to live in community. Nevertheless, because our first parents rebelled against God's good providence for them and we are complicit in continuing that rebellion, we do not live well together. We fight, we bicker, we envy, we kill. By our very God-given nature we are social creatures meant to love and live together—developing culture in society as we fulfill the creation mandate. But by our very sinful nature we sabotage love and community by seeking to dominate our fellow image-bearers (Deuteronomy 30:19). We have distorted our *imago Dei* and fractured the divine relationship with God and horizontal human relationships with each other.

We need each other. We cannot live peaceably with each other. And yet in the protoevangelium we get a first glimpse at God's ultimate plan for reconciling his rebellious children to himself and to each other. Only through the redemptive work of Jesus Christ on the cross will the serpent's head be crushed and the curse finally undone.[15] In the meantime, life will be marked by pain, toil, conflict, and death, though mingled with joy, love, music, and laughter. Attempts to overcome the curse entirely by our own efforts will fail, as a later passage in Genesis (Genesis 11:1-9) will illustrate through the quixotic Tower of Babel project. Finally, we draw from the Genesis account the idea that while God's ultimate plan for reconciliation is the cross, creational life in the body does not go on "pause." Rather, politics, law, and culture have a preserving and developing role to play until the eschaton arrives and Christ returns. For better or for worse, the Hebrew Scriptures undeniably speak to the political, and God's covenants seem to perform more than one purpose in not only preparing for the Messiah but also promoting and preserving an earthly and limited but nevertheless valuable political existence. The law cannot

---

[15] See note above regarding Luke 24:27 concerning a Christocentric reading of the Old Testament.

bear the salvific burden that some of God's people mistakenly attributed to it but choosing even an earthly life meant choosing to live by God's law (Deuteronomy 30:19).

We draw from Genesis, then, several insights relevant for Christian thinking about both the political realm and the natural law:

1. God has created human nature and set it apart as something special, made in God's image.
2. The rest of creation is also valuable, and God calls human beings as his image-bearers to preserve and creatively develop it.[16]
3. We are persons made to live in community. It is not good for man or woman to live alone.
4. We are fallen sinners and don't live well together.
5. God's ultimate plan to reconcile us to him and to each other is accomplished through the work of Jesus on the cross and fulfilled at his return.
6. In the meantime, as we will see confirmed in the passages to come, earthly politics is a God-ordained means of restraining evil and promoting creational goods.

In our next passage we will see these lessons further developed by the very Son of Man anticipated by the protoevangelium in Genesis.

Matthew 22:15-21: "Give back to Caesar what is Caesar's, and to God what is God's." In this passage, a group of overly ambitious Pharisees attempt to put Jesus in a tough spot by asking him an explicitly political question. After some passive-aggressive flattery, the Pharisees ask Jesus whether it is right to pay taxes to Caesar. This was not just a wonky question about good public policy. Israel was under the boot of a harsh Roman foreign occupation, and there was a range of Jewish responses to this—from nationalist zealots who violently resisted the occupation to collaborating tax collectors whose job it was to support their oppressors at the expense of their fellow Jews. We do well to keep in mind that both

---

[16]See Andy Crouch, *Culture Making: Recovering Our Creative Calling*, expanded ed. (Downers Grove, IL: InterVarsity Press, 2023).

zealots and tax collectors numbered among Jesus' own disciples. If Jesus answers that it is right to pay taxes to Caesar, then he will infuriate and alienate those who strongly resent the Roman presence in Israel. If he denies the legitimacy of paying taxes to Caesar, he crosses not only the Romans but their Jewish collaborators as well. He gives his enemies ammunition to interfere with his ministry, and while Jesus was hardly one to fear confrontation, he did consider the timing and circumstances of when he would cause a ruckus.[17] So not for the first time or the last, a religious leader is put in a tough spot by a political question. He is in trouble if he says yes, and he is in trouble if he says no.

Our familiarity with Jesus' famous answer threatens to dull its brilliance. After asking them to show him a coin,[18] Jesus asks whose image is on the coin. "Caesar's," they respond, and Jesus performs a proverbial mic drop in instructing them to "Give back to Caesar what is Caesar's, and to God what is God's" (Matthew 22:21). Matthew tells us they were amazed and went away.

As clever as the trap was, Jesus' response was remarkably wise. In asking for a denarius, Jesus gets to the heart of the matter of politics and authority, as coinage was then and remains now a marker of political sovereignty. There is a reason Roman emperors fashioned their coins complete with their own pictures and had these coins put into circulation. Modern American currency also bears the images of our political heroes, and defacing money is a crime still policed by the Secret Service.[19] As Augustine's teacher Ambrose of Milan said, Jesus' Jewish audience would not have missed the deeper meanings of his response.[20]

---

[17]Think of all the times when Jesus says "My time has not yet come . . ."
[18]Not surprisingly, Jesus had no money on him, it seems.
[19]Destroying legal tender violates Title 18, Section 333 of the United States Code, which says that
  whoever mutilates, cuts, disfigures, perforates, unites or cements together, or does any other thing to any bank bill, draft, note, or other evidence of debt issued by any national banking association, Federal Reserve Bank, or Federal Reserve System, with intent to render such item(s) unfit to be reissued, shall be fined not more than $100 or imprisoned not more than six months, or both.
  The law is policed by the Secret Service.
[20]Ambrose of Milan, "Sermon Against Auxentius," in *From Irenaeus to Grotius: A Sourcebook in Christian Political Thought*, ed. Oliver O'Donovan and Joan Lockwood O'Donovan (Grand Rapids, MI: Eerdmans Publishing, 1999), 74.

The first takeaway is the obvious one. Caesar's image is on the coin, representing Caesar's authority in the political system that provides, however rough by our modern standards, public goods, services, justice, and stability. Caesar has some sort of claim on the resources with which the government maintains a system of law and order. In other words, government holds legitimate authority and rightly places certain obligations on those under its care. As we have already intimated, government is a part of God's plan to preserve the good and restrain evil until this present age is concluded and history ends. Jesus here indicates the legitimacy of government, and of paying taxes, something he confirms in another passage in which he could but does not claim an exemption from the temple tax as the son of God (Matthew 17:24-26).

The conclusion that government as such has a legitimate role to play would not strike Jesus' fellow Jews as remarkable in any way. Much of the Old Testament presupposes this truth. When prophets challenge political leaders in the Hebrew Scriptures, it is because they are ruling unjustly, not that they are ruling at all. That Jesus' interlocutors can produce Roman coinage tells us they have accepted some degree of Roman rule just by being implicated in the use of the oppressors' economic system. Jesus' acknowledgment of government authority in principle, then, may not have been surprising, even if his nod to Caesar and the particular Roman government was. Nevertheless, there's another more subtle lesson to be drawn from this famous interaction.

If the first half of Jesus' answer tells us something about earthly government and Caesar's authority, what about the second half? "Give back to Caesar what is Caesar's" seems straightforward enough, but what about "give to God what is God's?" On first read this might strike us as paradoxical. Doesn't everything belong to God (see Psalm 24:1)? What can possibly be given to God that he doesn't already have? In one sense this is true. But might some things belong to God in a particular, special way?

We think so. Just as God declared that all of creation was very good but also set apart human beings as relating to him in a special way, so we can say that all of creation belongs to God but that human beings belong to God in a particular way. Note the parallel Jesus draws here between what belongs to Caesar and what belongs to God. We can identify Caesar's legitimate claim to tax the people's property by his image seen in the coins. So it is with giving to God what is his. What—or rather, *who*—bears God's image? Jesus' Jewish audience would see his allusion to the Genesis narrative that we discussed above. Men and women bear God's image, and thus all human beings belong to God in a special way. Caesar has a legitimate claim on the money that bears his image; God has a special claim on us as we bear his image.

We believe this adds a powerful corollary to the relatively straightforward teaching that the institution of government is legitimate: *the scope of legitimate governmental authority is limited*. The government can act on its claim to tax some of our goods, but it cannot act as if human beings belong wholly to governments. Jesus' stark distinction between what is due to God and to Caesar punctuates this point, challenging the divine lineage attributed to Caesar in the denarius's inscription.[21] Human beings are subject to a higher authority, we belong to him in whose image we are made, and thus when governments mistreat human beings they interfere with a power beyond their authority and their reckoning. And someday they will be held to account for it. All earthly governments are rightly understood as *relative to and secondary to God's divine governance*.

We understand Jesus in this passage to be building on the truths of the early chapters in Genesis. First, government has a legitimate role to play in our lives, and some political conclusions seem to follow from this (e.g., taxes might be too high, but taxation isn't intrinsically wicked; anarchism is incompatible with Christian teaching). Second, governmental claims on human beings are limited as we belong to God. We might add a third claim here, that governments exist for human beings rather than human beings existing for the purposes of governments. But the relationship between God, governments, and human beings is a thorny one, and we

---

[21] The Roman denarius bore the inscription: "Tiberius Caesar, son of the divine Augustus." See www.bibleref.com/Matthew/22/Matthew-22-20.html. Accessed May 14, 2024. Thanks are due to David Vander Laan for the reminder of this additional context.

need what is perhaps the most famous biblical passage on politics to develop our treatment of it more fully.

Romans 13:1-7: "For the one in authority is God's servant for your good." If government has no authority over us, then we need not worry about our duties toward political officials. The same thing follows if government is our ultimate authority, as posited by totalitarian regimes. But if government can have some legitimate authority underneath the ultimate authority of God, then we are faced with the thorny task of determining at what point our loyalty to our earthly authorities must give way to God's ultimate authority over us as image-bearers. The well-known encounter between the authorities and the apostles that culminates in Acts 5:29 demonstrates that God's authority ultimately trumps human authority.[22] However, the opening seven verses in Romans 13 make a strong corresponding case for the God-ordained authority of magistrates, described by Paul as "God's servants" or "God's ministers" no less than three times in this passage.

We won't pretend to offer a comprehensive treatment of all the different ways this passage has been interpreted, as this has been hotly contested ground for Christian thinkers for quite some time. Nevertheless, because we think Scripture is God-breathed and remains authoritative for believers today, we can draw some lessons from Paul's robust endorsement of the governing authorities, who have been established by God.

First, this passage echoes Jesus' teaching that Caesar has a legitimate role. Paul expands on this by pointing out that with this ruling authority comes our obligation to "be subject to" the government. As already noted, this is not an absolute obligation, but it is nevertheless a strong one and for several reasons. God has established these authorities, and it is their role to act as "God's servant for our good," and this includes

---

[22]"We must obey God rather than human beings!" It's true that this refusal is made to the Sanhedrin, which was a religious authority, but we must remember that the distinction between religious and political authorities was not as clear as our modern arrangements. The Sanhedrin had a version of a police force and the power to arrest and imprison the apostles.

acting as "agents of wrath to bring punishment on the wrongdoer." It follows then that our motivation to obey stems not only from our recognition of God's delegated authority but also from our very natural fear of being punished for doing wrong. Paul explains that we pay taxes because the magistrates govern full-time, which implies Paul views the task as so important that those carrying it out should not be distracted by other means of making a living. Finally, Paul goes beyond the monetary and encourages us to pay honor and respect, if they are owed.

Notable Christian thinkers have understood Paul's teaching differently. Luther and Calvin, for example, interpret Paul to mean that ordinary Christians subject to a vile tyrant can pray for relief and disobey orders to betray the faith, but cannot take up arms to overthrow the "magistrates" whom God has appointed.[23] Other Christians later interpreted the passage in another way, arguing that Paul defines the magistrates who act as God's servants by affirming what is right and punishing what is wrong. If there are tyrants in power who invert this formula by affirming wrong or punishing right, the reasoning follows, then one plausible interpretation is that they are not the magistrates Paul has in mind to whom we categorically owe taxes, respect, and honor.

We don't need to settle this debate to glean that the government's mandate from God involves upholding justice, serving with authority for our good, and punishing evil. Notably, the fact that Paul is writing to Christians living under a pagan regime suggests that the categories of good and evil here are creational more than redemptive; that is, even non-Christians will at least in part understand and operate within shared moral frameworks with Christians.

This passage also reinforces what Jesus affirmed in Matthew: government places legitimate claims on those under its care, including (in principle) taxes that Christians should pay. We also think this passage's

---

[23]Calvin hints at an idea that his successors would develop, namely that lower magistrates might resist tyrannical rule by virtue of their own public authority. See *Institutes*, bk. IV, chap. XX, especially secs. 22-32, 668-76. Martin Luther, "On Secular Authority," in *Luther and Calvin on Secular Authority*, ed. Harro Höpfl (New York: Cambridge University Press, 1991), 39.

mentioning of the sword is not, contra some of our pacifist brothers and sisters, merely metaphorical. Rather, Paul's teaching in Romans maintains continuity with the Old Testament assumption that governments must at times employ coercion to provide justice and stability through restraining evil. The idea of what Luther calls "office"—the unique, divinely appointed authority for justified power given to rulers—arises from Paul's distinction between individual, private vengeance (prohibited in Romans 12) and God-ordained use of just force by rulers in Romans 13.

Another wrinkle emerges from this passage when we apply it to our contemporary context. While many and perhaps most Christians reading this passage have lived in political regimes such that the magistrate or political sovereign was an external figure, Christians living in constitutional democracies or republics relate differently to those governing authorities. Whereas Luther and Calvin would understandably see the magistrates as perched at the top of the governing pyramid of sorts, and thus conclude that opposition to kings and queens is paramount to opposing that which God has instituted, we Christians in Western-style democracies find ourselves differently situated.

For when American Christians in particular consult their own founding political documents, we discover the political sovereign is "We the People," indicating not so much a top-down approach but rather a recognition that elected political officials act as "public servants" to further the common good, authorized by the delegation of power derived from the consent of the governed. Thus, the political authorities are not "out there," external to us, but rather we make up part of the grounding political sovereignty that then empowers those public officials at the local, state, and federal level. All citizens exercise political authority.

Christians should draw three crucial lessons from Romans 13 when applied to the contemporary American political context.[24] First, we are called to *yield* to political authority. That is to say, following the above

---

[24] Which is not to say these are the only lessons to draw from this passage.

reading of Matthew 22 and other passages in Scripture, political authorities have a limited but legitimate claim on our obedience and support (see also 1 Peter 2:13-17, Titus 3:1). We obey peace officers, pay our taxes, and honor our elected leaders not only because we fear the costs of not doing so, but because honor and taxes and respect are due to them, and our consciences testify that this is the case.[25]

Second, we are called to *wield* that same political authority. When we consult our particular political context, we find that as citizens of a constitutional democracy in which authority derives from "We the People," we are part of the human sovereignty that gives our political institutions their legitimacy. This "wielding" of political authority will look different for different people. Not everyone will run for office or serve as a judge. But even the most ordinary citizens in our political system can act in their official capacity in voting, serving on juries, paying taxes, and petitioning the government. In democratic systems, we the people simultaneously govern and are governed; we yield to government authority while we also wield political power. This means that we must all attend carefully to Paul's instructions to *rulers*, not just his instructions to those under the authority of rulers.

Finally, not only does Paul's teaching instruct us to yield to political authority, and in our case engage in modest ways to wield that authority, but by extension we recognize that in the plurality of our pre-eschaton society, citizens *share* that authority with neighbors who do not necessarily share moral convictions nor the underlying worldviews that give rise to those convictions.[26] Nothing in Paul's writings indicates he assumed Christians would be living in a predominantly God-fearing or Christian culture, and it is interesting that Nero was the Roman emperor when Paul penned the epistle to the Romans. If the above reading of this passage is sound, we are left with a fascinating, puzzling, and divine calling: how to live well as Christians in a pluralistic society in which

---

[25]This is not to say that such legitimate powers cannot be abused.
[26]For those who may not be persuaded that authority is shared, chap. 3 engages the question of plurality and its normative implications at significantly greater length.

God calls us to *yield* to political authority, *wield* political authority, and *share* that authority.

Conclusion

Given that the New Testament does not include a blueprint for politics, Christians of every generation have had to navigate these challenges, and our generation is no exception. Paul presupposes that his audience in Romans will understand what it means and why it is important for governments to commend and promote the good, punish evil, use coercion as a means, and receive the support necessary (taxes, honor, respect) to fulfill this calling. Moreover, these purposes for government in the service of human flourishing are universally intelligible. One does not have to be a Christian to understand and affirm government's dual role in promoting the good and punishing evil. God has not been stingy with the resources he has given us to fulfill this calling, and the natural law is part of his good provision for our and our neighbors' flourishing.

Yet Christians understandably will want to know how to understand the relationship between the biblical framework we claim as our foundation and the natural law approach we think contributes to applying sound norms and principles to real-life political and moral issues in our current context. We move to consider that very relationship in the next chapter, describing the witness of Scripture and the Christian tradition to the reality of the natural law.

2

HOPEFUL REALISM

An Evangelical Theory of the Natural Law

Hopeful Realism is an evangelical theory of the natural law.[1] It draws on the central biblical claims of Christian political thought articulated in chapter one to show how Scripture teaches that we are bound to the moral law and our flourishing depends on securing goods appropriate to our created nature. In that sense, Hopeful Realism stands well within the tradition of Christian natural law and shares with that tradition any number of theological, moral, and practical conclusions. Hopeful Realism is distinct in its relative emphasis on Scripture and its understanding of the importance of sin and the role of earthly politics, among other things.

We hope that this reasonably quick sketch of our theory shows both how Hopeful Realism stands well within the tradition of Christian political theology more broadly *and* bears the distinctive commitments and emphases that makes it recognizably evangelical. Following the magisterial Reformers, we find Saint Augustine of Hippo to be a particularly faithful and helpful guide. His attention to Scripture and understanding of the natural law in the context of creation, sin, and redemptive history offer a touchstone for the argument that follows.

---

[1] We gratefully acknowledge that in this chapter we draw on arguments and language initially developed in other contexts: Jesse Covington, "Augustine's Aspirational Imperfectionism: What We Should Hope for from Politics," *Public Justice Review* VII, no. 4 (2018); and Jesse Covington, Bryan McGraw, and Micah Watson, "Hopeful Realism: Renewing Evangelical Political Morality," *Public Discourse*, 2022.

Upon receiving a smaller helping of dessert compared to her sibling, a child wails, "That's not fair!" Watching a news story recounting the horrors suffered by kidnapped and enslaved Yazidis, we all are horrified by the terrible wrongs being inflicted on them. We are angry and indignant when we hear stories of severe child abuse: how could they do this? Our experiences of human life reveal that we know moral standards to be real and that they should govern our conduct, even as we observe so many stark departures from them. While construed differently according to cultural context (and other factors), moral goods like fairness, honesty, and respect for others' persons and property are valued across human societies, even as they are imperfectly observed. Thinkers have long suggested that these kinds of intuitions point us to the idea of natural law, but what exactly does that mean?

In the Christian intellectual tradition, the natural law has for centuries described a set of *stable, morally obliging norms for human action, grounded in a common human nature*. The basic idea is that we have a nature *oriented to the particular ends that are proper to us as human beings* such that we are obliged to pursue those ends and avoid what works against them. If we want to live well as human beings, there are certain things we should do and certain things we should not do. Not only is the moral guidance provided by natural law *obligatory for all* humans, it is also to some degree *accessible to all* humans. There are certain actions that all people ought to do and others that they ought not do—obligations that all people can at least partially understand, even if they come from different perspectives, commitments, cultures, and so on. In its traditional articulation, we know natural law primarily through *reason* and *conscience* (a view we will complicate a bit below). Examples of what we should know include (among many other things) the fairness required by equal human dignity, the obligation to preserve innocent human life and health, the importance of volition, association, learning—the very underpinnings to the examples of unfair dessert allocations, human rights violations, abuse, and much more.[2]

---

[2]For example, see J. Budziszewski, *Written on the Heart: The Case for Natural Law* (Downers Grove, IL: InterVarsity Press, 1997); Russ Hittinger, *The First Grace: Rediscovering the Natural Law in a Post-Christian World* (Wilmington, DE: ISI Books, 2007).

EVANGELICALISM AND NATURAL LAW

Among Christians, natural law most explicitly plays a central role in Catholic Social Teaching (CST), which emphasizes natural law's small "c" catholicity and commonality for all people. As Clark Cochran has put it,

> CST traditionally stressed the universality and rational accessibility of its principles.... The ideas of CST are neither exclusively Catholic nor applicable primarily to Catholic persons or Catholic nations. Rather, they are principles of human reason that orient the governance structures and the public purposes of any political system.[3]

Lisa Sowle Cahill similarly notes that the Catholic natural law tradition holds that "all people in principle can discern the basic requirements of justice" (providing the basis of the common good) even apart from Christian faith or special revelation.[4]

Thus described, natural law has long been central to Christian social and political ethics. It is grounded in the general revelation of creation and focuses on humans *as human*, rather than the recipients of the special revelation of Scripture or members of a believing community. As such, it offers guidance accessible and obligatory to all—not just co-religionists. This is vitally important for social and political ethics, as it provides a meaningful way to differentiate between obligations specific to the church and those common to all.

Without such distinctions, we run significant risks. On the one hand, believers may be tempted by some versions of Christian nationalism—up to and including integralism and theonomy—where what's right for the religious community isn't meaningfully differentiated from what's right for the political community.[5] Without such differentiation, the power of

---

[3] Clarke Cochran, "Life on the Border: A Catholic Perspective," in *Church, State and Public Justice: Five Views*, ed. Paul Kemeny (Downers Grove, IL: InterVarsity Press, 2007), 47-48.
[4] Lisa Sowle Cahill, "Catholic Social Teaching," in *The Cambridge Companion to Christian Political Theology*, ed. Craig Hovey and Elizabeth Phillips (New York: Cambridge University Press, 2015), 69.
[5] See Adrian Vermeule, "Integration from Within," *American Affairs Journal* II, no. 1 (Spring 2018): 202-13, (blog), February 20, 2018, https://americanaffairsjournal.org/2018/02/integration-from-within/; Rousas John Rushdoony, *The Institutes of Biblical Law*, vol. 1 (1973; repr. Vallecito: Ross House Books, 2020). To be clear, this is an approach we reject.

the state could compel compliance with the norms of a particular church. Imagine compulsory infant baptism or mandatory tithes, for example. On the other hand, drawing the distinction too sharply may suggest reserving all ethics for the Christian community alone, leaving politics only the will to power. Imagine a politics inhabiting a kind of moral vacuum, guided only by the unsteady judgment of the momentary majority (or something else). Both of these positions are in error, and Hopeful Realism instead seeks to ground social and political ethics in natural law.

Protestant social thought long relied on the natural law tradition for its social and political thought.[6] However, twentieth-century evangelicals became largely alienated from the tradition. Some of this likely reflected a degree of anti-Catholic sentiment, and there were also a number of specific theological disagreements, most importantly around the themes of commonality and accessibility. Evangelicals insisted on: "1) sin's damaging effects on natural human capacities, and 2) the necessity of special revelation through scripture,"[7] both of which suggested to evangelicals that the natural law tradition was theologically suspect. While many Protestant scholars (including a number of evangelicals) have argued this rejection is overblown and erroneous, evangelical natural law revivalism remains in its infancy.

As we have argued elsewhere, *evangelicals* can be characterized as "Protestant Christians who emphasize the unique authority of the Bible, the centrality of Christ to salvation, and the active response of the believer."[8] These distinctives highlight themes of *antithesis*—the difference or distance between Christians and non-Christians. The unique

---

[6] For some helpful historical accounts, see S. J. Grabill, *Rediscovering the Natural Law in Reformed Theological Ethics* (Grand Rapids, MI: Eerdmans, 2006); J. Daryl Charles, *Retrieving the Natural Law: A Return to Moral First Things* (Grand Rapids, MI: Eerdmans, 2008); David VanDrunen, *Natural Law and the Two Kingdoms: A Study in the Development of Reformed Social Thought* (Grand Rapids, MI: Eerdmans, 2010).

[7] Jesse Covington, "The Grammar of Virtue: St. Augustine and Natural Law," in *Natural Law and Evangelical Political Thought*, ed. Jesse Covington, Bryan T. McGraw, and Micah Joel Watson (Lanham, MD: Lexington Books, 2013), 167-94.

[8] Jesse Covington, Bryan T. McGraw, and Micah Joel Watson, "Introduction," in *Natural Law and Evangelical Political Thought*, ed. Jesse Covington, Bryan T. McGraw, and Micah Joel Watson (Lanham, MD: Lexington Books, 2013), ix-x.

authority of the Bible reflects antithesis between special revelation and general revelation: not only does special revelation in Scripture illuminate *beyond* general revelation (it tells us more), it *corrects* perceptions of natural revelation and speaks with greater authority than general revelation. Likewise, the centrality of Christ to salvation highlights human need apart from Christ and the gulf between human needs and human capacities based on our own resources: we all need Christ's atonement and empowerment and cannot resolve our deepest problems on our own power. Indeed, the depth of our need for salvation in Christ highlights the profound effects of the Fall: falling into sin carries with it a sweeping impact on human experience and capacities, including our rational and moral abilities. The upshot is that the distinctions of antithesis extend far beyond "mere" questions of salvation narrowly construed, impacting our assumptions, epistemology, and ability to live rightly—both individually and corporately. Antithesis highlights the stark and striking difference that God's gracious intervention in Christ makes for every part of life, the capacity to know and act rightly being just one aspect.[9]

Our effort to articulate a distinctively evangelical approach to natural law—what we call Hopeful Realism—attempts to account for this antithesis. We focus on how Scripture speaks both to the reality of natural law directly and how it informs other theological commitments as well. Of particular importance is our attention to the ways natural law helps us mediate a range of eschatological tensions in which some redemptive goods are realized in the here and now while others await realization in the new creation. Almost every Christian struggles to figure out what they might hope to achieve—politically and otherwise—in this age and what awaits the age to come. Our theory of the natural law does not by any means solve every question, but it can help.

We find Saint Augustine of Hippo particularly apt as a guide in this. Augustine consistently displays a deep commitment to the authority and necessity of Scripture. The Scriptures, he writes, "are the writings of

---

[9]Covington, "Grammar of Virtue," 167.

outstanding authority in which we put our trust concerning those things which we need to know for our good, and yet are incapable of discovering by ourselves."[10] Even apart from sin, Augustine is adamant about the unique illumination of Scripture, affirming that things can be "known in two different ways, in the Word of God, the 'daylight knowledge' as we may call it, and in itself, the 'twilight knowledge.'"[11] Augustine maintains that even when they do not understand Scripture, Christians must "ponder and believe that what is written there, even if obscure, is better and truer than any insights that we can gain by our own efforts."[12] Augustine is unequivocally a "biblicist" in the sense that Bebbington described as distinctive of evangelicals—emphasizing the necessity, centrality, and authority of Scripture.

Moreover, Augustine accounts for the deep impacts and implications of *antithesis*, so much so that he divides all humans into two cities defined by love of God (the City of God) and the love of self (the Earthly City).[13] For Augustine, the Fall and sin remain pervasive in human life, impacting ethics, epistemology, relationships, and more.[14] Indeed, Augustine draws striking eschatological contrasts, continually drawing attention to the distinctions between life inside of time and life in eternity.[15]

---

[10] Augustine, *City of God*, trans. Henry Bettenson, repr. ed. (New York: Penguin Classics, 2004), XI: 3, 431.

[11] Augustine, *City of God*, XI: 31, 466.

[12] Augustine, *On Christian Teaching*, trans. R. P. H. Green (New York: Oxford University Press, 1999), 34.

[13] "We see then that the two cities were created by two kinds of love: the earthly city was created by self-love reaching the point of contempt for God, the Heavenly City by the love of God carried so far as contempt of self." Augustine, *City of God* XIV: 28, 593.

[14] For instance, he writes, "The mind of man, the natural seat of his reason and understanding, is itself weakened by long-standing faults which darken it. It is too weak to cleave to that changeless light and to enjoy it; it is too weak even to endure that light." Augustine, *City of God* XI: 2, 430. Also:

> Even when we do see what is right and will to do it, we cannot do it because of the resistance of carnal habit, which develops almost naturally because of the unruliness of our mortal inheritance.... [T]hus we who knew what was right but did not do it lost the knowledge of what is right, and we who had the power but not the will to act rightly lost the power even when we have the will.

Augustine, *On Free Choice of the Will*, trans. Thomas Williams (Indianapolis, IN: Hackett Publishing, 1993), III: 106. Virtue is not even truly virtue for Augustine, absent rightly directed loves. *City of God* XVIII: 41, 819.

[15] This contrast remains a constant theme throughout *City of God*.

Despite this emphasis on antithesis, Augustine unequivocally stands squarely within the Christian natural law tradition. He affirms, "natural law is transcribed, as it were, upon the rational soul so that in the conduct of this life and in their earthly ways men might preserve semblances of workings of God."[16] This provides a kind of ethical commonality between believers and nonbelievers for Augustine. Even among the pagans, "the soul may appear to rule the body and the reason to govern the vicious elements in the most praiseworthy fashion."[17] Augustine thus stands in a special place in the tradition—a natural lawyer who takes deep account of Scripture and antithesis. Given this, we think a sound evangelical understanding of natural law will be demonstrably *Augustinian*.

It's no surprise, then, that the magisterial Reformers such as Martin Luther and John Calvin considered themselves Augustinian revivalists and also embraced natural law as true and central for guiding social and political ethics.[18] While better known for themes of antithesis, Martin Luther highlights the import of natural law for social life and political order.[19] Luther even cites Augustine as his authority for his claim that "unfettered reason, which is greater than all the laws in books . . . is so just a judgement that everyone is bound to approve it and find written in his heart that it is right."[20] Likewise with John

---

[16]Augustine, *Eighty-Three Different Questions*, trans. David L. Mosher (Washington, DC: The Catholic University of America Press, 1982) 53:2, 92. Elsewhere, he affirms:

> Then consider the law that is called the highest reason, which must always be obeyed, and by which the wicked deserve misery and the good deserve a happy life, and by which the law that we agreed to call "temporal" is rightly enacted and rightly changed. Can anyone of sense deny that this law is called unchangeable and eternal? . . . [N]othing is just and legitimate in the temporal law except that which human beings have derived from the eternal law. . . . [T]he notion of the eternal law that is stamped upon our minds: it is the law according to which it is just that all things be perfectly ordered.

On Free Choice I:11.
[17]Augustine, *City of God*, XIX: 25, 891.
[18]Mark Ellingsen, "Augustinian Origins of the Reformation Reconsidered," *Scottish Journal of Theology* 64, no. 1 (2011): 13-28; S. J. Han, "An Investigation into Calvin's Use of Augustine," *Acta Theologica* 28 (2008): 70-83; Grabill, *Rediscovering the Natural Law*.
[19]"Good judgement is not to be found in books, but from free good sense, as if there were no books. But it is love and natural law, with which all reason is filled, that confer such good judgement." Martin Luther, "On Secular Authority," in *Luther and Calvin on Secular Authority*, ed. Harro Höpfl (New York: Cambridge University Press, 1991), 42.
[20]Luther, "On Secular Authority," 43.

Calvin, who despite stark emphasis on sin and antithesis, also emphasizes the import of natural law.[21] Natural law is accessible to nonbelievers, Calvin argues, both so that they can serve as "God's instruments for the preservation of human society,"[22] and because of God's justice: "The purpose of natural law, therefore, is to render man inexcusable."[23] Contemporary Protestant natural law thinkers have accordingly located their project squarely in the tradition of the Reformers.[24] So to the extent that contemporary evangelicals seek to ground their theological tradition in the Reformation, looking beyond the Reformers back to Saint Augustine aligns nicely with the approach of the Reformers themselves.

Scripture on Natural Law

For Christians, the "Book of Scripture" is essential to salvation, obedience, and reconciliation to God. It interprets the created order, confirms creational norms, and corrects errors in the ways human beings perceive and appropriate those norms, errors themselves caused by sin and finitude. For an account of natural law to be meaningfully *evangelical*, it must be grounded in Scripture. It must reflect biblical teaching about the natural law.

What do the Scriptures of the Old and New Testaments teach about the natural law? The Bible teaches that natural law *exists* and *obliges all*, that natural law can be *assumed* even in the absence of special revelation, that much of the moral teaching of special revelation *overlaps* with natural law, and that special revelation *extends beyond* what the natural law teaches. We'll consider each of these in brief.

---

[21]"Since man is by nature a social animal, he is disposed, from natural instinct, to cherish and preserve society; and accordingly we see that the minds of all men have impressions of civil order and honesty. Hence it is that every individual understands how human societies must be regulated by laws, and also is able to comprehend the principles of those laws."
John Calvin, *Institutes of the Christian Religion*, trans. Beveridge (Grand Rapids, MI: Eerdmans, 1993), bk. II, chap. 11, sec. 13, 235.2: 235.
[22]Calvin, *Institutes*, bk. III, chap. 14, sec. 3.
[23]Calvin, *Institutes*, bk. II, chap. 2, sec. 22.
[24]Charles, *Retrieving the Natural Law*; VanDrunen, *Natural Law*.

First, *Scripture explicitly teaches that the created order is governed by a moral law which all humans can to some degree apprehend and to which all are subject.* Among the clearest examples is Psalm 19, where the first four verses highlight how the created order speaks to the existence and glory of the Creator:

> The heavens declare the glory of God;
> the skies proclaim the work of his hands.
> Day after day they pour forth speech;
> night after night they reveal knowledge.
> They have no speech, they use no words;
> no sound is heard from them.
> Yet their voice goes out into all the earth,
> their words to the ends of the world. (Psalm 19:1-4)

While the Psalm does not elaborate further content of what is revealed in creation, it is clear that the natural order provides accessible knowledge to all—including knowledge of God. For the psalmist, appeals to "knowledge" and "speech" suggest the rational intent within the created world. This provides the grounds for an account of natural law, even if its specifics are not fully developed.

Paul, in the letter to the Romans, develops the moral implications of natural knowledge of God the Creator:

> The wrath of God is being revealed from heaven against all the godlessness and wickedness of people, who suppress the truth by their wickedness, since what may be known about God is plain to them, because God has made it plain to them. For since the creation of the world God's invisible qualities—his eternal power and divine nature—have been clearly seen, being understood from what has been made, so that people are without excuse.
>
> For although they knew God, they neither glorified him as God nor gave thanks to him, but their thinking became futile and their foolish hearts were darkened. Although they claimed to be wise, they became fools and exchanged the glory of the immortal God for images made to look like a mortal human being and birds and animals and reptiles. (Romans 1:18-23)

Here, Paul elaborates that failure to give due glory to God—for which "people are without excuse"—leads to all sorts of idolatries and immorality. General revelation and creational morality are linked. Moreover, Paul continues in Romans 2 to describe how even Gentiles (those without access to special revelation) have knowledge of the moral law:

> Indeed, when Gentiles, who do not have the law, do by nature things required by the law, they are a law for themselves, even though they do not have the law. They show that the requirements of the law are written on their hearts, their consciences also bearing witness, and their thoughts sometimes accusing them and at other times even defending them. (Romans 2:14-15)

Scripture explicitly teaches that humans, unassisted by special revelation, have access to moral knowledge for which we are accountable. The natural law exists and is evident in the order of creation.

In addition to this, *Scripture assumes the natural law even for those without access to special revelation.* As J. Budziszewski has put it, "the Bible takes it for granted that we know certain large truths even prior to its instruction, truths apart from which this instruction would be incomprehensible. . . . Special revelation takes general revelation for granted."[25] A few examples will suffice. In Genesis 4 when Cain murders Abel, murder was already wrong and Cain knew it—prior to explicit prohibition in the Ten Commandments. The same is true of lust and violence in Genesis 6, drunkenness and dishonoring parents in Genesis 9, and adultery and sins of Sodom in Genesis 12 and 18. Even after the law of God is given to Israel through the Ten Commandments, surrounding nations are held accountable for certain sins that *they should have known better* than to commit. For example, in Isaiah 10:12-19, God's judgment is declared against Assyria's sins of pride. Likewise, the wickedness of Nineveh provides the basis for God's calling Jonah to go and call it to repentance, implying that the Ninevites should have known better. Paul's

---

[25]J. Budziszewski, *Evangelicals in the Public Square: Four Formative Voices on Political Thought and Action* (Grand Rapids, MI: Baker Academic, 2006), 31.

exhortations about governing authorities in Romans 13 assume some shared standards of good to be commended and evil to be punished—even for those living under Nero's rule. While more could be said here, Scripture clearly assumes that all people are responsible for keeping a moral law that is available apart from special revelation.

Significantly, Scripture also teaches that *the content of special revelation overlaps significantly with the general revelation of natural law*. That is, not all of the moral guidance that Scripture makes explicit is "new." Rather, it is consistent with what the natural law already revealed, even if in an imperfect or incomplete manner. For example, many of the prohibitions of the Ten Commandments in Exodus 20 are already assumed in the passages of Genesis cited above: dishonoring parents, murder, adultery, and so forth. Likewise, provisions for just exchange as found in Proverbs 20:10 ("Differing weights and differing measures—the LORD detests them both") and against exploitation as in Psalm 82:3 ("Defend the weak and the fatherless; uphold the cause of the poor and the oppressed") assume justice as a precept of natural law *and* confirm that God's character sides with justice. In this sense, Scripture's overlap with natural law provides illumination, confirmation, and clarity—but not necessarily moral guidance that is altogether new.

However, it is also clear that *the moral guidance of special revelation extends beyond natural law*, providing something better, more extensive, and more demanding than the obligations of the natural law. Again, while much more could be noted, three facets will suffice to illustrate this point. First, special revelation consistently takes place in the context of a unique covenantal relationship and imposes special obligations on those who participate in the covenant. Paradigmatic examples include circumcision in Genesis 17 and baptism in Matthew 28:19-20 and Acts 2:38-41. Second, special revelation highlights how God cares about the *heart*, not just behavior, making the demands of fidelity to Christ even more demanding than those revealed under the Old Testament, let alone natural law. For example, Jesus' litany of "You have heard that it was said . . . but I tell you that . . ." in Matthew 5 highlights how the movement of the heart away from God is the locus of sin, not just its outward manifestation in action. Third, the moral guidance of Scripture highlights the "more excellent way" of love, where all apparently right outward actions are meaningless if love is absent (see 1 Corinthians 13).

Scripture is thus inescapably necessary for Christians' moral life. In keeping with evangelical commitments to Scripture's final authority, Hopeful Realism prioritizes scriptural revelation over general revelation when an apparent question arises between them (though a fundamental consistency is also presumed). But while Scripture stands as our highest authority, there is much pertaining to human life that it does not speak about directly. Instead, Scripture presumes access to general revelation, including natural moral norms. This position about the relationship of natural law in general revelation to the authority of scriptural revelation is consistent with the classic natural law thinkers favored in the Catholic tradition as well as with the *sola scriptura* positions of the magisterial Reformers—who were no less committed to the idea of natural law. The norms of the created order are essential to rightly ordered creaturely life, but by no means replace God's revelation in Scripture by which God directs us to saving faith.

In sum, Scripture explicitly teaches that the natural law exists, that it is accessible to all, and that it is obligatory for all, such that all stand without excuse for rejecting the moral guidance apparent in creation. Moreover, Scripture *assumes* the precepts of the natural law, even when it does not always spell these out. Special revelation in Scripture confirms and reinforces the natural law, and Scripture extends further than the natural law in articulating the unique obligations placed on God's people. This distinction is essential in differentiating what is unique to the church from what is obligatory for all humans as humans. But given all of this, evangelical Christians can no more ignore natural law as part of general revelation than they can ignore Scripture itself. We turn now to how key evangelical theological commitments shape Hopeful Realism as a distinctively evangelical approach to the natural law.

Evangelical Theological Distinctives with Bearing on Natural Law

The goodness and intelligibility of the created order. A central claim of Hopeful Realism is that the created order is fundamentally good. That is, God's declarations of goodness at creation establish the truth that the created order participates in the goodness of its Creator, though of course the creation must neither be conflated with nor confused for the Creator. Its goodness means, however, that creation cannot rightly be spurned as "earthly" or "temporal" in a pejorative sense, nor can it be treated as "neutral." Rather, the creation is *good* and therefore worthy of being treated as such. Augustine famously emphasized this point repeatedly and crafted his argument about evil as privation of the good from it.[26]

Moreover, the goodness of the created order is not concealed or cryptic, but rather accessible. Hopeful Realism relies on the *intelligibility* of the created order, that God has rendered it accessible to human understanding. Recall Adam's task in Genesis 2, where he names the animals brought before him: he sees the animals, can distinguish each of them, and can discern and assign proper names that are suitable for each. Or consider our shared human sense perceptions: one person can invite a friend to look together at the beauty of the Grand Canyon or Yosemite's Half Dome, believing rightly that both are perceiving and enjoying the same reality. Empirical scientific inquiry depends upon shareable observation and repeatable experimentation: clear testimony to the intelligibility and shareability of the creation.[27] Perhaps it goes without saying, but affirming the intelligibility of creation does not entail that we enjoy *perfect* intelligibility or infallibility. Errors, distortions, and partial understandings can and do impact our perception and remain profoundly significant—we get things wrong all the time. However, those errors do not mean that creation is

---

[26]Augustine, *City of God*, XI: 22, 454. See also *On Free Choice* I: 26.

[27]It is striking that the practice of natural science arose and took hold in the Christian world, even as at times Christianity and science found themselves at odds. For a rather nice history of that interaction that avoids the trope of "war" between Christianity and science without smoothing over their sometimes difficulties, see Nicholas Spencer, *Magisteria: The Entangled Histories of Science & Religion* (London: Oneworld Publications, 2023).

unintelligible in some absolute or irreducible sense. The created order can be observed and understood in shareable ways.

The same is true—though perhaps less obviously—when it comes to certain types of philosophical reasoning. Logic—take for instance the law of noncontradiction (that A cannot be both B and not-B at the same time)—depends upon a shareable, intelligible order in the realm of ideas, no less than material reality. Significantly, these ideas include *moral* truths about what a good life entails, including norms of justice.

This is a central commitment of Hopeful Realism: moral norms are part of the created order and are intelligible to humans, a position philosophically described as *moral realism*. Moral realism is a necessary implication of Scripture's consistent assumption of natural law truths. Unlike *realism* as the term is used in international relations (to describe a narrow pursuit of national interest without adherence to moral standards), moral realism contends that moral standards are universal, intelligible, and part of the good, created order. Thus we use the term *moral realism* in the sense that the late philosopher Dallas Willard used it, as an aspect of epistemic realism, denoting that real and obligatory moral knowledge can be obtained, relied upon, and shared.[28] Indeed, the very concept of human beings as morally responsible agents at creation depends upon the existence of creational norms. For all the challenges of perceiving, sharing, obeying, and applying creational norms, we cannot escape the reality that we are bound by moral truths. We cannot wish away, ignore, or simply reconstruct these truths to our liking.

Within the natural law tradition, creational norms get described in terms of goods that can be discerned rationally. Their particular elements differ somewhat from author to author, but there is (as we might expect!) a good bit of commonality. Thomas Aquinas explains the first precept of the natural law as "good should be done and pursued and evil avoided.

---

[28]See for example, Dallas Willard, *Knowing Christ Today: Why We Can Trust Spiritual Knowledge* (Grand Rapids, MI: Zondervan, 2009); Dallas Willard, *The Disappearance of Moral Knowledge*, ed. and completed by Steven L. Porter, Aaron Preston, and Gregg A. Ten Elshof (New York: Routledge, 2018).

All other precepts of the law of nature are grounded in this one, such that all those things that are to be done or avoided pertain to precepts of natural law which practical reason naturally grasps as human goods." He then elaborates three kinds of goods, including biological goods of preserving life, animal goods of procreation and the raising of young, and uniquely human goods related to our capacity for reason: "to know the truth about God and to live in society."[29] These goods are largely consistent with the Greco-Roman philosophical tradition.

A slightly modified restatement of these goods offers a bit more clarity to their several aspects, particularly with respect to the place of human will and relationships. These latter two facets reflect a distinctively Augustinian cast to Hopeful Realism: human will and our relational (loving) nature is deeply important for Augustine's overall philosophy and theology. And so, Hopeful Realism posits that intelligible creational goods humans are obliged to pursue include these:

1. Physical goods: We ought to pursue and preserve animal (bodily) life, bodily integrity, physical health, reproduction, and so on.
2. Volitional goods: We ought to preserve and protect the responsibility and agency of individuals and groups for directing their thoughts, words, and actions.
3. Rational goods: We ought to pursue and preserve goods of education, contemplation, and the attainment of wisdom.
4. Relational goods: We ought to pursue and preserve social and religious life, manifest in families, associations, churches, and governments.

This articulation does not reflect any major departure from the Christian natural law tradition. It simply names specific goods, evident from the created order, that we can obtain real and obligatory knowledge about. So far, so good: this account has something of an Augustinian *flavor* (emphasizing our loves and will) but remains basically consistent with the broader natural law tradition.

---
[29]Thomas Aquinas, *Summa Theologica*, I-II, 94:2.

Redemptive-historical realities and antithesis. A firm commitment to the existence and accessibility of creational moral norms does not mean minimizing the consequences of the Fall. Instead, the present moment is part of a larger redemptive-historical context that features the goodness of creation, the major distortions introduced by the Fall, God's activity in redemption, and Christian hope for eternity. Augustine proves an especially helpful guide here. In tandem with his account of natural law, Augustine describes the radical changes incurred by the Fall. The Fall does more than divide us from God and damage our natural capacities. It also divides all of humanity into two groups of citizens, each defined by the objects of its loves. While sharing their humanity, these two groups are marked by their "mutually exclusive character" and "opposition."[30] The effects of the Fall—including this division of humanity—are central to the above description of *antithesis* in Augustine's thought.

Augustine describes human knowledge apart from Scripture as "twilight" as opposed to "daylight." Our capacities as knowers are already limited by virtue of being finite (the creature's knowledge is constrained compared to that of the Creator), and the effects of the Fall further impede our ability to attain reliable knowledge. He writes, "the mind of man, the natural seat of his reason and understanding, is itself weakened by longstanding faults which darken it. It is too weak to cleave to that changeless light and to enjoy it; it is too weak even to endure that light."[31] After the Fall, our epistemic and moral capacities are profoundly damaged.

While it is hard to overstate Augustine's account of the Fall's impact, its effects are not *fundamental*. Even with his emphasis on sin, Augustine remains unequivocal in affirming the basic and ineradicable goodness of all of creation. All things are created by God, proceed from God's goodness, and retain their essential goodness. Indeed, this basic assumption is central to Augustine's well-known account of evil: "There is no such entity in nature as 'evil': 'evil' is merely a name for the privation

---

[30] Robert Austin Markus, *Saeculum: History and Society in the Theology of Saint Augustine* (New York: Cambridge University Press, 1970), 60.
[31] Augustine, *City of God*, XI: 2, 430.

of good."[32] Good things, he maintains, can be put to bad use without altering the essential goodness of their substance. Augustine's understanding of evil maintains God's goodness and justice *and* the fundamental goodness of creation. God mercifully prevents "natural" knowledge from going *completely* astray.

Our lives within the fallen created order reflect the reality that we live in what Augustine calls the *saeculum*—inside of time—or what some have called "the time between the times." Christ has come "already" to inaugurate the Kingdom but has "not yet" come again to consummate it. The "already" and the "not yet" have important implications for Hopeful Realism, since the "already" is a basis for hope and the "not yet" calls for sober realism. The dynamics of our present age reflect this tension—a fact that is particularly important for Augustine's account of happiness.

Put succinctly, for Augustine, the greatest good of human flourishing is reserved for the life to come. Any account of the highest human good that locates our flourishing within this mortal life of the *saeculum* errs significantly. In other words, there is a stark "not yet" for the highest human good of eternity with God. No goods of the body or soul (or both of these) located within this life will suffice.[33]

This "not yet" has major implications for God's sovereignty in relation to time. Augustine unequivocally rejects what he calls the *libido dominandi*—the lust for domination—and the central focus on political power that goes with it. Unlike pagan Roman visions of political power, which impose by force types of peace that align with self-love, Augustine's vision of power is always motivated by love (for the good of the governed) and tempered by humility. Augustine's humility is driven by both epistemic and moral concerns. We lack perfect knowledge both because of creaturely finitude and because of sin, which impedes and corrupts natural human capacities ("twilight knowledge"). Likewise, even for those pilgrims who are journeying toward God through the grace of Christ, original sin continues to warp the will and render moral

---

[32] Augustine, *City of God*, XI: 22, 454.
[33] Augustine, *City of God*, XIX: 1-4, 841-59.

judgments suspect. So power is always to be tempered by humility and the limits of what is possible during the present age of the *saeculum*.

Of course, there is a significant "already" in Augustine's thought as well, as the goodness of God can indeed be experienced meaningfully in this life. This has two facets—one grounded in the ontological goodness of creation (which the privations of the Fall affect but do not obliterate) and the other grounded in the Christian hope of eternity and gracious foretastes of eternal fellowship with God. These two facets are perennially in tension: while real goods are genuinely accessible in this life, they are all limited, imperfect, and inflected by sin and suffering, all amid hope for eternity with God. Again, the structure of Hopeful Realism is evident in Augustine's account of creation.

In *City of God* Augustine brilliantly describes this complex relation of creational goodness, fallen distortion, and redemptive hope as applied to politics. However, this can easily be (and often has been) misconstrued. Augustine divides all of humanity into two "cities" defined by their ultimate loves: "We see then that the two cities were created by two kinds of love: the earthly city was created by self-love reaching the point of contempt for God, the Heavenly City by the love of God carried so far as contempt of self."[34]

Significantly, *neither of Augustine's two cities correlates with the political community*. Rather than being characterized in terms of *ultimate loves* of God or self, particular political communities find their definition elsewhere. Political communities—what Augustine calls "commonwealths"—are comprised of citizens of both "cities." While a particular political community can be associated with pagan worship and domination and therefore in some sense is an instance of the "earthly city" (as in the case of Rome), Augustine's "two cities" are heart orientations toward God or away from God, not a reference to a specific political community. Nowhere is this clearer than in Augustine's critique of and proposed alternative to Cicero's definition of a commonwealth.

---

[34] Augustine, *City of God*, XIV: 28, 593.

In *City of God*, Augustine rejects Cicero's definition of a commonwealth as too perfectionist. Cicero's account describes the commonwealth as "united by a common sense of right" (that is, justice), which Augustine argues is contingent on rendering to God *his* due in order to be truly just. Cicero's conception of a commonwealth thus requires a shared account of *theological* justice among a people—under which all people love God and neighbor perfectly.[35] But Augustine rejects this view for being too perfectionist, since this is only an apt description of eternal life with God, never the plural character of the two-city reality of the *saeculum*, where members of both cities share time and space. In other words, *a fully just political community is only eschatological*. For Augustine, the combination of the two cities in time makes it impossible to achieve full agreement about a theological vision for right-ordering. Thus, as long as commonwealths are composed of citizens with divergent loves, *political justice and the goods of earthly peace must always remain proximate rather than final*.

Unpacking the nature of such proximate political goods, Augustine articulates a vision for political life that might be termed a "third city." He proposes a redefined, nonperfectionist account of the commonwealth, describing it as composed of a mixture of members of the City of God (lovers of God) and the earthly city (lovers of self). It thus reflects the *plurality of ultimate commitments found among the two cities while occupying the same political space*. On this understanding, political bodies cannot unify around a shared conception of justice, since they do not concur on first rendering to God what is due him and then ordering all relationships accordingly. One consequence of this is that they cannot have any religious laws in common since they do not share ultimate loves.[36]

However, commonwealths consisting of both cities *can* share proximate loves and seek these together. Augustine lumps these proximate

---

[35] Augustine, *City of God*, XIX: 17, 881-83.
[36] Augustine rather infamously seems to undercut this claim with his willingness to use imperial power to rein in the Donatists. We take this to be an unfortunate anomaly rather than a reflection of Augustine's central ideas. For a discussion of this, see chap. 3.

goods under the term "earthly peace," which he describes as a "compromise between human wills about the things relevant to mortal life."[37] These "things relevant to mortal life" refer to *real creational goods* that each city uses for its own purposes—that is, each applies these goods to different ends. These temporal goods include

> the peace that consists in bodily health and soundness, and in fellowship with one's kind; and everything necessary to safeguard or recover this peace—those things, for example, which are appropriate and accessible to our senses: light, speech, air to breathe, water to drink, and whatever is suitable for the adornment of the person.[38]

These goods are clearly both *material* and *moral*; they consist of both provision and social ordering.

Earthly peace is grounded on the objective goodness of the created order, including material goods, shareable and knowable truths, and a common moral order. But not all commonwealths have equal clarity on these goods. Rather, commonwealths will vary by virtue of the objects of their loves: the better the things loved, the better the community. Communities can be more or less oriented toward the true conditions for flourishing, grounded in the order of creation.[39]

To sum up, the goodness of the created order makes possible the shared pursuit of real goods. These are material, moral, and social goods, relevant to our earthly lives and broadly shared among believers and nonbelievers alike. Put differently, the "common grace" of creational goods is offered to both Christians and non-Christians. But the stubborn (though ultimately temporary) impact of the Fall means that the ultimate ends to which these are directed will not be shared in this life.[40] The two cities—those who love God and those who don't—continue to inhabit

---

[37] Augustine, *City of God*, XIX: 17, 877.
[38] Augustine, *City of God*, XIX: 13, 872.
[39] Augustine, *City of God*, XIX: 21, 881-83.
[40] Some accounts of natural law construct goods as independent, objective, and freestanding. In contrast, an Augustinian account of natural law is both structural and directional. See Covington, "Grammar of Virtue."

the same age (the *saeculum*), sharing time and space as a nonperfectionist political community.

Conclusion

Hopeful Realism is shorthand for our Augustinian effort to bring together creational moral norms and redemptive-historical realities. We aim to acknowledge on the basis of Scripture the truth of the natural law as part of the created order while honoring evangelical distinctives that emphasize the impact of antithesis. People always and everywhere inhabit political communities marked by both (1) a shared interest in creational goods that are ordered to human flourishing but also (2) deep disagreement about the nature of that flourishing and thus the goods attached to it.

Many Christian accounts of politics emphasize one of these two—shared creational goods *or* antithesis—to the neglect of the other. The results are often harmful, leading to overstatements of commonality (think Niebuhr's "Christ of culture" type) or overstatements of distinction (think Niebuhr's "Christ against culture" type).[41] An evangelical account of natural law aims to provide meaningful moral guidance that makes neither sort of error.

How can we best order political communities in light of those realities? We turn next to describing the political principles we think flow from the ideas developed here, particularly as they relate to diverse, democratic contexts.

---

[41] H. Richard Niebuhr, *Christ and Culture*, expanded ed. (San Francisco: HarperSanFrancisco, 2001). Originally published in 1951.

3

HOPEFUL REALISM'S
POLITICAL PRINCIPLES

EVEN IF YOU ARE PERSUADED THAT a hopeful realist account of natural law is sound—that there are creational moral norms to which all are accountable, confirmed by Scripture and tempered by antithesis—major questions remain about the political implications of a hopeful realist approach to natural law.[1] For example, should government officials simply discern the natural law and compel all people to follow it using the coercive power of the state? More pointedly, does acknowledging the moral guidance of natural law as an organizing principle of social order mean giving up on the project of liberal democracy—understood as a *limited, rights-respecting government that is electorally accountable to the governed*? The answer, we believe, is a resounding no. A hopeful realist account of natural law certainly shapes how one approaches liberal democracy, but we show here that the two are far from incompatible.

In this chapter we articulate four broad political principles that follow from our account of natural law. What is striking about these principles is the degree to which they comport with certain understandings of a

---

[1] We gratefully acknowledge that several of the ideas in this chapter were originally developed and articulated in other contexts, namely Jesse Covington, "Augustine's Aspirational Imperfectionism: What We Should Hope for from Politics," *Public Justice Review* VII, no. 4 (2018); Jesse Covington, Bryan McGraw, and Micah Watson, "Hopeful Realism: Renewing Evangelical Political Morality," *Public Discourse* (2022). While much here extends beyond those initial efforts, we have drawn from arguments and language from both prior publications.

liberal democratic regime.[2] We do not mean to suggest that liberal democratic politics is a *necessary* conclusion of the natural law; that would prove too much. But we do think that the sorts of political communities suggested by Hopeful Realism fit well within a certain understanding of liberal democratic politics. This should encourage evangelicals who seem increasingly disenchanted with liberal democracy, discouraged by its excesses and moral failures. It is possible to be a faithful Christian in a liberal democratic order. It should also encourage our other fellow citizens who may be concerned by some evangelicals' political disenchantments, fearing an embrace of post-liberal alternatives.[3] Properly understood, Christian commitments to the natural law need not draw us into theonomy, integralism, or other sorts of illiberal politics.[4]

But Hopeful Realism is not simply an uncritical endorsement of twenty-first-century American liberal democratic politics. (Indeed, it may be at odds in certain respects with visions of democratic politics that aspire to remain abstracted from one's deepest principles.[5]) Hopeful Realism's political principles bring substantive moral principles to liberal democracy, looking to inform its structure and aims. In this respect, Hopeful Realism has real political teeth. Indeed, we believe that this approach can make liberal democracy both *qualitatively better* (i.e., providing better moral guidance to direct it) and *structurally more sound* (providing good principles to inform its commitments and organization).

The four principles that we explore here flow from our theological commitments and our understanding of natural law. They fit within the Christian natural law tradition, though they also reflect the distinctive

---

[2]As noted in the introduction, in contrast to contemporary popular usage of the term *liberal*, as political theorists we use the term *liberal democracy* to refer to *limited, liberty-respecting governments characterized by democratic accountability*.

[3]While we say more about some of what we mean by "post-liberal" in the pages that follow, as the name suggests, this term refers to approaches to politics that see moving away from limited, rights-respecting government as helpful, prudent, and in some cases morally obligatory for the sake of obtaining goods that are less accessible under liberal regimes.

[4]Theonomists argue that contemporary governments should generally rule in accordance with Old Testament law. Integralists generally maintain that the separation of church and state is misguided such that the (Catholic) church should provide guidance as an officially established state church.

[5]John Rawls, *Political Liberalism* (New York: Columbia University Press, 1996).

evangelical commitments we explored in the previous chapter. The four principles are these:

1. The common good and civic friendship: Shared human nature and creational context means that political communities seek to cultivate material, relational, and moral goods that are key building blocks of earthly peace and flourishing for all.

2. Confessional pluralism and religious liberty: Political communities are marked by a plurality of ultimate commitments requiring, among other things, institutional differentiation of church and state and protections for religious liberty.

3. Restraint and liberty: The goods of responsible human agency, the danger of power in the hands of sinners, and the importance of virtues like humility suggest an accountable government of limited powers and a deference to liberty as the default.

4. Democracy and decentralization: Citizen involvement in governance and decentralized power respect human agency, allow political decisions to reflect diverse community values, and keep "thicker" decisions closer to smaller subcommunities.

Augustine of Hippo will feature prominently in our development of these four principles. It is important to acknowledge that *Augustine is not himself a proponent of liberal democracy*. Hopeful Realism could be thought of as a development of his thought, but we are not claiming that Augustine himself would have endorsed these principles. Nevertheless, we do think that Augustine's theological commitments can provide a basis for understanding what a healthy democratic order looks like. In some sense, this is nothing new, as scholars have long enlisted Augustine in support of liberal democracy, though their approaches have varied a good bit. Some have approached this fairly optimistically, finding in Augustine deep political hope and expansive aspirations for liberal government.[6] Others have been less sanguine, finding in Augustine's

---

[6] Eric Gregory, *Politics and the Order of Love: An Augustinian Ethic of Democratic Citizenship* (Chicago: University of Chicago Press, 2008); Charles T. Mathewes, *A Theology of Public Life* (New

accounts of the Fall and human sin reasons for deep pessimism, caution, and political restraint.[7] We think that *both* strains of Augustinian political theology are important for a distinctively evangelical Hopeful Realism. With the optimistic Augustinians, we affirm the importance of commonality, shared goods, and hopeful aspirations to greater justice, all grounded in the shared goodness of the created order. And with the more pessimistic Augustinians, Hopeful Realism recognizes the depth and impact of the Fall, sin, and antithesis more broadly, with all this means for politics. Neither are neglected in the working out of Hopeful Realism's political principles.

Most centrally for this season, we see Hopeful Realism as compatible with a liberal democratic understanding of politics. It is worth reiterating: liberal democracy does not follow as a *strict logical necessity* from our theory's presuppositions any more than it does from Augustine's thought. Our political principles are grounded in and expand upon the Augustinian natural law commitments we described in the previous chapter. Christians can, and should, see a form of liberal democracy as a reasonably good instantiation of the sort of political order that our basic theological commitments and natural law implications suggest. What is more, those natural law arguments and their political principles can provide good grounds to propose and guide policies that will work to the flourishing of fellow citizens. Love of neighbor requires that we take this seriously.

The Common Good and Civic Friendship

In Monty Python's film "The Life of Brian," a group of anti-Roman zealots gather to plot their resistance. One of the zealots, Reg, notes that the

---

York: Cambridge University Press, 2007); John Von Heyking, *Augustine and Politics as Longing in the World* (Columbia, MO: University of Missouri Press, 2001); Michael Lamb, *A Commonwealth of Hope: Augustine's Political Thought* (Princeton, NJ: Princeton University Press, 2022).

[7] Robert Austin Markus, *Saeculum: History and Society in the Theology of Saint Augustine* (New York: Cambridge University Press, 1970); Reinhold Niebuhr, "Augustine's Political Realism," in *The Essential Reinhold Niebuhr: Selected Essays and Addresses*, ed. Robert McAfee Brown (New Haven, CT: Yale University Press, 1986), 123-41; Jeanne Bethke Elshtain, *Augustine and the Limits of Politics* (Notre Dame, IN: University of Notre Dame Press, 1996).

Romans have "taken everything we had." He then poses the ostensibly rhetorical question "What have they ever given us in return?!" Unfortunately for the momentum of his argument, this question is taken at face value, as his coconspirators proceed to catalog the many important goods that have come with Roman occupation: sanitation, medicine, education, wine, public order, irrigation, roads, a fresh-water system, public health, and peace. We're meant to laugh at how these many meaningful Roman goods undercut Reg's effort to stir up the resistance (he responds with a frustrated "Shut up!" to his coconspirators).[8] The humor of this scene makes an important point: the possibility of shared goods despite deep differences and even hostility. That is, it highlights the potential for genuinely *common goods* within a political community. Hopeful Realism's emphasis on the goodness and intelligibility of the created order provides a helpful theological starting point for a key political principle: fellow citizens can identify and pursue shared human goods as part of our political life, including certain types of rightly ordered relationships. This section describes these in terms of the common good and civic friendship.

First, it is important to recall what we argued in the last chapter, that Augustine's political theology describes politics as a *civic commonwealth*. This commonwealth is best understood as a "third city" composed of citizens of both the City of God and the earthly city (divided by their love of God and self, respectively). While the *ends* of the civic commonwealth are not ultimate, there are nevertheless real goods in view—goods of "earthly peace." The goods of earthly peace are the substance of what we describe here as the common good and provide the basis for civic friendship.

Earthly peace is grounded on the objective goodness of the created order, and it includes material goods (sufficient food, shelter, etc.), social goods (healthy families, friendships, institutions), and a common moral

---

[8] See the script at http://montypython.50webs.com/scripts/Life_of_Brian/10.htm, accessed February 15, 2023.

order (frameworks for justice, temperance, etc.). All of this assumes a certain epistemic realism: shareable truths about these goods are accessible to human knowledge. An Augustinian Hopeful Realism is confident that all humans, no matter which of the two "cities" they belong to, can aspire to know more about reality, to act increasingly in accord with the virtues, and to profitably engage with the goodness of material creation.

As creatures who are part of an intelligible creation, we humans share a basic nature as embodied, rational, moral, and relational souls. As such, we are oriented toward a discernible range of goods that we have in common. That is, certain goods are important for human flourishing. These inescapable commonalities of the created order make up much of the "stuff" of politics, despite the mixed composition of all political communities. While he insists that such goods are proximate and not ultimate, Augustine describes the shared goods of politics as constitutive of "earthly peace"—a "compromise between human wills about the things relevant to mortal life."[9] As was mentioned in the last chapter, for Augustine, the "things relevant to mortal life" involve *real creational goods*. He describes the temporal goods of earthly peace thus:

> The peace that consists in bodily health and soundness, and in fellowship with one's kind; and everything necessary to safeguard or recover this peace—those things, for example, which are appropriate and accessible to our senses: light, speech, air to breathe, water to drink, and whatever is suitable for the adornment of the person.[10]

Here, the goods of "earthly peace" point to common creational goods that extend beyond material necessities. They are moral and social, not just material. And the last chapter's list of goods includes aspects that are implicated by safeguarding or recovering other goods—such as rational and volitional goods. To be sure, Augustine is clear that those who love God and those who do not will use these goods for divergent purposes.

---

[9] Augustine, *City of God*, trans. Henry Bettenson, repr. ed. (New York: Penguin Classics, 2004), XIX: 17, 877.
[10] Augustine, *City of God*, XIX: 13, 872.

Each applies these goods to different ends. But the goods themselves are an important area of commonality. This suggests that political communities can identify and pursue common goods. Augustine exhorts Christians to seek earthly peace in politics with the expectation that improvement is possible in terms of real, objective goods, both material and moral. Societal unity can be increased, basic human needs can be better met, wars and coercion can be reduced. Augustine's vision for politics is a far cry from only restraining the worst sins and making life bearable while waiting for eternity (though such restraint is included). His vision for politics aspires to a greater earthly peace through the common creational goods that make human well-being possible.

A word about the *moral* aspect of this is in order: we maintain that common moral goods can provide important guidance for a liberal democracy. Along with the classical tradition, we affirm here that political communities are organized with justice in view, but we do so once again informed by Augustine. On the one hand, Augustine is adamant that political commonwealths composed of Christians and non-Christians in the *saeculum* of this life will not have a shared sense of theological justice that renders to God what is due him.[11] Nevertheless, he remains persuaded that even pagan virtues have a great deal in common with Christian virtues. He credits pagan philosophy with perceiving "truths about the nobility of virtue, about love of country and loyalty in friendship, about good works and all things belonging to an upright character," despite being aimed at the wrong ends.[12] This means that political aspirations for greater justice—of increasingly rendering to each what is due—are possible, albeit tempered. Contrary to pessimistic interpreters of this tradition, Augustine offers a meaningfully hopeful vision of politics as striving for greater justice and human flourishing.

Augustine does not cede unlimited scope to antithesis: both cities continue to operate in the context of a shared material, moral, epistemic, and

---

[11] Augustine, *City of God*, XIX: 21, 881-83.
[12] Augustine, *City of God*, XVIII: 41, 819; Jesse Covington, "The Grammar of Virtue: St. Augustine and Natural Law," in *Natural Law and Evangelical Political Thought*, ed. Jesse Covington, Bryan T. McGraw, and Micah Joel Watson (Lanham, MD: Lexington Books, 2013), 176-77.

social order, such that Christians can and should seek improvements in the earthly peace that consists of these goods. Significantly, such aspirations serve to constrain the scope of moral pluralism—the range of competing and potentially incommensurable visions of the good. Augustine's emphasis on antithesis and a limited political commonwealth does not lead him to make moral pluralism absolute. Political goods, including justice, can and should be pursued and (imperfectly) realized as part of the common goods of earthly peace.[13]

In one sense, suggesting that there are basic, shared political goods is not a particularly novel proposition. The prospect of shareable epistemic and moral frameworks is presupposed in Scripture. First Peter 2:12 suggests something similar: "Live such good lives among the pagans that, though they accuse you of doing wrong, they may see your good deeds and glorify God on the day he visits us." As we noted in our introduction, Matthew 5:16 states, "In the same way, let your light shine before others, that they may see your good deeds and glorify your Father in heaven." Likewise, modern political thinkers from across the ideological spectrum affirm the idea that there are common material, social, and even moral goods that can be grasped by a wide range of people, though they frame these somewhat differently.[14] Suffice it to say that the notion of shared goods of the sort that Augustine describes as belonging to earthly peace not only predates Augustine but has persisted to this day.

---

[13]Oliver O'Donovan, among others, disagrees, maintaining that anything called "justice" in the context of politics must be *theological* justice, for Augustine. See Oliver O'Donovan, "The Political Thought of City of God 19," in *Bonds of Imperfection: Christian Politics, Past and Present*, by O. O'Donovan and J. L. O'Donovan (Grand Rapids, MI: Eerdmans, 2004), 48-72. We maintain that the broader arguments that Augustine makes in *City of God* suggest something rather different, where the form or structure of justice may be shared between the two cities, even if its direction or telos is not.

[14]For example, John Rawls lists "rights, liberties, and opportunities, and income and wealth" as "chief primary goods," going on to include self-respect among the "social primary goods." He then includes "health and vigor, intelligence and imagination" as additional primary goods. See John Rawls, *A Theory of Justice* (Cambridge, MA: Harvard University Press, 1999), 54. Likewise, John Finnis lists these as "Basic Forms of Human Good": practical reflection, life, knowledge, play, aesthetic experience, sociability/friendship, practical reasonableness, and religion. See chap. IV in J. Finnis, *Natural Law and Natural Rights* (New York: Oxford University Press, 1980).

To some extent, all political communities seek the creational goods that humans have in common. Indeed, the peace that these goods provide is the raison d'être of the state. However, admitting there are real goods that are truly common does not lead to any automatic policy conclusions. Just as recognizing the moral goods of marital fidelity does not necessarily lead to policy conclusions that criminalize divorce, so too with recognizing the good of bodily integrity and provision of basic needs and policy questions around healthcare, poverty relief, and so forth. (We will describe a framework for practical judgments applying these natural law principles in chapter four.) This is true for multiple reasons, including the contingency of limited resources, the difficulty of moral judgment, interaction with other goods, and divergent loves among members of a political community. Nevertheless, goods can be recognized as *common* (even if debated) and hence become the subject of the "compromise of wills" that Augustine refers to as the domain of politics.

Our primary point here is that commonality about shared creational goods persists. While there will not be absolute agreement within a political community about such goods or how best to promote them, our core claim remains unequivocal: *difference and plurality cannot be totalized*. Human goods—material, moral, and social—are real, inescapable, and necessary for human flourishing, and they are the primary subjects of political life. This political principle of orientation toward the common good has substantive objects. That is, rather than simply asserting formal or process goods for *how* conclusions are reached, the common good—relying on the created order—draws on truth and goodness as vital categories. Hopeful Realism therefore maintains an unshakeable commitment to the true and the good as *real, accessible,* and *shareable* (even if such access and sharing are imperfect and partial). In other words, however much limited by antithesis, there must be something toward which the political community aspires. Despite the discomforts of making such claims in contexts increasingly wary of substantive claims (and of course such claims may be abused), nevertheless *conviction* about real goods (material, moral, and social) and a *commitment* to seek those goods for others remains indispensable to the "hopeful" side of Hopeful Realism.

For example, this approach would counsel a persistent pursuit of justice in regard to human dignity, whether injustices are broadly recognized within the culture (as with racism or human trafficking) or not (as with abortion). Rooted in a creational theology and motivated by a redemptive vision, "earthly peace" must have *content* in terms of real goods—content that helps to secure the conditions in which human flourishing is possible for all.

This commonality opens the door to the possibility of real civic friendship, the mutual rendering of proximate justice in community. This is not the robust fellowship of teleologically aligned pilgrims with shared ultimate loves. But neither is it a thin, constructivist contract about what self-interested individuals find mutually willable. Instead, it involves shared visions of the good that shape political pursuits. These are often the result of compromise, not the full vision of any one group. But the subjects of the compromise are proximate loves for real creational goods that are willed for self and others, even if for different ultimate reasons.

In its minimalist form, such civic friendship may originate with simple co-belligerency—where those who disagree about most things may nevertheless work together for a single particular end, building commonality through pursuit of a common end. A small-town coalition to limit industrial cannabis development may bring together the deeply religious, secular ecologists, and those with business interests in regular meetings over food to strategize on shared ends focused on the good of the community. But civic friendship may also manifest in thicker forms ranging from neighborhood associations bringing neighbors together on a regular basis to long-term, relationally engaged initiatives from disparate groups—such as the LGBTQ groups working with religious organizations to find a mutually honoring path toward policy solutions. In each case, civic friendship works toward shared creational goods in relationship with others.

Confessional Plurality and Religious Liberty

A vital implication of Hopeful Realism is that every political community is also marked by a *plurality of ultimate commitments*. Inside of time, both cities are mixed up with each other and cannot be authoritatively sorted prior to the last judgment. In one sense, our claim here is just *descriptive*: within the redemptive-historical reality prior to Christ's return, all commonwealths include members with mixed (and competing) ultimate loyalties. This grounds the irreducible two-cities composition of every civic commonwealth, meaning that the boundaries of the political community simply cannot be the same as an ecclesial or faith community. In another sense, though, this plurality of ultimate commitments carries important *normative* implications for individual and institutional religious liberty. Looking at Augustine will help trace the connection between these two, even though he himself does not offer a fully developed theory of religious liberty and indeed has a complicated history on the question. Nonetheless, Augustine is helpful for understanding the theological underpinnings for our claims in favor of religious liberty.

As we noted in chapter two, the two-cities composition of political communities is central to Augustine's understanding of political justice. Indeed, this inescapable reality leads him to offer his theologically nonperfectionist account of a "commonwealth." As we have noted, Augustine critiques Cicero for offering a definition of the commonwealth that assumes a *shared sense of justice* among a people. Anything worthy of the name *justice*, he maintains, requires rendering to God his due: "Justice is found where God, the one supreme God, rules an obedient City according to his grace."[15] Because Augustine is pessimistic about the possibility of *theological* justice in politics, he rejects Cicero's perfectionist account of the commonwealth: "By this definition people amongst whom there is no justice can never be said to

---

[15]He continues: Thus, "an association, or people, of righteous men lives on the same basis of faith, active in love, the love with which a man loves God as God ought to be loved." *City of God*, XIX: 23, 890.

have a commonwealth."[16] Augustine's alternative definition of a "commonwealth" is decidedly *imperfectionist*. It focuses on the shared objects of love that are possible in a given context—a more flexible and variable understanding of the political community.[17] This coincides with Augustine's stark contrast that the heavenly city and the earthly city cannot share any religious laws.[18] He even qualifies Christians' political obedience, endorsing it only "so far as may be permitted without detriment to true religion and piety."[19] Groups with divergent ultimate loves should not share religious laws, and Christians' political obedience is limited.

We should acknowledge that Augustine himself, in his role as bishop of Hippo, did not consistently observe this principle—and Christians have unfortunately used his example to deny others liberty in the subsequent centuries. After years of strife between Catholic and Donatist Christians, Augustine advocated the use of force to compel Donatist compliance and adherence to Catholic doctrine. This aberration in relation to his overall theological framework could be explained either as simply an inconsistency arising from his exasperation with the Donatists or perhaps by the church's civil role at the time and his sense that the Donatists' willingness to use violence needed restraining. Regardless, we treat Augustine's response to the Donatist controversy as an aberration and rely on what we think of as his more fundamental theological account for our argument.[20]

Augustine's two-cities construction provides the theological basis of what neo-Kuyperians (and others) call "confessional pluralism." This view posits that the plurality of ultimate commitments, inside of time, warrants legal and political protection.[21] Put differently, Augustine's

---

[16] Augustine, *City of God*, XIX: 22, 883.

[17] Augustine, *City of God*, XIX: 24, 890.

[18] "The Heavenly City could not have laws of religion common with the earthly city." *City of God*, XIX: 17, 878.

[19] Augustine, *City of God*, XIX: 17, 878.

[20] Peter Brown notes the tempered views of the mature Augustine regarding the relationship of church and empire. See Peter Brown, *Augustine of Hippo: A Biography* (Oakland, CA: University of California Press, 2013), 338-39.

[21] *Plurality* may be a more apt term than *pluralism*, as it is accounting for the place in redemptive history, not providing an ideological framework in the ilk of other "-isms."

theological claims end up in a type of *imperfectionism*: religious plurality as such should not be forced into unity through state power. To do so is a theological mistake in that it wrongly collapses the eschatological future with the present in what has been called "immanentizing the eschaton" (drawing on the work of Eric Voegelin).[22] It is also a practical mistake in that using the power of the state in that way is simply bound to go astray. Indeed, such efforts almost inevitably end up suffering from the *libido dominandi*—the lust for domination and control—rather than exhibiting love of neighbor.[23]

This provides theological grounds for limiting state establishments of religion since it refuses to conflate the Christian community with the political community. For example, it rejects any effort to set up a confessional state, like recent movements in Catholic integralism. It likewise rejects an effort to mandate a stringently secular public realm, where religious institutions, language, or rationales are prohibited. It also points to the value of protecting citizens' own liberty of religious conscience and practice, whether they are Christians or not. All persons must obey their conscience, even if the state attempts to impose mandates to the contrary. The relation of conscience and political authority is, we recognize, often a thorny and difficult question (one we explore further in chapter eight), and we do not mean to suggest that individuals and groups can merely *assert* any claim of conscience, regardless of its content. No political authority can neutrally accommodate *every* "good conscience" claim. Sometimes there really are zero-sum conflicts in play. But political communities that ride roughshod over conscience claims and do not at least attempt to accommodate and protect them profoundly threaten the goods of human flourishing.

Recognizing the implications of a commonwealth full of divergent ultimate commitments does not prescribe one particular approach to

---

[22] Eric Voegelin, *The New Science of Politics: An Introduction* (Chicago: University of Chicago Press, 1987).
[23] Micah Watson, "Another Meditation on the Third Commandment," *Perspectives on Political Science* 46, no. 1 (2017): 43-50.

either the shape of institutional structures (i.e., the precise limits on religious establishments) or the extent of individual liberties. But it does suggest that both are central principles that should inform the scope and limits of political power. The divergent ultimate loves within a commonwealth will only be finally addressed at the Last Day, not in the next election or court decision. Protecting this sort of plurality is a key political good.

Restraint and Liberty

One implication of the basic goods of human rationality, relationality, and agency is the importance of *liberty* as a principle that reflects and protects these human goods. That is, none of these goods is likely to be secured in the absence of some degree of social and political liberty and limited government. Likewise, *restraint* follows directly from valuing liberty and especially in light of human sinfulness. If power is always wielded by finite, sin-prone humans, limiting power becomes a central concern. Both facets—liberty and restraint—require some elaboration.

Even apart from the real dangers of consolidated power, liberty matters in its own right. For people to exercise their capacities—described as creational goods in chapter two (volitional goods most obviously, but also relational, rational, and physical goods)—individual and corporate political liberty must be protected. Hopeful Realism's emphasis on the doctrines of creation affirms the plurality of social life in ways that extend the principle of liberty beyond individual liberty (though this is certainly included). What some have called the "creation mandate" or the "cultural mandate" describes believers' calling in the world as including the development of social life in different sectors, each with their own authority. Families, businesses, science, the arts, and so forth all have their own spheres of development for which they are responsible.[24] This is not an unusual claim within the tradition of Christian political thought: the Catholic principle of subsidiarity

---

[24] A. Kuyper, *Lectures on Calvinism* (Grand Rapids, MI: Eerdmans, 2000).

recognizes these intermediate institutions, as does the Reformed principle of sphere sovereignty.[25] This understanding of creational goods and a plural social life informs the hopeful realist emphasis on liberty: government should exercise caution in extending its power over individuals and other structures of social life and should only do so with due justification, deferring to liberty as the default (more on this under "democracy and decentralization" below).

This deference to liberty and the need to justify intrusions upon it produces a corollary to the principle of decentralization, articulated more fully below. Not only do the concerns of the civic commonwealth "thicken" as they get closer to the local, but the concerns of social life are more specific and robust in their particular and distinct manifestations. And significantly, none of these can simply be reduced to the political. The pluriformity of society—manifest in everything from families, businesses, clubs, schools, and far more—warrants protection from the intrusions of government. A rancher's co-op in South Dakota will pursue goods and concerns that vary widely from those of a dance hall in Miami or a conservation club working to reduce coral depletion in Hanauma Bay. This does not preclude regulation, but it acknowledges the need for such regulation to be justified and weighed against the independent value and creational grounding of social structures. Indeed, the coercive nature of politics makes it particularly dangerous, since it risks intruding on other aspects of social life in ways they cannot return in kind.[26]

This leads us to the importance of restraining power. Restraint of power is an essential feature of Hopeful Realism, due to our distinctively evangelical assessment of human knowledge, goodness, and abilities. These lead us to reject the epistemic and ethical optimism of perfectionist political visions for the same reasons that Augustine rejected Cicero's

---

[25]See chap. 8 of David T. Koyzis, *Political Visions & Illusions: A Survey & Christian Critique of Contemporary Ideologies*, 2nd ed. (Downers Grove; IL: InterVarsity Press, 2019). We recognize that the principle of subsidiarity is important for other Christian traditions as well.

[26]See chaps. 7–9 of Koyzis, *Political Visions*. For a broader argument about associations and pluralism that is broadly similar to ours (without the natural law framing), see John D. Inazu, *Confident Pluralism: Surviving and Thriving Through Deep Difference* (Chicago: University of Chicago Press, 2018).

account of the commonwealth: until the eschaton, perfection is impossible. Two means of restraining power are worth noting here: first, cultivating virtues that resist the abuse of power, and second, structuring governments such that they do not rely wholly on the successful cultivation of virtue.

As one of us has argued elsewhere, a number of virtues are central here, especially as they relate to the limits of politics, human finitude, and the effects of the Fall.[27] First among these is *humility*: Hopeful Realism counsels a deeply humble assessment of our moral rectitude in the use of power and of our ability to enact sweeping changes without bad unintended consequences. Likewise, *prudence*—and with it a commitment to incremental change, accountable power, a suspicion of perfectionism, and compromise—is vital. Moreover, a certain *detachment* from guaranteeing outcomes (implicit in ethical commitments that take means just as seriously as ends) is key. That is, we have to trust that God will accomplish his purposes in history, rather than succumb to the temptations of what Augustine called the *libido dominandi*—the lust for power—in which we seek ultimate control and attempt to exercise godlike power over history and those we are called to love.

This bears emphasis and points toward the structural aspects of restraint. Augustine is acutely aware of how the *libido dominandi* impacts political power. Roman imperial power consistently set itself up in God's place, seeking to exercise godlike power. And it is not just Rome: Augustine's understanding of original sin—a key feature of evangelical emphasis on *antithesis*—persuades him that no human (or collection of humans or political structures) can quite entirely escape this. Virtue is important but insufficient. Restraint requires institutional arrangements and commitments that attempt to rein in the discretionary exercise of power, precautions that will sound very familiar to anyone acquainted with liberal democratic politics.

---

[27] Covington, "Augustine's Aspirational Imperfectionism."

Consider first the idea of the rule of law. The idea that fixed, known rules will govern—rather than the arbitrary rule of an individual—offers a vital check on the *libido dominandi*. This certainly will not prevent all abuses—far from it—but a commitment to the rule of law is a key means of restraining political power. Likewise, common liberal democratic institutional features like the separation of powers, checks and balances, and the like all flow from a tempered assessment of human nature. James Madison's *Federalist* no. 51 argument for checks and balances as a means of maintaining a separation of powers springs from his dim assessment of human's moral rectitude: if men, rather than angels, are to hold power, one *must* provide structural means of checking their ambition.[28] What Madison means by ambition here reflects a deeply Augustinian concern with the *libido dominandi*. Finally, liberal democracies rely on the idea of *accountability*—that governments need to be answerable for their actions. At a basic level, this is the idea that rulers can be removed from office and are responsible to the voting public.

Are these particular features—particularly those associated with Western democratic constitutionalism—*necessary* conclusions of Hopeful Realism? That is, does an evangelical natural law approach to politics *require* this specific form of constitutionalism? This has been suggested elsewhere.[29] We do not make this claim here, though it warrants further exploration (namely, what alternatives could instantiate the sort of restraint that is called for?). Rather, we affirm that Hopeful Realism highlights the wisdom of these approaches to restraining government for securing liberty. An evangelical approach to natural law points to the wisdom and goodness of key features of a liberal democratic order.

---

[28]Madison writes: "If men were angels, no government would be necessary. If angels were to govern men, neither external nor internal controls on government would be necessary. In framing a government which is to be administered by men over men, the great difficulty lies in this: you must first enable the government to control the governed; and in the next place oblige it to control itself." Alexander Hamilton, John Jay, and James Madison, *The Federalist*, ed. George W. Carey and James McClellan, 2nd ed. (Indianapolis, IN: Liberty Fund, 2001), no. 51 (James Madison).
[29]Nicholas Wolterstorff, "Theological Foundations for an Evangelical Political Philosophy," in *Toward an Evangelical Public Policy: Political Strategies for the Health of the Nation*, ed. Ronald J. Sider and Diane Knippers (Grand Rapids, MI: Baker Books, 2005), 140-62.

DEMOCRACY AND DECENTRALIZATION

Hopeful Realism affirms that the creational goods of earthly peace contribute to the common good and therefore calls for a particular kind of politics. Real material, moral, and social goods can provide the basis for substantive political agreement and action. However, acknowledging that such goods exist does not automatically lead to determinate policy conclusions. Humans, as responsible agents, will need to work these out, which we think requires both *democracy* and *decentralization*. As the preceding section argues, human agency within the created order requires liberty. One implication of this agency is the democratic principle that members of a community can exercise their agency together in discerning the shape and direction of that community. In this sense, then, the capacity for agency gets worked out as a call for self-government, both as individuals and as communities.[30]

Of course, individuals and communities will vary in their understanding of what makes for a good life and their willingness to agree on it, both because of human finitude and different ultimate commitments. It is not just that we disagree about what ultimately matters in life; this disagreement means that within the *saeculum* there is significant variation in which earthly goods may be shared in a given place and time. As we've noted before, Augustine is confident that political communities—commonwealths defined by their shared objects of love—can be better or worse. When a people's "shared objects of love" are better, the commonwealth is better. When shared objects of love are worse, the commonwealth suffers.[31] Thus, the shared goods of earthly peace may be more or less robust, more or less well developed, and so on, depending on the political community in view. While not a fully articulated democratic principle, this nevertheless has an important democratic element: *the ends of the political community vary by virtue of the people within it and the objects of their love.* A political community at some level

---

[30] As we have already noted, while Augustine informs this effort, our argument here goes beyond where Augustine himself would go.
[31] Augustine, *City of God*, XIX: 21.

inevitably reflects the people, and the shared objects of love vary among different peoples.

An example may be helpful here. The 1957 case of *Roth v. United States* resisted the idea of a single national standard for identifying obscenity as a category of expression subject to regulation despite First Amendment guarantees. *Roth* held that obscenity could be assessed by asking whether "to the average person, applying contemporary community standards, the dominant theme of the material, taken as a whole, appeals to prurient interest."[32] The community standards aspect of this assessment recognizes that different communities will hold and live out different values that can and should be reflected in their regulatory schemes.

Thus, a central task of political communities is to *work out*—in a manner that respects human dignity and agency across a range of social structures—what aspects of the common good can and should be pursued in a given political context. This requires deliberation and compromise, not just imposition. Augustine describes political rules as a "compromise between human wills about the things relevant to mortal life."[33] Compromise increases the variation yet further, highlighting the reality that *political communities will differ in significant ways*. This is why Hopeful Realism affirms the principle of democracy, where amid the plurality of a political community, commonwealths need to work out their compromise of wills on which shared objects of love may be pursued.[34] This does not specify any particular sort of democracy or give direction on any of a host of other important questions.[35] It simply points toward the idea that political ends should reflect the loves and wills of those within it in ways that respect the particular character(s) of the people within that community.

Significantly, though, the process of working out democratic judgment and compromise in any particular context will still grapple with real

---

[32] Roth v. United States, 354 U.S. 476 at 489.
[33] Augustine, *City of God*, XIX: 17, 877.
[34] Gregory, *Politics*.
[35] For example, this does not specify a preference between direct versus representative democracy, or agonistic versus deliberative democracy, etc.

moral content and guidelines. The parameters of any particular community are not *simply* contingent on whatever happens to be mutually willed by all members of the community. To the extent that those within the political community can reach what John Rawls called an "overlapping consensus"[36] on important moral and political matters, these should be informed by *true moral claims grounded in human nature and the order of creation*. But the degree to which the people in a community can reach consensus and the degree to which the community manifests those truths about human flourishing will inevitably depend to some degree on the people in the community themselves. Hopeful Realism's claim in favor of democracy prioritizes the responsible agency of the people in any community and their understanding of the good as they attempt to secure the goods necessary for human flourishing.

This democratic principle points us in turn to *decentralization*. While larger political communities may be necessary and can have important shared ends, the extent of agreement about shared goods and objects of love across a larger community will inevitably be thinner and less substantive, simply due to the diversity of interests within it. In contrast, the civic commonwealth "thickens" as it moves closer to the local, as shared objects of love increase in scope and the compromise of wills includes more robust goods of earthly peace. This concept has significant affinity with the Roman Catholic and Reformed principle of subsidiarity, though we need not endorse (or reject) the ontological hierarchy associated with this that extends beyond the political.[37] The bottom line is that thicker, more robust conceptions of the good should be politically operationalized at the level of smaller communities rather than larger ones. For example, a prohibition of explicitly racist business practices (a rather "thin" and minimalist account of flourishing) might make sense at a broader policy level, while the details of the moral vision of the good life—including sexuality—to be incorporated into primary school curricula might better account for local norms.

---

[36]See his *Political Liberalism*, Lecture IV, 133-72.
[37]For a helpful orientation, see chaps. 7–9 of Koyzis, *Political Visions*.

This is an important principle in our current moment. Too often, political solutions—offered through a centralized authority—are regularly seen as the primary means of solving our most pressing problems. Decentralization cuts against the popular grain. But for communities divided by their ultimate loves, we would do well to think seriously about how political power can be decentralized in ways that help preserve the relational and volitional goods we have highlighted. Centralization lures us with the promise of clean and final decisions, and no doubt there are times and places where certain types of centralization may and should provide for important goods—especially where collective action problems or other intervening variables may inhibit local efforts. But even a touch of Augustinian realism should make us wary, as consolidated power is more susceptible to the *libido dominandi*, given the heightened opportunities it offers for our sinfulness to manifest as exploitation and control. Decentralization and democracy enable responsible agency and minimize the risks of persistent sin harnessed to centralized power.

Conclusion

To reiterate, we argue that the basic principles of a hopeful realist approach to politics include these:

1. The common good and civic friendship: Our shared human nature and creational context means the earthly peace that governments seek to cultivate includes material, relational, and moral goods that are key building blocks of human flourishing. These can and should guide the substantive ends at which even a liberal democratic order aims. Indeed, liberal democracy needs such guidance in order to remain grounded in the created order and not be directed only by the momentary will of the majority.

2. Confessional pluralism and religious liberty: Human communities are marked by a plurality of ultimate commitments until the eschaton, requiring institutional differentiation of church and state

and protections for religious liberty. This key feature of liberal democratic orders is *essential* to a hopeful realist understanding of politics.

3. Restraint and liberty: The goods of responsible human agency, the danger of power in the hands of sinners, and the importance of virtues like humility, prudence, and detachment all suggest a government of limited powers, exercised with accountability, and a deference to liberty as the default.

4. Democracy and decentralization: Citizen involvement in governance and decentralized power respects human agency, allows political decisions to reflect distinct and varied community values, and aims to keep "thicker" decisions closer to smaller subcommunities.

To be sure, these principles are general and leave much to prudence and contextual factors that would guide particular applications. Nevertheless, they reveal that a commitment to the natural law is not at all incompatible with participation in liberal democracy. Quite the contrary. Rather, Hopeful Realism provides a framework for how political compromise might work with integrity. Moreover, it provides significant guidance for the structure and limits of a liberal democratic order. We are persuaded that this guidance strengthens, rather than weakens, such an order. How Christians might then participate in that sort of order, and how they might make judgments about particular issues or political dilemmas, is where we turn next.

4

MAKING HOPEFUL
REALISM PRACTICAL

IN ONE SENSE, THIS BOOK EMERGED from a conversation one of us had with a friend in church who expressed her exasperation at the political choices she had in an upcoming election and wanted some help in thinking through what she should do. Observation of our students in the classroom and various churches in our orbit suggested similar needs. We had already put together a conference and an edited volume dedicated to questions around whether and how evangelicals might appropriate the natural law tradition. But that work did not go very far in thinking about how to *apply* natural law principles within a political context like ours. This book thus serves a twofold purpose: (1) it describes a theory of natural law politics that reflects evangelical theological emphases and distinctions; and (2) it shows how such a theory can work practically within a pluralist liberal democratic order. We turn to the second task in this chapter. Below, we lay out a framework with which Christians can translate the relatively broad moral and political principles we described in chapters two and three into practical judgments. This framework can help with thinking about particular policy issues, give guidance for voting, suggest whether and how to support causes with time and money, and much else. The second half of the book puts this framework to use in considering a range of relatively controversial issues, and we hope that evangelicals (including our friends in church) will find both the principles and framework useful as they grapple with their own sometimes difficult and exasperating political choices.

First, note something important: *the Hopeful Realism framework does not on its own always produce definitive results.* Or to put it another way, it does not—or at least it does not always—produce a single definitive result. It is not some algorithmic machine into which we as Christians can feed data or even a set of moral claims and then receive back a single, fully orbed answer to which all reasonable and faithful people must agree. That's just not how moral and political reasoning generally works. While of course some policy questions have a clear and definitive answer, even well-meaning and well-informed people will often come to different conclusions while working within the same basic moral and political framework. Sometimes, this is just on account of our limits as finite creatures: we can only know so much about any particular case. But we will also sometimes simply weigh the facts of cases differently. This might be because of our own particular experiences but also simply because we have an intuitive sense that a trade-off should go one way as opposed to another. Our judgments about particular situations and competing goods are simply not identical—a reality that reflects our moral agency. And finally, we should never forget that we are sinful creatures, all too willing to bend our reasoning in the service of our own interests. We may not be the rational creatures that philosophers sometimes suppose us to be, but we are surely "rationalizing" creatures who are capable of thinking our way into some quite bad conclusions if it makes life a bit better for us. So the present volume offers this framework with some modesty as to what we can expect from it.

This has important implications for what we do with our moral and political judgments. Too often, Christians (and others, of course) get ahold of a set of moral or ideological rules and then use them to bludgeon others (and themselves). Anyone with a passing familiarity with contemporary social media culture can recognize this. Alternatively, for some, seeing others act like modern-day inquisitors makes them leery of asserting clearly almost *any* serious or controversial moral or political claim. Modesty and humility are not the same thing as being unwilling to make strong and even controversial moral claims. Indeed, having reasonably modest expectations can help us to see more clearly when we *should* have full confidence in our conclusions. It is vitally important that we strive to get at the right answers to our moral and political questions. If we grasp our own and others' limitations, we can get at those answers while also remaining realistic and modest about where we and others eventually land. We can thus proceed confidently in making our moral and political judgments while also figuring out how to live politically with others who come to other conclusions. It might very well be the case that rooting our judgments in a robust sense of what Scripture *and* nature teach about us will provide a better means of finding common ground than the alternatives. We should not be naive here, but neither need we despair. Hopeful Realism offers sound reasons to believe that there are good answers to even our most contentious and difficult problems and reason to expect that some number of our fellow citizens, family members, and even church members will come to think differently than we do. By rooting our political judgments in our best understanding of what Scripture and nature teach about our common life in the created order, we can embrace judgments in confidence without falling into the sort of demonization of others that characterizes too much of our public discourse these days. The framework we offer below creates a way to do just that.

Hopeful Realism's Framework for Political Judgments

As we have argued in previous chapters, almost every Christian tradition accepts the notion that God's creation includes a moral law that all persons are subject to and that is a key aspect of their flourishing. But in addition to the worries about how we know the substance of that law and whether it is compatible with liberal democratic norms, one clear challenge to making use of natural law theories is figuring out how to get from basic principles to particular policy judgments. It sometimes can seem as though the natural law's basic principles are so basic and abstract that they do not do much in the way of directing our political action, at least not in the kinds of controversial cases where we need the most help. It is one thing, after all, to suggest that any reasonably just political order will look to protect its citizens against murder and assault. No one disputes that. But the succeeding chapters take on issues like public intervention in the economy or when and how to go to war, and these sorts of issues raise quite different questions. There is a lot more space for reasonable disagreement and it is simply harder as a practical matter to connect our first principles to on-the-ground political judgments. This chapter's framework helps bridge that gap.

The first thing to do is to ask, what are we actually doing when we are making political judgments? The answer is this: when we make any political judgment, we are making judgments *about the relative value of particular goods*, like the goods associated with family life, education, employment, worship, and much else. If you were to decide, for example, to vote in favor of a proposal to use tax monies to refurbish a dilapidated building in your community's downtown, you might describe that judgment as deciding in favor of the good of *beauty* (if your interest is in preservation of a certain aesthetic environment) or perhaps *economic well-being* (if you think that the refurbished building will provide economic benefits). If you decided to vote against it, perhaps your interest is also in the good of economic well-being, albeit having come to a different conclusion about the building's economic prospects.

Almost any view of the natural law, ours included, frames its argument in terms of goods, and in particular in terms of how particular goods do or do not relate to human flourishing. Recall our earlier discussion about how theories of the natural law are inextricably tied to understandings of human nature and human flourishing.[1] In one sense, the natural law

---

[1] When Christians use the terms *human flourishing* or *human goods*, they can sometimes mean rather different things. For instance, some use the terms to describe "natural" goods like health, education, and friendship—goods that are shared in some sense by believers and nonbelievers alike. Others, however, use the terms more expansively, to also include reconciliation to God and right relationship with him. We hold that indeed this latter understanding reflects *full* human flourishing and, further, that the "natural" goods in the former are themselves also only *fully* realized when they are properly related to God. It may seem like a rather fine distinction,

just is our reasoned understanding of how goods do and do not contribute to human flourishing and natural law political theories *just are* arguments about how certain sorts of social and political institutions and practices secure and protect—or undermine and neglect—those goods. Given this, our framework proceeds in three steps: (1) we first identify what the good (or goods) at issue are in any particular political issue and how that good (or goods) relates to human flourishing; (2) we then identify the options for securing that good, think through how the different options secure the good, affect other goods, and comport with our political principles; and (3) we finally identify prudential considerations that inevitably come into play in making these judgments.

Step 1: *Identifying the good or principle and how it relates to human flourishing.* It might seem obvious that the first thing we need to do when applying our natural law principles is figure out what sort of good is actually at issue. In a surprising number of cases, the resolution to a political dispute can hinge on how people understand what it is they are actually disputing (i.e., the good in question). For example, in abortion, those in favor of abortion rights think what's at issue is the right of the woman to a sort of bodily autonomy. In contrast, for those opposed to abortion rights, what is at issue is the good of life for the unborn child. It is no accident that one of the most famous arguments in favor of

---

but it carries with it some rather important implications for our project here, most notably with respect to the obligations and limits for ordinary political authorities in relation to citizens' *full* flourishing—i.e., their salvation.

As one of us has argued elsewhere, an Augustinian approach to virtue includes both what we would call "structural" and "directional" aspects. See Jesse Covington, "The Grammar of Virtue: St. Augustine and Natural Law," in *Natural Law and Evangelical Political Thought*, ed. Jesse Covington, Bryan T. McGraw, and Micah Joel Watson (Lanham, MD: Lexington Books, 2013), 167-94. In thinking about morality, *structure* refers to the universal standards to which all goodness must conform (to echo C. S. Lewis's description). These standards, while necessary for virtue, are not sufficient for it, since what looks like virtue can be motivated by self-loving pride and thus in that respect be vice. True virtue is also rightly *directed*, enabled by grace, motivated by love of God, and grounded in union with Christ. The same is true with "flourishing" or "human goods" as we use them here: they have both structural (creational) and directional aspects, though the two are obviously deeply connected. To be clear, when thinking about our ordinary political orders and their relation to flourishing, we mean the structural (or creational) aspect. We do not think political orders have a role to play in salvation, except insofar as creational goods like peace, security, and sustenance make that more or less possible.

> ## Applying Hopeful Realism
>
> ### Step 1: Identifying the good or principle and how it relates to human flourishing
> Working with the categories of physical, rational, volitional, and relational goods, we should try to figure out which good or set of goods is primarily implicated in a political question.
>
> ### Step 2: Discerning and choosing among our options
> We then survey the range of options we might have to address that political question and look to discern which makes the most sense by asking the following questions:
>
> - Question One: Which of the options is most likely to secure the primary good in question in a manner consistent with our political principles?
> - Question Two: Which of the options helps to secure other goods at issue without harming other goods, violating our political principles, or both?
>
> ### Step 3: Applying prudential considerations
> We then think through the relevant prudential considerations in considering how we might best pursue our chosen option in our particular social and political context.

abortion rights acknowledges that the unborn child has indeed a right to not be killed but evades that point by making the inquiry entirely about the woman's right to bodily autonomy.[2] Getting clear on the good (or goods) that are *actually* at stake turns out to matter a lot.

This requires being a bit more systematic than one might expect, but it will help discipline our thinking and make for better judgments. To help organize our reflections on this, we can start with the four categories of goods introduced in chapter two (physical, rational, volitional, and relational) and outline how each relates to human flourishing. These categories can help us think through whether some posited good is, in

---

[2] See Judith Jarvis Thomson, "A Defense of Abortion," *Philosophy and Public Affairs* 47 (1971): 3-22.

fact, a good at all, whether it has any reasonable connection to human flourishing, and eventually how we can frame our deliberations in the steps that follow. It is important to recognize here that these categories are meant to sharpen our thinking about goods and human flourishing and are drawn both from observations about what seems common to human life and from what Scripture teaches. Innumerable scholars and thinkers—Christian and otherwise—have devised similar sorts of frameworks, and while there is not space here to compare our approach to those of others, what appears below fits reasonably well within the broad tradition of natural law.[3]

Physical goods. Just a moment's reflection on what a good human life looks like makes clear that it includes an irreducible physical component. We are physical creatures who breathe, eat, sleep, think, and act as embodied beings. Few serious persons would claim that our lives have gone well in the absence of reasonable physical health or if we are subject to starvation, assault, maiming, or killing.[4] In Christian theology, both the fact of the Incarnation and the importance of Jesus' bodily resurrection— without which Paul says our faith is "futile" (1 Corinthians 15:17)— confirm the importance of bodies and physical goods to our well-being.

Plato is sometimes described as thinking otherwise. In *The Republic*, Plato has Socrates attempting to persuade a group of young Athenian noblemen that they should be just even if it costs them everything, including being horribly maimed and even killed. Aristotle criticizes him on this point in *Politics*, thinking the claim obviously unreasonable. To the degree that they actually disagree, we would be on Aristotle's side: happiness requires certain physical goods. But it's worth noting that Plato is keen to describe all the ways in which the most excellent

---

[3]Other than obviously Aquinas, see also J. Finnis, *Natural Law and Natural Rights* (New York: Oxford University Press, 1980); Russell Hittinger, *The First Grace: Rediscovering the Natural Law in a Post-Christian World* (Wilmington, DE: ISI Books, 2007); J. Budziszewski, *The Resurrection of Nature: Political Theory and the Human Character* (Ithaca, NY: Cornell University Press, 1986).
[4]Given the rapid spread of medically assisted suicide, it is important to note that just because our physical well-being is crucial to our flourishing, it does not follow that significant physical suffering provides grounds for suicide. For a thoughtful reflection in this regard, see G. Meilaender, *Bioethics: A Primer for Christians* (Grand Rapids, MI: Eerdmans, 1996).

persons—the philosopher-kings and queens—would have to have their bodies carefully trained and kept healthy if they are to fulfill their assigned roles.

Augustine similarly sometimes gets associated with disdaining our physical selves, and there are certainly reasons why some interpreters read him as thinking that our embodiment is a sinful burden. And sometimes it is, as in our *sinful* and *finite* embodiment we find ourselves drawn to ways that work against our good. Paul's distinctions between "flesh" and "spirit" are not really reducible to body and soul—that unfairly imports a kind of dualism into Paul's thinking (as Augustine notes[5]). But "flesh" is not just a metaphor. It denotes how the sinful nature impacts our embodied life, particularly idolatries of the senses. No one can read Augustine's *Confessions* and miss how much he struggled against his own flesh-ness. But neither did he adopt some caricatured gnostic-like Platonism of thinking our "true" selves are just disembodied spirits. Indeed, if we attend to the most famous chapter in *City of God*, book XIX, there Augustine levels critique after critique of stoicism (which *does* devalue embodied life) on the grounds that it cannot deliver a true accounting of human flourishing partly because it neglects embodied suffering. And he makes clear in the same chapter that the "earthly peace" described in chapters two and three is itself tied up with our physical selves.

Of course, that points to a crucial truth we must not forget: attending to the embodied nature of human flourishing does not mean that human flourishing is simply *reducible* to our physical well-being or that it acts as a kind of trump card when it comes into conflict with other goods. We all recognize that there are times when the obligation to do the right thing—to live well—can mean sacrificing our physical well-being, and Scripture clearly teaches that physical goods are not the end-all-be-all of human flourishing. No one who follows a man who gave himself up to a gruesome death on a cross should believe that. But Christ's body restored in the resurrection points beyond the cross to a renewed, embodied life.

---

[5]Augustine, *City of God*, trans. Henry Bettenson, repr. ed. (New York: Penguin Classics, 2004), XIV: 2-5 (548-55).

So, the general point stands. *Our physical well-being matters* for our flourishing, and it matters for this present project in at least two respects: first and foremost, it enables us to engage creation—including acting as agents; and second, it acts as a bulwark against unjust oppression.[6] We will briefly describe each in turn.

Physical goods matter first insofar as our bodies are a primary interface with creation—as regards enjoyment and agency. When Adam is placed in the garden in Genesis, he is quite clearly put there for certain purposes. For our purposes here, agency is especially important. Adam is to do more than just while away his days enjoying the view (though he is also just as clearly given leave to simply *enjoy* creation as such). God gives him what becomes known in some theological circles as the "creation mandate" or "cultural mandate," as noted in chapter one: he is to fill, subdue, and develop the earth. For the church father Irenaeus, this is a command to participate in the completion of creation.[7] He and Eve have tasks to do, tasks which continue, albeit in drastically altered form, after their Fall and expulsion from the garden. Adam and Eve are then, among other things, created to be agents, creatures with the capacity to reflect, choose, and act of their own accord—sometimes to disastrous ends, but also sometimes to remarkable ones. They were (and we are) *agents*, and our capacity for agency is intrinsic to what it means to be a human being.[8] Significantly, however, this agency is not a "freestanding" good, but rather one that is directly tied to image-bearing: our agency in creation, while it can be misused, is designed to follow the example and character of our Creator.

For some, invoking agency may raise all sorts of alarm bells, and understandably so. For all too often, an overemphasis on human agency can

---

[6]This is by no means meant to be an exhaustive account of the significance of embodiment to flourishing. We do not denigrate other aspects of the goodness of embodiment in terms of beauty, sensory pleasure, etc. Nor would we minimize the way that God can use physical suffering for good in the lives of believers.

[7]See C. Gunton, *Christ and Creation* (Grand Rapids, MI: Eerdmans, 1992).

[8]To avoid any misunderstanding on this point, what we mean here is that agency is a part of being a human being, not that any human being who lacks (or loses) the capacity for agency thereby ceases to be a human being.

lead to the sort of person John Stuart Mill celebrated in *On Liberty*: the sovereign person who lives only by his or her own lights, who is happy to experiment with the full range of moral choices, and who only owes to others what he or she has *chosen* to owe.[9] It can sometimes resemble more like what the serpent offers to Eve—to be "like God, [choosing what is] good and evil" (see Genesis 3:5)—than what any Christian should regard as true flourishing. But the suspicion of agency is misplaced precisely because Mill mischaracterizes what agency actually *is*. Agency is not just acting independently of one's context in every respect. That is impossible, at least insofar as you end up bumping up against others. It is, as the sociologist Christian Smith has described, the capacity to reflect and act toward reasonable and good ends in the context of already existing moral, social, and political structures.[10] Or, to put it a bit more theologically, it is the capacity to reflect and act as embodied creatures within a good, if fallen, creation—not independently of that creation. The very nature of the creation mandate assumes (and indeed requires) agency in response to God's commands.

This is how most decent parents think about what they want for their children, that they grow up to be responsible adults, able to care for themselves and those around them. That requires more than mere potential. It requires investment: attention, care, education—never mind food, water, shelter, and so on. To be able to exercise agency in some fashion, human beings require, at least, access to a range of basic physical goods. While we can imagine scenarios—say, a severe drought requiring rationing—such that we might be justified in not providing a particular person water, there is no plausible argument for preventing someone in general from accessing water for their basic needs. To do otherwise would be little different in practice than simply killing them outright. Thus social orders quite plausibly have obligations to prioritize access to these sorts of goods.

---

[9] John Stuart Mill, *On Liberty* (Indianapolis, IN: Hackett Publishing, 1978).
[10] C. Smith, *Moral, Believing Animals: Human Personhood and Culture* (New York: Oxford University Press, 2003).

Agency requires more than just having material resources available to us. We must also have the ability to exercise that agency—namely, a type of freedom. One must not be prevented from fulfilling the creation mandate. If there is a consistent claim across the long tradition of Western moral and political thought, it is that *tyranny* is a particular and particularly intolerable evil. Tyranny is not just finding yourself oppressed by another person or political order. It is the kind of oppression in which we are put under the un-tender mercies of someone's arbitrary will.

Alexander Solzhenitsyn won a Nobel Prize for his *Gulag Archipelago*, where he catalogued the horror at the heart of the Stalinist Soviet political order. Millions found themselves subject to arbitrary arrest, torture, imprisonment, and death. No one truly knew whether they were vulnerable because the system's victims were picked out sometimes almost at whim. The sheer physical terror of hearing the boots of the secret police coming up the stairs of an apartment building at night and not knowing if they will stop at your door is not, to put it mildly, conducive to human flourishing.

If tyranny, especially as it treats our physical bodies, is indeed incompatible with human flourishing, we can infer some things about the kinds of immunities against attack, coercion, or disablement that are proper to us. We often describe these immunities in the contemporary world with the language of "rights." What we often mean by "rights" language is that we all have claims against others in that they may not, morally speaking, breach those immunities. Absent some very good reason, one person may not assault another walking across the park. These sorts of immunities and their associated rights tend to be absolute. Some physical goods are so basic to our well-being that they almost always imply categorical prohibitions like the proscription of murder.

Here, too, misconceptions around the idea of rights cast these sorts of immunities in a bad light. The perfectly defensible immunity we might have against unwanted medical treatment, for example, gets taken by some to a near unlimited right to demand physician-assisted suicide (PAS).[11] This is a real danger, but it emerges from the same misunderstanding as before with respect to what it means to be an agent. Again, too often we think about human agency merely in terms of individual autonomy, where the person is freed from external constraints to act according to his or her subjective will. On that account, rights are little more than social conventions assigned to protect whatever interests we might assert. But if agency is in fact much more like the view we briefly described above (the capacity to exercise responsibilities for genuine goods within a specific community), then rights are something quite different. They are better understood as immunities that protect the social and personal space necessary for us to reflect, choose, and act toward genuine goods. And insofar as those rights protect our physical selves, they make possible our capacity to act as agents in ways that further and indeed partly constitute our flourishing.

Rational goods. In his magisterial reflection on law, Thomas Aquinas defines law as a "rule of reason promulgated by one who has responsibility for a community towards the common good" and the natural law as our "participation in the eternal law."[12] The eternal law is how God orders all of creation and everything "participates" in that law by acting according to its nature. A rock "participates" in the eternal law by acting like a rock, subject to the laws of physics, chemistry, and the like. We participate in the eternal law by acting according to our nature as rational beings with the capacity to learn, discern, and choose what is good and then to act on those choices. As bearers of the divine image, we imitate God's ordered reason (to the extent possible) as part of our nature. The natural law according to Aquinas, then, just *is* the set of norms and obligations entailed by exercising our nature properly: understanding, choosing, and acting toward our proper end, proper in the sense of

---

[11]See Ronald Dworkin et al., "Assisted Suicide: The Philosophers' Brief," *The New York Review of Books*, March 27, 1997, www.nybooks.com/articles/archives/1997/mar/27/assisted-suicide-the-philosophers-brief/.

[12]Thomas Aquinas, *Summa Theologica*, I-II, Q. 91. A2. From *Aquinas on Law, Morality, and Politics*, trans. Richard J. Regan, 2nd ed. (Indianapolis, IN: Hackett Publishing Company, 2002), 18.

constituting our flourishing as natural creatures.[13] For us to live well, we must develop the capacity for what the tradition calls "practical reason," the capacity to choose well what we are supposed to do, as well as the corresponding capacity to act on those (good) choices. In the way we have described things, this means pursuing the sorts of goods that help us discern choice-worthy ends (rational goods) and being able to act toward those ends (volitional goods).

A range of late-modern Protestants have expressed some skepticism about the rational-goods aspect of the natural law precisely because they think that it on the one hand underestimates the effects of sin on our rationality and on the other, tends toward a moral autonomy that is incompatible with our status as creatures dependent on God. These are fair worries and exploring them will help illuminate what we mean—and don't mean—by rational goods.

The second worry, the moral autonomy concern, was discussed a bit above, but it's important enough to return to it again. In Genesis, we learn some of the deepest truths about human beings, among them that we are created in the image of God and that we are all heirs of a Fall, where our first parents broke with God and then with one another. But for what end did they break that fellowship? Well, consider how the story is related:

> Now the serpent was more crafty than any of the wild animals the Lord God had made. He said to the woman, "Did God really say, 'You must not eat from any tree in the garden'?"
>
> The woman said to the serpent, "We may eat fruit from the trees in the garden, but God did say, 'You must not eat fruit from the tree that is in the middle of the garden, and you must not touch it, or you will die.'"
>
> "You will not certainly die," the serpent said to the woman. "For God knows that when you eat from it your eyes will be opened, and you will be like God, knowing good and evil."

---

[13] Aquinas argues that we are also bound by a divine law that orders us to our supernatural ends, what he calls the beatific vision, a full communion with God. This divine law is revealed to us in the life, death, and resurrection of Christ and in the teachings of Scripture.

When the woman saw that the fruit of the tree was good for food and pleasing to the eye, and also desirable for gaining wisdom, she took some and ate it. She also gave some to her husband, who was with her, and he ate it. (Genesis 3:1-6)

What does it mean to "be like God, knowing good and evil"? For a range of modern philosophers—Rousseau and Kant among them—it means awakening to a kind of moral autonomy, a capacity for discerning and choosing what is good (and evil) for ourselves. Indeed, for them, the story is hardly a "fall" at all. It is, rather, a story of us achieving our humanity through moral autonomy. But for Christians, it cannot be that. It is clearly disobedience to God, for which Adam and Eve are severely punished, as are the rest of us.[14] To aspire to moral autonomy by ignoring our fundamental dependence on God is in fact rebellion, against both God and our nature. Securing, or pursuing, rational goods does not mean securing or pursuing moral autonomy as such.

It is thus tempting to dismiss the rational goods and suppose them to be relatively unimportant (or even problematic), especially when many in our liberal societies too often employ arguments around those goods to justify unlimited abortion rights or disturbingly expansive schemes of physician-assisted suicide. But our flourishing does clearly involve our capacity for rational reflection and choice-making—and the former serves to guide and limit the latter. The remarkable things that even the fallen human mind can create are surely the gift of a good Creator. Or consider the way that even the *idea* of a moral law carries with it the sense that it is given to creatures who can and do have the responsibility to make the right choices.[15] There may be less distance between human beings and other animals in terms of rational capacities than Aquinas or others in the tradition have supposed,[16] but we can clearly observe that

---

[14] A marvelous exploration of this idea of the "original sin" and its uses (and misuses) across history is Alan Jacobs, *Original Sin: A Cultural History* (New York: HarperOne, 2008).
[15] This is reflected even in the Mosaic code, where offenses are treated differently based on whether volition was part of the offense.
[16] See Caitrin Keiper, "Do Elephants Have Souls?" *The New Atlantis*, Winter/Spring 2013, www.thenewatlantis.com/publications/do-elephants-have-souls.

we are distinct in our capacity for reflection and choice. Our *nature*—and thus our "participation in the eternal law"—is wrapped up in *reflecting* and *choosing*. What's more, it also seems clear that while Scripture shows the poverty of an untrammeled moral autonomy, it also shows again and again how God allows people to make meaningful choices. We are not automatons. Even in the garden, after all, Adam and Eve are granted space and time to make their choices, to admittedly fateful ends.

Human flourishing thus is tied up in some important sense with *our capacity to reflect on and make choices about our ends*. To live well involves choosing well and things that help develop our ability to do that thus are important to our well-being. In ways similar to the discussion of physical goods, we have to take seriously the idea that human persons need their liberty protected so that they themselves can rationally discern goods and make choices about their own lives. Even those like Aquinas, whose religious liberty credentials are relatively weak, emphasized the importance of the liberty of conscience.[17] Societies that overly constrain individual and corporate liberties do real damage to human flourishing, even sometimes when done in the name of that same flourishing. Of course, our sinfulness and finitude make it hard for us to know fully what is actually good. Even Christians who have access to Spirit-illuminated special revelation in Scripture see through the glass darkly (1 Corinthians 13:12 KJV). And so what one person thinks is an oppressive constraint on human liberty is for another a reasonable reflection of human knowledge of what is truly good. We cannot flesh out here the proper limits our theory of the natural law would suggest with respect to our political liberties, though we will try to model in our subsequent chapters just how Hopeful Realism can help us all work through these often quite vexing moral and political judgments. For now, note that the protection of our liberty is essential in

---

[17] Aquinas upheld the inviolability of religious conscience but also thought that the political authority could reasonably punish heretics within the church as they (or their parents) had already made their choice. See his *Summa Theologica*, II-II, Q. 10.8. For an argument showing how early Christians articulated a robust view of religious liberty, see Robert Louis Wilken, *Liberty in the Things of God* (New Haven, CT: Yale University Press, 2019). See chap. 8 of this book for our argument about how the natural law points to a rather strong view of religious liberty.

that it shields our capacity for reflecting and choosing well, since these capacities are part of our nature as human beings.

That, of course, prompts the other worry, that in focusing our attention on human beings' rational capacities for choosing toward our flourishing, we underestimate the effects of sin on our cognitive and volitional abilities. It's all well and good to say that we are the sorts of creatures created with rational capacities to choose what is good, but quite clearly, we make errors all the time, sometimes horrible ones, and sometimes on purpose. What sense does it make to organize our moral and political reflections in terms of a set of goods about which we frequently err? Aren't we just set up for failure, and maybe in our failure end up profoundly harming ourselves and others? A skeptic here might suggest that Scripture doesn't just teach that humans are given some important degree of choice but that they also reliably and persistently choose poorly.

We are indeed sinful and are all too often gravely mistaken about what is good for human persons. This afflicts even those who emphasize the natural law. Two responses might help here, though. First, if, as Christians believe, sin truly affects us all, this includes political leaders, and this counsels in favor of limited powers for government and a relatively expansive set of liberties for citizens, since there's no reason to think that those who hold political power are particularly graced with a better understanding than the rest of us. This doesn't mean they know nothing, but it does suggest a degree of modesty occasioned by a recognition of our limits. Augustine suggests that Scripture provides vital illumination for Christians who study it with faith, but that even then our knowledge remains partial and sometimes simply mistaken. Whether political leaders are Christians or non-Christians, we just cannot assume infallible guidance that would justify the denial of liberty as such.[18]

---

[18]For an excellent discussion of how this concern for human fallenness shaped the framing of the American political order, see Robert Tracy McKenzie, *We the Fallen People: The Founders and the Future of American Democracy* (Downers Grove, IL: InterVarsity Press, 2021). See below for our argument that human sinfulness and finitude provide good grounds for the protection of human liberty.

Second, and just as importantly, it is a mistake to go from an acknowledgment of human sinfulness to absolute pessimism about what we can know and how we can come to know it. Modesty is not the same as skepticism, and it is quite possible to cultivate the goods necessary for us to get better in this respect. Even a non-Christian teacher of logic would recognize meaningful standards for students' instruction and improvement in their use of their rational capacity. Augustine would describe the occluded knowledge of non-Christians as "twilight knowledge": they can see things, just not clearly or fully, since "twilight" is not darkness. And as Christian teachers, we can all attest to the ways that careful study, biblical analysis, theological training, and participation in a community of learners can cultivate our capacity to discern truth, including choice-worthy ends. There is no sure formula, and this book can hardly even scratch the surface of what sort of education and formation in virtue is needed for its success. But consider the state of our online discourse. Could we describe it as anything other than mostly an example of what a *vicious* exercise of our rational capacities looks like? And can't we imagine ways we can and should do better? We need not be naive optimists to believe that there are goods worth pursuing and that the exercise of our rational faculties can enable us to obtain true knowledge and to make good choices that contribute to our and others' flourishing.

Volitional goods. Our calling to fulfill the cultural mandate by imitating God and developing the created order involves *choices and acting on them*. Making choices, exercising our human creativity—even Adam's naming of animals—necessarily involves more than just our rationality. It involves the exercise of our will, or volition. This is true even when a choice is not between good and evil but between multiple good options. To the degree that we have a role to play in developing creation (Scripture begins with a garden and ends with a garden-city), it should be clear that we are created to exercise our agency, making volition a key human good.[19] It is simply a part of who we are supposed to be.

---

[19]The relative importance of human agency in God's redemption of creation is, of course, a matter of great dispute, even among Christians who might seem to agree on almost everything. For our

Making Hopeful Realism Practical

Post-Fall, of course, we have to consider additional variables. Sometimes, even when we know what we are supposed to do, we nonetheless choose not to make ourselves do it. Sometimes it's trivial, eating some food that we know isn't healthy for us. Sometimes it's terribly significant—say, defrauding a customer or cheating on a spouse. In such moments it isn't that we're seeing through the proverbial glass "darkly." We see quite clearly enough. We know what we are supposed to do. We are burdened with divided wills, as we do the things we should not do and don't do the things we should (Romans 7:15-20). To this dilemma, what we call volitional goods can speak, as these are goods describing the right use of our will. They are the goods associated with the action that comes on the heels of choosing and, ideally, joining the two together for our and our neighbors' good.

Think of the best person you know, the person whose character is unimpeachable, who always seems to do and say the right thing, even when it comes at some significant cost—or even when it doesn't even matter all that much. Philosophers and theologians would say that he or she inhabits the virtues appropriate to a human being.[20] What they mean is that a good human being possesses a set of habits that makes it likely that he or she will do the right thing when faced with some choice. When offered the opportunity to pad their wallet a bit by deceiving a customer, they demur. When they see another in need, they act. Virtues do not turn us into mechanistic automatons who just always do the right thing. It is, remember, in our nature to make choices. Virtues just make it possible for us to make the right choices for the right reasons and then act on those choices.

People do not come to inhabit the virtues just willy-nilly. Some people, of course, seem to have natural inclinations that make the acquisition of

---

part, we think indeed that we do have some important role to play, though clearly under God's providence. But even if you disagree about that, it is hard to imagine how we could understand ourselves as created without agency.

[20]Bear in mind the distinction in note 1 above with respect to the structural and directional aspects of virtue. Here, the structural aspect is most clearly in view. But rightly understood, the virtues are directionally motivated by love of God and enabled by grace.

this virtue or that one easier, in much the same way that some people find it easy to run, throw a ball, or play an instrument. But no one becomes virtuous simply by accident; they are trained into it. Take children, for example. Almost every parent experiences the mild (or severe!) shock of having their children reflect back to them their own habits, tics, and figures of speech, sometimes happily and sometimes not. All parents worth their salt, moreover, look to help shape their children—teaching, encouraging, reproving—such that they become the sorts of adults we hope they will become. What's true about parents and children is true in general: we come to inhabit (or fail to inhabit) the virtues to some very great measure because of the ways we have been formed.[21]

We are here just recapitulating a longstanding tradition that has its roots in both classical Greek philosophy and Scripture. Aristotle is, of course, the most notable classical source: his *Nicomachean Ethics* is a staple of college philosophy courses and largely has set the terms for how we think about virtue, but no reader of Scripture can miss how Proverbs and other texts offer similar lessons. There are better and worse ways of living, and good character—virtues—are key to the better. But neither the classical nor biblical traditions teach that we can just do this on our own, bootstrapping our way into the good life. For that, we have the never-ending and never-fruitful "self-help" industry that feeds our illusions of autonomy. Children cannot become virtuous simply being left to their own devices. They need parents to guide and shape them and we need others to guide and shape us as well. A somewhat simple way to understand this is that human beings, when faced with a choice to act in one way or another, never simply choose *ex nihilo*. We are not wholly determined by our context, but we are all always profoundly influenced by our context: our already existing character, history, institutional incentives, and so on. In making good choices—treating others with integrity,

---

[21]Of course, this outside-in description of formation addresses structural aspects of virtue and does not always "work" even in this limited capacity. But the fact that it sometimes does is why Augustine can say that pagan virtues can be virtually indistinguishable from Christian virtues in how they manifest themselves. In a more fundamental and ultimate sense, however, only the transformation of the heart by grace and its reoriented loves makes true virtue possible.

exhibiting courage, remaining faithful to our commitments, and so forth—we are putting into play habits or inclinations that themselves have been built up over a long period of time. And that doesn't just happen by accident. It is, at least in part, the product of institutions—families, schools, churches, associations, and so on—that work to make us into who we are, or at least who we can be.[22] So when we think about volitional goods, we should think about institutions and their role in developing our character. Whether more formal institutions like schools, churches, civic groups or more informal ones like a workout group, they go some distance toward shaping us and making us more likely (or unlikely) to be virtuous, to be capable of acting toward our and others' good.

Relational goods. In chapter one, we noted that right from the beginning, God judged that it was "not good" for Adam to be alone. When the apostle John attempts to describe his vision of the consummated Kingdom of God in Revelation, the picture is, tellingly, of a great assembly worshiping God and of a new Jerusalem set within a new heavens and new earth. This picture of the redeemed creation makes clear that what it means to flourish *fully* as a human person is not a solitary endeavor nor is it simply an exercise in internal reflection. Lewis's imaginative description of hell in *The Great Divorce* incisively brings that point home, suggesting that eternal punishment is a deeply lonely affair.[23] Jesus' teaching on the greatest commandments confirms we are built ultimately to love God and love one another. Flourishing necessarily involves a web of human relationships and means of sociality, and relational goods are those goods that enable the sorts of institutions, associations, and the like that make that relational flourishing possible and even more likely.

There has been a good bit of attention paid of late to what the economists Angus Deaton and Anne Case have called the "deaths of despair."[24]

---

[22]See Yuval Levin, *A Time to Build: From Family and Community to Congress and the Campus, How Recommitting to Our Institutions Can Revive the American Dream* (New York: Basic Books, 2020).
[23]Perhaps the most striking picture there is that of Napoleon, alone at the edges of hell, pacing and muttering to himself. Lewis's description follows on from his teacher George MacDonald, who said in a sermon, "The one principle of Hell is 'I am my own.'"
[24]Anne Case and Angus Deaton, *Deaths of Despair and the Future of Capitalism* (Princeton, NJ: Princeton University Press, 2020).

The striking rise in the United States of suicides, drug overdoses, and other similar deaths over the past decade or so has been significant enough to measurably depress average life expectancy. The UK government appointed a "Minister of Loneliness" in 2018 to combat the widespread phenomenon of its citizens having essentially no real human relationships.[25] American teenagers seem less likely to engage in all sorts of risky behavior—dangerous driving, illicit drug use, promiscuous sex—but exhibit much higher rates of anxiety, depression, and suicidal ideations largely (perhaps) because they're just not leaving home as much.[26] To the degree that these are all connected, they are all rooted in the loss or absence of relationships, in the deep interpersonal ties that pull together and sustain families, friendships, neighborhoods, and much else. And, indeed, it is increasingly clear that a key feature of life satisfaction is the presence of deep, meaningful relationships—not higher income, status, or whatnot.

This should not be surprising. A moment's reflection makes obvious the importance of the kinds of relationships we all enjoy (or wish we could enjoy) within families, friendships, and other kinds of associations. Human beings are obviously social creatures. The odd exceptions are classic cases of exceptions proving the rule. Christians more than anyone should not be surprised by that. We worship a triune God whose very essence is relational, and we are called into the collective "body of Christ." Human beings are created in the image of the relational God. This means it is intrinsic to our nature to relate to others. One rather Augustinian way of understanding this is that we are fundamentally *loving* creatures, called to love God and love others in God. We are relational and our flourishing depends on how our relationships are oriented and structured.[27]

---

[25]Ceylan Yeginsu, "U.K. Appoints a Minister for Loneliness." *The New York Times*, January 17, 2018, sec. World, www.nytimes.com/2018/01/17/world/europe/uk-britain-loneliness.html. The appointment of Tracey Crouch was in part a response to studies that suggested large numbers of people in the United Kingdom did not have regular conversations with anyone.

[26]Jean M. Twenge, "Have Smartphones Destroyed a Generation?" *The Atlantic*, September 2017, www.theatlantic.com/magazine/archive/2017/09/has-the-smartphone-destroyed-a-generation/534198/.

[27]To be sure, describing this "good" in terms of loving God and loving others in God makes explicit the directional aspect of this good (as opposed to just structural). But the directional

Making Hopeful Realism Practical

Of course, not all relations are good and conducive to our flourishing. We are all too aware of the ways in which abuse, manipulation, and exploitation can do profound damage. Nonetheless, since we are relational beings our relationality is intrinsic to our well-being. It is essential for helping us cultivate virtue and providing crucial means of acting effectively. Below is a brief sketch of what each means in turn.

The above discussion outlined how both rational and volitional goods help us develop the capacities, habits, and inclinations appropriate to being a good human being. The means to attaining those goods are often, if not always, relational. We simply are not equipped to become virtuous on our own; we need other people to help us along. Parents and families are the most obvious and ubiquitous example: the evidence is overwhelming that children who grow up in intact, stable families with two parents do much better than others, to the degree that some scholars have (perhaps somewhat tongue-in-cheek) proposed that if we're serious about inequality, we might have to think about dispensing with the family.[28] And we all recognize the ways teachers, coaches, pastors, and the like can help make us into functioning, flourishing adults.

In the second volume of *Democracy in America*, Alexis de Tocqueville, the great nineteenth-century French chronicler of American democracy, marvels at the American habit of joining together in all manner of associations. This brings any number of benefits, including moral formation. But these associations crucially make it possible for people to act as agents in a democratic world. Humans are defined in some way by our capacity to act as agents. In a mass democratic society, this becomes challenging—well-nigh impossible—if each person acts as a mere individual.

---

aspect is by no means limited to this good. It still applies to physical, rational, and volitional goods described above.

[28] See Harry Brighouse and Adam Swift, *Family Values: The Ethics of Parent-Child Relationships* (Princeton, NJ: Princeton University Press, 2014). To be clear, Brighouse and Swift do not commend the abolition of the family, but they do argue for giving the state a lot more authority over children because of the ways parents can confer "advantages" to their children. For a compelling argument about the importance of parents to well-being, see Melissa S. Kearney, *The Two-Parent Privilege: How the Decline in Marriage Has Increased Inequality and Lowered Social Mobility, and What We Can Do About It* (London: Swift Press, 2023).

We need one another in order to resist or effect change: "we" can act effectively where "I" will just flounder. To the degree that such agency is indeed a part of our nature and thus flourishing, it is with our relation to one another that we can be (and do) what we should.

Step 2: *Discerning and choosing among our options*. Once we have a good sense of what good or goods are at stake with a particular political issue and how securing (or failing to secure) those goods would bear on our and others' flourishing, we then need to identify our options and how to choose between or among them. In some sense, this is the most fraught and challenging part of the Hopeful Realism framework, as here we must grapple with and choose what tradeoffs we think are correct, and there is no straightforward or easy way to make those judgments. But judge we must, and to do it well requires bringing to bear the resources of both special and general revelation on two distinct questions: (1) Which of the options is most likely to secure the primary good in question in a manner consistent with our political principles? and (2) Which of the options helps to secure *other* related goods without harming other goods, violating our political principles, or both? Before explaining these two questions and how to answer them, we should explore what it means to bring the resources of special and general revelation to bear.

First, consider special revelation, especially as it relates to the created order. What does Scripture teach about goods relevant to all humans as humans? Consistent with how we have framed Hopeful Realism above, we start with Scripture to see if there are more or less clear teachings that inform how to evaluate the options at hand. Sometimes, Scripture will simply be silent on a particular matter, but often we can learn a great deal by attending to the biblical text. Take, for instance, the relatively easy question of who has authority to impose physical punishments on criminals. It is well-nigh impossible to offer a scriptural argument that gets around Romans 13, where Paul very clearly teaches that it is the relevant political authority who "wields the sword," not any private person or corporation.

Making Hopeful Realism Practical

Of course, looking to special revelation involves more than mere "proof-texting." Scripture is often clear, but it also often requires patient, searching inquiries that inevitably involve theological, philosophical, and other sorts of resources to understand what it reveals about God's nature and purposes. Consider, for example, the "cultural mandate" we cited earlier, which describes God's command to Adam to fill and subdue the earth, exercising "dominion." What that means is not a matter of straightforwardly reading the account in Genesis and then grasping as obvious that human beings have responsibilities rooted in creation to build out communities—in all their wild and remarkable diversity—that will respond to that mandate. Similarly, when Jesus says that he has come to "fulfill the law" without changing the law, while pretty clearly freeing us from judgment under the law, what does that mean for how we understand lessons drawn from Israel's example? These are not straightforward or easy questions to solve.[29]

Second, we turn to general revelation to see what it offers as regards the options available in a particular context. As noted in chapter two, Scripture itself teaches that Christians should look to what nature and our reason can tell us about our flourishing. We think that we can only really understand nature through the eyes of Scripture, but that does not mean that nature itself does not have anything to teach us. In attempting to discern among options, bringing the resources of general revelation to bear means employing our reason as best we can. But what does that mean? Well, in general, it means to offer arguments (or reasons) drawn from common observations from the world around us. But that is but the barest gesture at an answer, for what it means to employ our reason is hotly contested, to the point of some denying it has much utility at all. For present purposes, it seems enough to try to understand the world around us and employ our rational capacities to make judgments about what that understanding might imply for our lives.

---

[29]For an especially involved effort in that direction, see Oliver O'Donovan, *Desire of the Nations: Rediscovering the Roots of Political Theology* (New York: Cambridge University Press, 1996).

We should recognize, though, that we are not on our own as we bring our reason to bear. The English essayist G. K. Chesterton once suggested that if we were to come across a fence in a pasture, we should be reluctant to remove it even if we could not see why it was there. At the very least, it at one time served some purpose and likely continues to do so. The same is true of many, perhaps most, of our social practices and institutions, and in thinking about what general revelation might teach us, one important clue has to be what others have traditionally believed. In the natural law tradition, there is a consistent effort to work through what is called the "law of nations" (*jus gentium*) as a means of discerning the content of the natural law. The idea is that we might be able to identify practices that have emerged in different parts of the world that have important commonalities, and that those commonalities could suggests that they contribute to human flourishing. It probably goes without saying, but of course these practices can turn out to be dreadfully wrong—and they have too often done so. Not only are we all too likely to pick and choose which "common practices" are common with an eye toward our own self-interest, but sometimes what is "common" is just wrong. Enslavement is the most obvious example, perhaps, but there are plenty of others. On the other hand, we can sometimes save ourselves a great deal of grief if we decline to embrace every new "advance" that comes down the road. The traditional convention that children generally do better with intact families with both parents was a generation ago challenged as outmoded, even oppressive, but today is recognized as an obvious truism. Tradition can certainly be wrong, but if we first treat it as the accumulated repository of human judgments, we can benefit from our forebears and make better, if always imperfect, judgments of our own.

To *choose* among our options is often the most challenging part of making moral and political judgments. Sometimes we are faced with a number of different good options, and it can be agonizing to foreclose one in favor of another. Other times, we are compelled to accept tragic losses one way or another and must decide which of those losses we are willing to endure. To help navigate these dilemmas, we can ask two questions: which of our options is most likely *to secure* the good in question and which of the options is most likely to *not damage* other important goods, all with an eye toward how the options would fit with our political principles. Below is a brief sketch of what we mean by each.

Question One: Which of the options is most likely to secure the primary good at issue in a manner consistent with our political principles? Our first question is pretty obvious, though it may help to explain what it means to secure a good in a way consistent with our political principles. Say that the issue at hand is how best to organize primary and secondary education for children. This obviously has implications for the development primarily of rational and volitional goods, the latter since schooling goes some distance toward shaping children's moral character. Imagine that we had three options on the table: (1) leave it solely to private individuals to fund and organize children's education (generally the situation prior to the nineteenth century); (2) make it an exclusively state-run affair; or (3) employ some sort of public-private hybrid (like in most democratic societies). Both (1) and (2) would run afoul of our political principles. The former fails because it probably doesn't even really aim at securing the common good in that it would inevitably leave some significant part of the population without access to education, especially the sort of education that would prepare children to live well in the modern world. The latter fails because it doesn't make space for modes of education that differ from what a secular state might offer.[30] That is, it violates the liberty and restraint principle in that it needlessly centralizes education at the cost of protecting pluralism.

Sometimes, none of the options available actually *violate* one of the principles. Then, the analysis looks to see if one of them fulfills them better than the others. Take the education question again, and suppose that we consider three versions of the hybrid model: (3a) where the state

---

[30]Here, ironically enough, John Stuart Mill is quite the ally in his deep distrust of government-directed education and its tendency to suppress liberty. For a well-considered Christian argument in favor of educational pluralism, see R. McCarthy et al., *Society, State, and Schools: A Case for Structural and Confessional Pluralism* (Grand Rapids, MI: Eerdmans, 1981).

runs public schools for everyone and private groups are free to run their own schools with moderate degrees of regulation (the model that largely obtains in the United States currently); (3b) where the state runs public schools and provides limited funding to private schools through aid monies; or (3c) where the state runs public schools and funds private schools equitably on a per-student basis. None of these seem to obviously violate our political principles and all three have their advantages and disadvantages, but it seems plausible to argue in favor of (3c) on account of its better protection of "confessional plurality." The details in the options would matter a great deal, so this is not an argument per se for (3c) but is just meant to be illustrative of the process.

Question Two: Which of the options helps to secure other goods at issue without harming other goods, violating our political principles, or both? This second question really asks us to look at the sort of knock-on effects a policy choice might have. No one can ever anticipate all of a given policy's effects—unintended consequences are very much a real thing—but for those we can anticipate, we should evaluate our options along two lines. First, would one policy over another help secure other goods not primarily at issue? Consider again the second set of education options above. The primary good is the education of children. Suppose evidence suggesting that some forms of religious schools actually did better than their counterparts at cultivating their students' capacities for civic engagement and social responsibility. That would be a point in favor of (3c).

Suppose, though, that we had evidence that private religious schools increased racial segregation and racial animus. (We do not have evidence in that direction, for what it's worth.) That would most obviously tell against (3c), since that option would harm what we are calling relational goods as well as work against the common good. Of course, policy options can always be tweaked to mitigate negative effects, but we should not miss the fact that there are rarely simple wins when it comes to trying to find solutions to thorny social and political issues. And so the question often isn't whether a policy in question will or will not cause any harms; it's what sorts of harms it will likely cause and whether those harms are worth the expected benefits. One of the reasons economic analysis can be such a powerful tool in thinking about tradeoffs is that it focuses our attention on those tradeoffs along a common metric, usually money. But for noneconomic questions or issues with a mix of economic and noneconomic metrics, knowing exactly how to make the tradeoffs is especially difficult—and we are skeptical that there is a foolproof or straightforward way of doing so. Indeed, even within economics, judging tradeoffs is not nearly so straightforward as we might suppose, since burdens and benefits fall differently on different people and there are, in fact, a range of "economic" outcomes to consider, not all of which are commensurable. The difficulties are magnified when trying to compare goods that are even less comparable. Nonetheless, in discerning which options we might choose (for or against), these are the sorts of considerations to which we must attend.

Step 3: Applying prudential considerations. The last point above brings out something that bears developing. As the previous discussion has hopefully made clear, Hopeful Realism does not promise a ready-made machine into which we can feed our questions and get indisputable answers. To some questions—should there be a broad right to an abortion?—we think Hopeful Realism, as with any natural law argument, will give a clear answer. (It is no, in case you were wondering.) To many other questions, its answers will be much less definitive and concrete. The very things that make our view of natural law "realist"—human finitude and sinfulness and the imperfectionism of all human institutions—just mean that the answers available are correspondingly modest.

We apply this modesty through a final part of this practical framework: prudence. Prudence has long contributed to almost every system of moral and political reflection, though in contemporary parlance it has often been reduced to little more than a utilitarian cost-benefit analysis. Thinking about the relative balance of costs and benefits matters a great deal in making our practical political judgments, but prudence properly understood has a much richer and more robust meaning. In this richer sense, it is the process through which we properly relate means and ends.

Consider the question of undertaking military action to defend an ally against unjust aggression. Repelling an unjust invasion is most certainly a legitimate end, and there would be a range of means available to accomplish that end. How do we choose the most proper means, and what sorts of considerations are involved?

First, we must choose means that do not conflict with the stated end, in this case the establishment of a just peace. Choosing a means that precludes that peace—say, by launching brutal attacks on the aggressor's civilian populations and engendering implacable hostilities—would simply be acting in a self-contradictory manner. Or, in another way of putting it, we are compelled to choose means that are *consistent* with the ends we are pursuing. This is true in a broad sense in that just as we should never choose evil ends neither should we choose evil means: the "lesser of two evils" is still evil and not a choice any serious natural law thinker would countenance.[31] It does not mean we cannot consider very hard or very terrible actions—bearing responsibility in a broken and sinful world does not allow us to escape that dilemma—but it does mean we do not choose to do moral evil, full stop. Choosing means consistent with our (just) ends also more particularly leads us to means that direct us to the particular ends in question. Securing a just peace requires fighting in ways that do not preclude that peace.

Second, we must be attentive to how multiple goods will inevitably interact and figure out how to balance them properly. We mentioned this above in talking about evaluating options, but it is worth repeating: few political judgments involve only a single political good, especially controversial or difficult judgments. They are often controversial or difficult just in that they do not admit of straightforward resolution, they lie at the nexus or a tangle of interacting goods, or both. The properly prudent action takes those interactions into account and makes the best available

---

[31]Of course, sometimes when we say "lesser of two evils" what we mean is that one outcome or one action is less "terrible" than the other, not that it's morally evil as such. The distinction between these ideas matters a great deal. See chap. 7 for a more extensive discussion in the context of the just war tradition.

tradeoffs among them. As should be clear, this is not an easy task. Indeed, it will often be the most difficult aspect of the framework.

In light of these complexities, three considerations are worth keeping in mind. First, if one of the goods you are trying to balance is truly a genuine good, then whatever action you choose cannot simply disregard that good. In the case above, in order to defend your ally, you might actually have to put civilians at risk, but no defensibly just action will simply disregard the fate of noncombatants. Second, sometimes one of the actions under consideration will have deep, far-reaching consequences—positive or negative—for a range of other goods. We could call these "structural" consequences in the sense that they involve changing some aspect of the basic structure of the social order, which inevitably has all kinds of knock-on effects on the possibility of securing other goods. When thinking about tradeoffs among goods, paying especially close attention to these sorts of consequences makes a great deal of sense. Finally, it is often said that "sunlight is the best disinfectant," that transparency and publicity can forestall various sorts of moral corruption. That might be oversold, but at least when making our political judgments and especially the sorts of tradeoffs we're describing here, we can discipline ourselves by asking how we would react if those judgments and their accepted tradeoffs were made public. The idea is not that everyone would be happy or even agree but that others would understand them as reasonable, given the constraints we might find ourselves under. These considerations do not guarantee success and certainly do not make for easy decision-making, but they can, we think, help us discern how different options might affect goods beyond the primary one in question.

Conclusion

Critics of the natural law tradition have sometimes faulted it for a lack of practical direction. It is true that any reasonable natural law theory will recognize that recommending particular actions in particular societies means becoming less definite in our conclusions. Every just political order must attempt to prevent and punish murder, but what that looks like in any one society will differ significantly, depending on its social and political context. But for Christians, if it is indeed true that Scripture directs us to a set of moral and political claims about what human beings are and what we owe one another, then we are obliged to think about and act on how to bring those claims to bear in our own pluralist democratic context.

Hopeful Realism advances a framework to help us do just that. Though it does not, as we have been at pains to note, always or even often deliver indisputable conclusions about what one should think and do politically, we do believe that it offers a helpful guide for Christian moral and political reflection—and actions that one might then take. To summarize, we propose working through three broad steps: (1) first identify what the good (or goods) at issue are in any particular political issue and how that good (or goods) relates to human flourishing; then (2) identify the options for securing that good, think through how the different options secure the good, affect other goods, and comport with our political principles; and finally, (3) identify prudential considerations that inevitably come into play in making these judgments. We now turn to showing what this looks like with four discrete and controversial political issues.

PART II

APPLICATION

5

ECONOMICS

In the preceding chapters, we have argued that evangelical Christians have good theological and biblical reasons to frame their political activities in light of what we are calling Hopeful Realism, a theory of the natural law that is itself shaped by distinctively evangelical commitments. We offered in turn a set of political principles that follow on from that theory and a framework to put those principles to work within a liberal democracy like the United States. In these next four chapters, we put that framework to use in showing how Hopeful Realism can help Christians navigate some quite difficult and controversial political issues. The goal of these chapters is not to suggest that every faithful Christian should necessarily come to the same judgments nor even that embracing Hopeful Realism will mean that everyone ends up in the same place politically. Rather, *the goal is to model how we think evangelical Christians can reason about political matters in light of both general revelation and Scripture's insights about the created order.* Politics is a messy business, and it involves—as our framework itself emphasizes—plenty of moral and prudential judgments that well-meaning and faithful people can and do disagree about. Well-meaning and faithful people should take seriously their own biblical and moral commitments and bring those commitments to bear in ways that encourage the flourishing of all. These next four chapters show the promise of Hopeful Realism in just that regard.

We begin our practical discussions with an area that is not often the focus of contemporary natural law thinking: economics.[1] It might seem a strange place to begin, given that in contemporary American politics, natural law typically gets deployed in the context of "culture war" issues like abortion, marriage, and the like. While Hopeful Realism does have something to say to those issues, we very much believe that it speaks to the full range of political questions. And indeed, in the natural law tradition, what we think of as "culture war" issues have historically not occupied center stage, in large part because they were not as much in contention as they are today. But economics, and in particular how a society organizes the production and distribution of goods and services, by necessity is always and everywhere a live political issue. (Politics has often been described as "who gets what, when, how," after all.[2]) It certainly is in our day, as Christians endorse a wide range of basic approaches and particular policy choices.

This chapter will not settle those disputes—far from it—and we approach these questions with some modesty. Offering more complete answers requires a degree of technical expertise and a broad range of knowledge that escapes all but a few. But in focusing on a particular issue—here, whether and how the state ought to support families with children—we hope to illuminate how Hopeful Realism works in practice and point to some broader economic principles that an evangelical theory of the natural law should endorse.

What Is Economics About?

In keeping with the framework we described in chapter four, we start by considering what economics is actually about, or in our terms, what sorts of goods does economic life look to secure or protect? It may seem a bit pedantic, but the place to start is with the word *economics*, which Aristotle

---

[1] A clear exception to this is Mary L. Hirschfeld, *Aquinas and the Market: Toward a Humane Economy* (Cambridge, MA: Harvard University Press, 2018).
[2] Harold D. Lasswell, *Politics: Who Gets What, When, How* (1936; repr. Potomac, MD: Pickle Partners Publishing, 2018).

defines within his discussion of *oikonomia* in his *Politics*. There, Aristotle sketches out the parameters of what is required to maintain the "household," or the basic necessities people need to live and live well. At its most basic, economic systems should provide what we have called "physical goods"—food, water, shelter, and so on, without which human lives are simply not possible, never mind flourishing. (It is worth noting here that these are also some of the goods that constitute Augustine's goods of earthly peace.)

It is tempting to stop here and suggest that economics *is just* about these basic material goods—and then to suppose that economic systems that produce *more* of those goods are better than those that produce *less*. And all other things being equal, that seems plausible: who would not want more rather than fewer material goods (i.e., wealth)? Don't these goods help secure the conditions for human flourishing, and won't more goods make for more flourishing? Well, other things are rarely equal, and we can all call to mind people who possess tremendous material wealth but in no sense would we consider them exemplars of flourishing human beings—sometimes precisely *because* of how they acquired that wealth or how they use it. The same holds true of societies more broadly: societies need a measure of wealth to function at all, and while poverty is hardly a boon to flourishing, thinking that economics is *only* about material wealth makes a serious mistake.

To put it in the language of a Hopeful Realism framework, the economic order obviously matters for physical goods but has important implications for rational, volitional, and relational goods as well. For a human being to cultivate the broader set of goods we described in chapter four, they need to be embedded in well-functioning institutions and practices. No one gets skilled at choosing and acting in favor of good ends on their own. We need families, schools, churches, associations, and much more, and those require resources. Sometimes, they don't take much: families can provide a robust, nurturing environment even in the absence of significant wealth, obviously, and there are plenty of very wealthy institutions that work to malform their members. Material provision is necessary for those institutions to function, but just as important is the relationship of those formative institutions to the wider economic order and how that relationship makes possible some sorts of institutions and not others. Imagine, for instance, an economic order that made it all but impossible for a broad range of voluntary associations to flourish—and just how such an order would impoverish the possibilities for securing rational, volitional, and relational goods. So we might say that economics is primarily about securing physical goods but also that, because of the role economics plays in other parts of our lives, *how* an economic order secures those physical goods matters for the rest of them as well.

In Search of the Common Good

None of this would have surprised Aristotle and none of it should be especially surprising today. Economics is about more than just wealth. One way that natural law accounts of economics have traditionally parsed these relationships is to suggest that *economic life ought to be organized around the common good*, a claim that we endorse, though with some qualifications discussed below. The idea of the common good is one of those things that gets tossed around so much that one suspects its everyday usage means little more than whatever one happens to like.[3] But it does have a genuinely distinct meaning in the context of economic life and one that we should find attractive and instructive.

One way to put it is that, even in the context of a social order marked by a wide plurality of commitments, there is a set of creational goods necessary for individual and collective flourishing and that these together constitute what we call the common good. Or, alternatively, we could describe the common good as a state of affairs in which each person can flourish and all people can flourish together. What's not to like? As we have noted, human beings need a measure of material goods just to survive, and any economic order that denied or made access to basic goods like water, food, and shelter extraordinarily difficult for some

---

[3]Recall from chap. 3 how we described the principle of the common good and civic friendship: "Our shared human nature and creational context means that the earthly peace that political communities seek to cultivate includes material, relational, and moral goods that are key building blocks of a common human flourishing."

people would be clearly unjust.[4] More to the point, if one could imagine an economic order that both reflected and supported human flourishing across a population, it's hard to imagine what objections there might be.

Suppose one is looking for an economic system in which the production and distribution of goods and services are such that all people have a reasonable opportunity to flourish. That is probably a definition that almost everyone would endorse. We here cannot offer anything like a full-fledged economic theory, but by working through two rather distinct alternatives that we do not endorse—libertarian and statist approaches—one can get a reasonably good grasp of how Hopeful Realism might speak to our economic life.[5]

Take first what we can call statist economics, economic orders that are organized primarily to benefit the state, vis-a-vis both the rest of society and other states. As will become clear, we think this has significant moral and practical problems, but for many there is a kind of intuitive attractiveness, at least insofar as they conflate the success of the state with the good of the society more broadly. Today there's less straightforward valorization of the state as the engine of economic well-being than perhaps there used to be, but there is certainly on both the American left and right a renewed sense that a powerful state is necessary for national economic and social success.[6]

Mercantilism—one of the chief targets of Adam Smith's *Wealth of Nations*—provides a clear example of statist economics. Here, European nation-states imposed trade and tax regimes on their colonial territories as a means of enriching the home country. Similarly, Russia's current economic order is designed mostly to benefit the power of the state and

---

[4] To be clear, we can imagine situations—say, a severe famine—where this would not necessarily apply.
[5] It probably goes without saying, but few thinkers and even fewer ordinary citizens fit nicely into any one of these ideal-type categories. But they're nonetheless useful for sharpening our analytical understanding.
[6] It is one of the oddities of our contemporary moment that the trade policies of presidents Biden and Trump are indistinguishable in the main. There are, of course, significant and important differences between progressives and populist conservatives as to what they want the state to *do*, but it is striking that both want to strengthen the state and make it more central to American economic life.

in particular the political and corporate powers that run it. Of course, every national government looks to benefit itself vis-a-vis other countries and the political institutions we describe as the "state" have an almost inevitable inclination toward increasing their own authority vis-a-vis society, sometimes (maybe often) with the hope of benefiting that society through that authority. And as we will suggest below, it is exceedingly unlikely that an economic order can genuinely be self-regulating or operate effectively without some sort of centralized authority. States everywhere exercise significant power and influence on their respective national economies and do so not just because power-hungry politicos want control (though some do). Rather, even if sometimes the cure is worse than the disease, the increased power of states reflects in part attempts to solve particular problems of economic or social life.

But some state economies are organized so far in this direction that it becomes clear that they are committed above all to enriching the state or an elite ruling class *at the expense of* other states or of their own citizens. No one, for instance, can read anything about Russia's current economic order and conclude otherwise, nor could they of Russia's Soviet or other state socialist predecessors.[7] And this points to the two chief problems with statist economics: *they are designed to enrich some at the expense of others, and they just don't work well in the long-term (in terms of securing the common good).*

There's a certain sort of college-dorm atheist argument out there suggesting that Christianity exploded in popularity in the fourth and fifth centuries because Constantine and his successors put political weight behind the faith. And no doubt, there is some truth to that claim. But as Rodney Stark and others have suggested, there is a more plausible historical cause, namely that Christians were willing to attend to those cast off by Roman society, even amid waves of deadly plague.[8] For Christians

---

[7]The relative wealth and ease that goes along with running state socialist economies speaks to this. When Fidel Castro died in 2016, *Forbes* magazine estimated his personal wealth at around $900 million. Per capita income in Cuba at the time was about $7,400.
[8]R. Stark, *The Rise of Christianity: A Sociologist Reconsiders History* (Princeton, NJ: Princeton University Press, 1996).

have ample, even overwhelming, scriptural reasons to both care about and care for the poor and the outcast. Not only does Jesus himself deliver some of the most chilling condemnations of those who do *not* care for the poor, hungry, and imprisoned (Matthew 25:31-46), but the Old Testament is likewise replete with prophetic condemnations of those who exploit the vulnerable and encouragement to treat all with fairness and justice.

Some have taken these sorts of passages to mean that market economies and the inequalities they seem almost inevitably to produce are fundamentally out of step with Christian convictions. Or, alternatively, that markets rely on the pernicious inflammation of appetites and thus reshape us in vicious ways.[9] There is no doubt that markets *can* do and have done this—there is a reason Scripture warns us so sternly about how corrupting the love of money can be. But what often follows on from these critiques, the idea that the state should then take the central role in the economic system, proves deeply flawed.

One way to argue the point is to say that statist economies just don't deliver the goods. They are not, as Adam Smith showed long ago, means of prosperity. No one surveying the wreckage imposed by state socialist economies over the last century or so could really think otherwise.[10] But that is not *really* where they err, for even if they did manage to produce some degree of general prosperity, they still offer significant moral risks, ones that both Scripture and the natural law illuminate.

Consider again Aristotle's *Politics*, where he powerfully describes how the shape of economic life plays an important role in our individual and common flourishing, an argument that undergirds much of our own thinking about the common good—and our critiques of markets. Aristotle here makes a rather neat distinction between public and private and

---

[9] See Daniel M. Bell, *The Economy of Desire: Christianity and Capitalism in a Postmodern World* (Grand Rapids, MI: Baker Academic, 2012); W. T. Cavanaugh, *Being Consumed: Economics and Christian Desire* (Grand Rapids, MI: Eerdmans, 2008); Eugene McCarraher, *The Enchantments of Mammon: How Capitalism Became the Religion of Modernity* (New York: Oxford University Press, 2021).

[10] The now classic argument in favor of what the authors call "open" economies as opposed to statist ones is Daron Acemoglu and James A. Robinson, *Why Nations Fail: The Origins of Power, Prosperity, and Poverty* (New York: Crown Business, 2012).

relegates economic activity to the private, making it largely the province of women and slaves. Since those two categories of people are not, on his telling, truly capable of flourishing as full human beings, they are given the task of producing for the household, freeing the men (free men, at least) to cultivate the virtues necessary for human excellence.

This is the moral danger posed by statist economies, namely that they are *designed* to benefit some through the exploitation of others. Christian critics of markets sometimes believe that is precisely what markets do—and there are no doubt places and times where that is true. (See our discussion of libertarianism below.) But the danger seems much more marked with statist economies, where political and economic power get joined together. Our critique of moral optimism about state power is rooted in one of the distinctively evangelical features of Hopeful Realism: the effects of the Fall. It is hard to credibly imagine a social order in which political authorities have extensive economic power and do not use it for their own benefit and to the exclusion of others' well-being. If what Scripture teaches—and the natural law confirms—is that the common good is indeed to be common to all, then we can reasonably reject robustly statist alternatives to market economies.[11]

Hopeful Realism's framework shows why statist economics fail by neglecting both volitional and relational goods. Statist approaches are certainly not always framed with exploitation in mind, but they do end up being exploitative nonetheless.[12] Even if statist economics turned out to

---

[11] Note here that this does not at all represent a critique as such of economic systems with large welfare or regulatory systems. Scandinavian economies, whatever else we might think of them, are not in the main exploitative. But they avoid this precisely because they do not centralize decisions about the production and distribution of goods and services. They are relatively free economic orders where individuals and groups can decide for themselves how to employ their resources. The Heritage Foundation's Index of Economic Freedom has Finland, Sweden, Norway, and Denmark all within the top 12 in the world—and all well above the United States (#25). See www.heritage.org/index/pages/all-country-scores, accessed April 16, 2024.

[12] Cf. Pope John Paul II's acute analysis: "The root of modern totalitarianism is to be found in the denial of the transcendent dignity of the human person who, as the visible image of the invisible God, is therefore by his very nature the subject of rights which no one may violate—no individual, group, class, nation or State." "Centesimus Annus," delivered May 1, 1991, www.vatican.va/content/john-paul-ii/en/encyclicals/documents/hf_jp-ii_enc_01051991_centesimus-annus.html, section V, 44.

be more productive in generating wealth (contrary to historical evidence), statism would still be a problem because it doesn't take seriously enough how the exercise of human freedom is integral, not just instrumental, to our flourishing.

An example might help flesh out what we mean here. We are all three college professors and (for a season) parents of college students ourselves. Students finishing up college can find themselves just a bit stressed about their next steps. Which jobs to apply for (and accept) is a constant source of conversation and is obviously important—and not just to twenty-two-year-olds! And these are, at least in part, economic questions, just like questions of where to live, with whom to live, how to get around, and so on. A social world in which those decisions were largely not yours to make is one in which human flourishing—no matter your degree of personal comfort—is diminished. A world in which people cannot largely decide for themselves how to trade, truck, and barter except as directed by their political superiors is not just bad materially. It leaves them without effective agency and thus runs contrary to human flourishing. This is why statist economics runs afoul of Hopeful Realism.[13]

We might suppose, then, that if statist economics is a problem morally, then its opposite would be better. Libertarian economics, broadly understood as an economic order that looks to maximize individual opportunities by freeing individuals from a wide range of social and political constraints, suggests that the resulting social and economic order is both more prosperous and fairer than its statist alternatives. It has long gotten a respectful hearing among conservative Christians in the United States (though less so elsewhere), especially during the Cold War.

There are some good reasons for thinking that libertarianism beats the (statist) alternative—both practically and morally. It is clear that the

---

[13]Though we have not the space to develop it here, this is part of the reason that Hopeful Realism stands well within the main body of natural law arguments endorsing a natural right to private property. See Thomas Aquinas, *Summa Theologica*, II-II, Q. 66, in Thomas Aquinas, *Summa Theologica* (New Advent, LLC, 1920), https://www.newadvent.org/summa/. Aquinas's argument here is relatively practical, namely that a regime with private property better cares for resources and makes for a more peaceful society. But that possession has its end, namely the flourishing of all, and so can be curtailed or shaped toward the common good.

advent of market economies, where decisions about production and distribution are made by private actors, has over the past few hundred years produced the greatest global expansion of wealth and decline of extreme poverty the world has ever seen. Even Marx, no libertarian for sure, appreciated the productive power of markets (and, correspondingly, individual choice).[14] And while it is certainly the case that market economies also produce significant inequalities within nations, the most striking trend of the past thirty years or so has been the decline of inequalities *among* nations, clearly itself a product of globalization and the libertarian economics sometimes associated with it.[15]

What's more, we should not underestimate the degree to which some forms of libertarian economics trade on the scriptural affirmation of private property and other biblical claims. It would, of course, be anachronistic to claim that the Bible is libertarian (or, for that matter, that the Bible is socialist). But it is no accident that libertarian economics emerges out of the Christian world. Consider how Scripture affirms the right to private property in its commands against stealing and even covetousness in the Ten Commandments. There are no jeremiads against private economic activity as such, and there is even a picture of a redeemed creation in which "everyone will sit . . . under their own fig tree, and no one will make them afraid" (Micah 4:4). Even the early church in Jerusalem's pooling together of resources validates their common *voluntary* commitments, not the sort of centralized coercive economic order statists of various stripes propose.[16] The point is not to sacralize market economies

---

[14]Cf. Karl Marx and Friedrich Engels, *The Communist Manifesto* in Karl Marx, *Selected Writings*, ed. Lawrence H. Simon (Indianapolis: Hackett Publishing, 1994), 157-86.

[15]For a chart showing the remarkable growth in global GDP, see https://ourworldindata.org/grapher/world-gdp-over-the-last-two-millennia. For one showing the decline in global inequality, see https://ourworldindata.org/global-economic-inequality#global-income-inequality-increased-for-2-centuries-and-is-now-falling.

[16]The early church, as recorded in the book of Acts, quite clearly pooled their resources and gave to each as they needed. And, similarly, we would affirm that the provision of aid is an integral part of the church's mission in the world. But to jump from that to the idea that the economic order in general should be organized similarly is simply to make a theological mistake of confusing norms appropriate to the church and those appropriate to the world (or creation, even). As Acts 5:4 records, Peter's words to Ananias regarding his property are telling: "Didn't it belong to you before it was sold? And after it was sold, wasn't the money at your disposal?"

or the particularities of our current American economic regime—far from it!—but merely to affirm that the traditional natural law argument in favor of private property is quite congruent with the teachings of Scripture.

Nonetheless, Hopeful Realism is not a brief for libertarian economics, for at least two important reasons. For inasmuch as market economies are more productive than the extant alternatives, they are not always productive for *all*—and certainly not for all to the same (or even similar) degree. Some—the very young and very old, the severely disabled or ill—can be left without provision from the market in large part because they don't have sufficient agency to effectively participate in the market. While of course in principle a libertarian economic order need not leave such people (and others) entirely in the lurch since there is always the possibility of private provision for them, the historical record strongly suggests that leaving economic resources entirely in private hands risks the well-being of some to a degree that we should reject. Indeed, Scripture again and again and again commands those with power and authority to care for those who cannot care for themselves—and, seemingly, not just as a matter of charity, but of justice.[17]

Just as importantly, though, libertarian economics as such has very little to say about the ways those markets can permit and even encourage plainly immoral ends. In this sense, at least, the idea that markets corrupt and inflame our desires seems quite right. It took concerted political power, after all, to end the slave trade, never mind chattel slavery, and in our own day, there are great fortunes to be made through selling pornography, sex, mind-altering substances, and much else that runs afoul of any decent sense of flourishing. It is not that markets are uniquely bad in this respect—the Soviet Union had unconscionably high rates of abortion, for example—but because markets allow unscrupulous people to profit by

---

[17]The question of who is to be helped, how they are to be helped, and who is responsible to help is a complex one—hence the discussion later in this chapter. But no one can read Scripture honestly and come away without recognizing that some, often described as "widows and orphans," deserve help and that those who refuse to give it act unjustly. For an excellent discussion of the Old Testament's attention to those whom he calls the "lowly ones," see Nicholas Wolterstorff, *Justice: Rights and Wrongs* (Princeton, NJ: Princeton University Press, 2008).

catering to the worst of human appetites, they can actually induce people to make worse moral choices than they might otherwise have made. To put things in the terms of our framework, libertarian economics runs the risk of leaving some without reasonable access to basic physical goods and creates incentives for the cultivation of vice that inevitably undermines people's ability (or inclination) to pursue with integrity the rational, volitional, and relational goods we've described previously.

There are good reasons, then, to reject both statist and libertarian accounts of economic life, but leaving the analysis there raises two important problems that our framework is meant to help solve. First, it seems to leave Christians at risk of landing in the "mushy middle," in practice unable to say all that much about economic life except what it should *not* look like. That's not unhelpful, but in a world where pure libertarianism is more thought than practiced and statist economies are hardly more attractive, we should hope for more. And second, it seems to leave little practical guidance: one can see, if only broadly, the sorts of principles that are attractive, but it's hard to see what that looks like closer to the ground. To address these problems, we turn to a set of current American policy debates and see what our principles might say about them.

The Common Good Applied

In the midst of the COVID-19 pandemic, the US Federal Government funneled a lot of money to states, companies, and individuals to keep them afloat financially while public health authorities imposed restrictions on social and economic life. One important piece of those policies was a dramatic expansion of the federal Child Tax Credit (CTC), increasing from $2,000 per child up to $3,600 per child and directly paid into household bank accounts. Those expanded payments ended at the end of 2021, and President Biden's administration proposed a raft of measures to make that tax credit permanent and expand other sorts of financial support payments to families with children. There followed, accordingly, a rather robust debate about family support policies. Hopeful

Realism can illuminate productive ways to think about whether and how the government ought to provide financial support to families with children. More importantly, doing so will help tease out some broader principles that can inform our thinking about other economic policy questions and model how Hopeful Realism can contribute to these sorts of debates.

Public aid to families with children has long been a hallmark of the American social welfare and tax system. Whether it is dependent tax credits, Aid to Families with Dependent Children (AFDC), Temporary Aid to Needy Families (TANF), food stamps, free or reduced school meals, mandates for family and medical leave, and so on, both federal and state governments have taken a number of steps to ease the financial and personal burdens of raising children and reduce the number of children raised in poverty. Some of these efforts are simply straightforward transfer payments, putting cash in parents' accounts to help them with the expenses of raising children. At first blush, these might not seem to implicate the kinds of questions we expect Hopeful Realism to address. But proposals for expanded parental leave or subsidized childcare or even just straight-up transfer payments are inevitably about more than just sending money to parents and children. They are about visions of the common good. And all of these efforts (or proposals) inevitably shape the character of those families by influencing the choices they make. AFDC, for example, was widely criticized for what amounted to a marriage penalty and incentives to nonmarital childbearing. Who can access childcare subsidies influences all sorts of career-family choices. And so on.[18]

The point here is relatively straightforward: decisions about whether and how to provide public support to families with children inevitably end up encouraging some kinds of nonmonetary outcomes and discouraging others, in addition to whatever straightforward economic outcomes

---

[18]The classic critique of American welfare policy is Charles Murray, *Losing Ground: American Social Policy, 1950–1980* (New York: Basic Books, 1984). Murray's argument, which proved crucial for the significant changes in the welfare system in the mid-1990s, is not, of course, uncontroversial.

the policies may be trying to achieve. And, thus, though it might not be its primary purpose, the question of public aid to families with children also implicates rational, volitional, and relational goods in addition to the physical or material ones. Not only do those programs impact whether and what sort of food a child might eat; they also impact who they eat it with, how they do in school, who cares for them, and much else.

Recall that chapter four suggested our analysis goes in three steps: (1) identifying the good or principle in question and how it relates to human flourishing; (2) choosing among our options by discerning which option is most likely to secure that good while also not damaging other goods, all within the boundaries of our political principles; and (3) applying our prudential considerations. When we think about evaluating the different options sketched out below, the ways in which assistance affects the full range of goods previously identified presents a challenge for making choices and especially identifying tradeoffs. To keep things workable, we focus on a few specific goods, suggesting that we should evaluate our options with an eye toward considering: (1) their effect on the material resources available to children and their families; (2) how the structure of those options will support and reshape the institutions necessary for the development of children (family, neighborhood, secondary associations); (3) how the different options would affect parents' prospects, both financial and otherwise; and (4) how the different options would affect the broader economy. No real-world proposal will be unreservedly positive along all four aspects, but getting clearer on all of these will help us think through the very real tradeoffs that are necessary.

What are our options? Let us consider three that run the gamut—from one where the state significantly displaces the family to one where the state offers little to no assistance. First, we might consider what we could call the "Plato" option. In *The Republic*, Plato has the dialogue's chief character Socrates propose how a properly just city would handle marriage and family among its elite rulers.[19] He suggests (457c-461e) that to

---

[19]Plato, *The Republic*, translated by C. M. A. Grube (Indianapolis: Hackett Publishing, 1992).

forestall the possibility that the city's rulers would be more concerned with their own family's welfare than the city's, they would simply not have personal families in any meaningful sense. Rather, the whole city would be considered one's family. Children would be raised together by the community, quite independent of their parents. It seems utterly implausible that any modern democratic state would simply arrogate to itself the full responsibility for raising children, but ideas and policy proposals in that direction are not nearly so far-fetched as we might imagine. Harry Brighouse and Adam Swift, for example, certainly do not suggest abolishing the family as such, but they do argue for rather severely restricting the scope of parental authority with an eye toward social equality and children's autonomy.[20] Others have suggested outlawing religious high schools (so as to detach children from their parents' views, especially their religious ones),[21] and Denmark requires many of its non-European immigrants to place their children in state-run daycare, largely to inculcate in those children proper "Danish" values.[22]

Note that all these proposals are meant to address what their authors genuinely believe to be significant problems in modern liberal societies, especially the social inequalities generated by the wide variety of families children inhabit. That is, they look to restructure the relational and material conditions of families to give children relatively equal and similar opportunities, going some distance toward effectively making children first the wards of the state. It is worth noting that efforts in these directions will, for some children, carry genuine benefits. To the degree that they improve some children's opportunities through the provision of material goods and even escape from abusive families,

---

[20] Harry Brighouse and Adam Swift, *Family Values: The Ethics of Parent-Child Relationships* (Princeton, NJ: Princeton University Press, 2014). On their account, parents would not have much to say about their children's education nor participation in religious communities nor be able to act in a way that conferred any significant advantage to their children. They would have the right to read to them at night, apparently, though they should feel a bit guilty about it.
[21] See Ian MacMullen, *Faith in Schools? Autonomy, Citizenship, and Religious Education in the Liberal State* (Princeton, NJ: Princeton University Press, 2007).
[22] See Ellen Barry and Martin Selsoe Sorensen, "In Denmark, Harsh New Laws for Immigrant 'Ghettos.'" *The New York Times*, July 1, 2018, sec. World, www.nytimes.com/2018/07/01/world/europe/denmark-immigrant-ghettos.html.

there might indeed be gains, at least for some.[23] But it is just as clear that these proposals would run afoul of important political principles—and would hardly be attractive to anyone outside the rarified air of the faculty philosophy colloquium.[24]

First, and perhaps most obviously, such proposals run up hard against Hopeful Realism's commitments to liberty and political restraint. Families, whether they are of the "nuclear" sort most common in the United States or of the more extended sort common elsewhere, are the most basic social institution and are grounded in the order of creation. And while public law has always shaped the family to some degree, largely supplanting parents in order to achieve some sort of social goal is hardly in keeping with the idea of a relatively modest government. More to the point, these sorts of proposals are explicitly designed to *centralize* not just resources but also *control* with an eye toward shaping the *character* of the people—especially the children—within families. The sort of centralization and hostility to pluralism inherent in those ideas is just as much of a problem—going against the principle of confessional pluralism and religious liberty. This approach treats the people as a moldable creature of the government rather than the government as a servant of the people.

If the "Plato" option is not attractive, perhaps its converse, a libertarian-minded model, might fare better. Here, at least, there is no centralization nor attempt to homogenize, but a model that simply leaves families on their own comes with its own problems. Though this is arguably more conceivable than the "Plato" option, it is still rather unlikely and undesirable. There are good reasons all developed democratic countries offer some level of assistance to families. Though it would be a mistake, as we

---

[23] Though it's not clear that things would always work out as the authors suppose, they imagine that their programs would "free" children from the tutelage of putatively bad religious parents. But as one of us has suggested in other places, it might also work to "free" children from the tutelage of the devoutly secular as well. See Bryan T. McGraw, "Liberal Multiculturalism and Confessional Religious Education," *Political Studies* 63, no. 5 (2014): 1087-1102.

[24] That's not to say that the faculty philosophy colloquia—and their subsequent publications—cannot do real harm, since on occasion those outside the guild actually read them and take them seriously.

just argued, to think raising children is simply a social project, that does not mean that how children are raised is without social consequence. Obviously, if a country had some significant number of children who were raised without the benefit of a decent education, the affection of parents (or if not able, other caregivers), and consistent provision of basic goods, both those children and the broader community would struggle to flourish.[25] Perhaps it is the case that a libertarian economy would solve these sorts of problems on its own, but to date no libertarian economy has ever quite been attempted. And in any case, there are actually existing problems that do need addressing, even if they cannot be entirely solved. To leave those unaddressed is to essentially endorse a system in which some significant number of children will be excluded from even a reasonable shot at flourishing, and that violates our commitments to the common good and the equality implicit in human dignity.

So, neither the "Plato" model nor libertarianism does so well according to Hopeful Realism's criteria, but of course neither are they especially real live options. Much more plausible are a set of proposals put together by a joint working group of individuals associated with the Brookings Institution and the American Enterprise Institute, DC-based think tanks on the center-left and center-right, respectively.[26] These proposals focus on redirecting public resources toward families with children twelve and under and reflect a pretty good consensus among the eminent scholars who participated. Among the proposals, the working group agreed on (1) increasing material resources to families by expanding the CTC, increasing food stamp benefits, and perhaps increasing subsidies for unemployment benefits and childcare; (2) strengthening incentives for marriage by reducing or eliminating marriage penalties in means-tested public support programs and engaging in

---

[25] Richard Reeves's recent book on boys is a good example of this. Reeves very ably describes the rather terrible outcomes for boys in particular that the decline of the family in the United States has caused: lower graduation rates, increased criminality, suicide, etc. See Richard Reeves, *Of Boys and Men: Why the Modern Male Is Struggling, Why It Matters, and What to Do About It* (Washington, DC: Brookings Institution Press, 2022).

[26] AEI-Brookings Working Group, "Rebalancing: Children First," February 8, 2022, www.brookings.edu/articles/rebalancing-children-first/.

education and public advocacy encouraging marriage itself; and (3) improving educational access by providing adequate resources (especially to poorer areas), investing in preschool programs, and offering more school choice.

We have not the space nor, really, the expertise to judge how effective these proposals would be in terms of particular economic and social outcomes. But we can say something about how they might fare with respect to the four criteria we described above. If put into action, these proposals would clearly devote more public resources to families, especially those of few means, and would do so in ways that comport with our political principles. Whatever other effects they might have, they would certainly improve the immediate economic well-being of those families. It is also plausible to think that they would also have broader positive economic effects, since healthier, better educated children are better for the economy. It is also unlikely these proposals would wreck the economy.[27]

What is less clear is how these proposals as a whole would affect institutions of civil society, including the family, and how they would affect parents' lives as well. The report addresses how various environmental and neighborhood effects matter for children's well-being, and it devotes one of its four chapters to the need for stable, intact, and nurturing families. So the authors clearly *want* the proposals to work positively on both counts. But it is, perhaps, a bit tricky to see whether this is, in fact, the case.

Consider a key issue that the report largely punts on, namely federal financial support for childcare. At the end of chapter one, the report mentions childcare, noting that "federal spending on childcare is low, which works against promoting both the goal of increasing employment and the goal of improving child development." But it doesn't offer a recommendation for significantly increasing that spending nor a recommendation for how that spending might be structured. It is an interesting

---

[27]It may be worth noting that the proposals were developed with a close eye on their budgetary implications and so are meant to be rather fiscally careful.

omission, because federal support for childcare has been a central part of our country's family policy discussions at least since President Biden proposed a significant expansion of federal support for childcare in April 2021.[28] No doubt the intellectually diverse working group could not quite agree on what to propose in this area, and so they avoided specificity. Why would they disagree to that extent? It's hard to say just from reading the report, but we might surmise that it's not so much because of the *amount* of public support (since that can be dialed up or dialed down to fit budgetary realities) but because the *structure* of the support has any number of ramifications for how that support would affect parents' prospects and the choices those families might be incentivized to make.

In one sense, public subsidies obviously would improve parents' financial prospects by making affordable childcare available. The cost of childcare is a challenge for most working parents, and especially for those of modest means. But how to structure that support and the strings that come with it can make a significant difference in how a Hopeful Realism approach might evaluate the policy. (Set aside the questions of quality, availability, etc.) Under President Biden's proposals, childcare subsidies would only be available to families where parents are working and only useable in certain sorts of state-licensed daycare centers. This would mean, of course, that there would be more incentives for both parents to work (perhaps full-time), which would improve the economic resources available to those households (a good thing) though perhaps at the cost of caregiving (a bad thing). Limiting where a parent could take those subsidies would also mean, though, that more informal networks of care—extended family, friends, neighborhood groups, and so on—would be ineligible. These elements should, we think, give us pause, not because parents should not work or because more formal daycare is bad as such. But in pushing that direction, the administration's proposals have the likely effect of both undermining

---

[28]See www.whitehouse.gov/briefing-room/statements-releases/2021/04/28/fact-sheet-the-american-families-plan/. The proposals did not make it through Congress and the administration proposed them again in 2022 and 2023, to no success so far.

those informal care networks and incentivizing parents' economic well-being over the care of children.

Here is the concern. As Lyman Stone has pointed out, significant numbers of Americans already choose to opt out of the labor market to care for children and clearly prefer informal care networks.[29] In terms of their childcare choices, the data suggests that they make those choices in part because they value the sort of care their informal networks provide. They would prefer to have friends, relatives, or neighbors care for their children. Some parents opt out of the labor market, moreover, and essentially sacrifice wage income to care for their children. Neither of those choices, especially to the degree that they are choices, are at all unreasonable.[30] Indeed, these choices may strengthen family life and improve the experiences of children.

While it is true the administration's proposals would help secure financial resources to many families that need them (given the high cost of childcare), they do so in a way that plausibly damages other goods, namely the family and social institutions that are necessary for the wellbeing of children. Just to be clear, the point here is not that putting children in any childcare setting is necessarily damaging to children and families. The point is that when families have made the judgment that informal care networks or opting out of the labor market altogether is better for their children (and families), creating strong incentives for those families to act otherwise plausibly acts against those families' chosen best interests. Additionally, in limiting where those childcare subsidies can go, the proposals are at odds with our principles of confessional pluralism, liberty, and decentralization. It would not be difficult—or unjust—to include informal care networks in the subsidy program and, as Stone points out, any number of countries already provide

---

[29]Lyman Stone, "More Choice, Fewer Costs: Four Key Principles to Guide Child Care Policy," Institute for Family Studies, May 20, 2021, https://ifstudies.org/blog/more-choice-fewer-costs-four-key-principles-to-guide-child-care-policy.

[30]Sometimes, they aren't choices, of course, but are driven by economic factors—the high cost of institutional childcare or the relatively low wages available to the parent. But Stone's data pretty clearly suggests that it is not just economics driving the parents' choices.

support for parents who are not in the labor market. The proposals unreasonably tilt against these parents' choices and thus make them to that degree unattractive proposals.

Note here, finally, the ways in which the proposals run up against some important prudential considerations. Decisions about childcare are fraught with all sorts of very particular and very local kinds of considerations. Almost all parents in our day make and revisit complex judgments about what works best for their family as a whole and their children in particular, and policymakers that try to impose their own judgment—that children are better off in formal care settings and that more parents should be in the labor market—are hardly exhibiting the sort of modesty that our argument for prudential considerations commends. There are genuine tradeoffs here, but if we're truly interested in protecting volitional and relational goods in ways consistent with liberty, restraint, and decentralization, they are ones that, really, only parents are responsible for making.

Conclusion

In some respects, the discussion above may seem a bit like a tempest-in-a-teapot (though perhaps not for parents who struggle to combine careers and care for children). But it both illustrates, we hope, the sort of analysis Hopeful Realism should encourage and some of the broader principles it can bring to bear on questions of economic policy. Clearly, the most central principle Hopeful Realism would commend is that the goal of economic policy is pursuing something like the common good, a state of affairs where all can flourish and all can flourish together. This means that while of course economic policy rightly concerns itself with the conditions for the development of material wealth, it does so in the broader context of considering the conditions for the development of human well-being more fully. Few people, we suspect, actually disagree with that idea, though they might very well contest the sense of flourishing that Hopeful Realism advances.

But as the saying goes, the devil really is in the details, and in a world where resources are relatively scarce, there are inevitably all kinds of judgments to be made, ones that involve tradeoffs, sometimes tragic ones. In the childcare subsidy case above, the judgments are not so much tragic, but they can be difficult—and one cannot suppose that they can be made reliably well by centralized authorities. And that's the second principle the case above illustrates, that when faced with the inevitable tradeoffs inherent in economic decisions, it is better in general to empower those closest to the decision and those who must most clearly bear its consequences. To be clear, this is not a back-door path to libertarianism: political authorities have a responsibility to exercise judgment when they (rightly) decide that some activities cut against or support the common good. But we contend that those political authorities should take special care in recognizing their own limitations and exercise that authority less rather than more.

No doubt, some fair-minded readers will not find *our* particular judgments quite compelling, and we are happy to acknowledge that our treatment above is not meant as a full-blooded analysis of what is a complex set of interlocking issues. But we hope that the chapter illustrates how the Hopeful Realism framework can help us think through economic issues: first, at a more general level regarding what kind of broad commitments we hold; and then, second, at a more particular level where we think through the kinds of policy tradeoffs we should be willing to make. No natural law theory will tell us the exact mix of economic policies a country or state or locality ought always to pursue. But it can—and should—help us see morally where particular policies or even broader principles can either help or hurt (or both, truth be told) our ability to flourish together.

6

MARRIAGE, SEX, AND THE FAMILY

IN 2018 THE CITY OF PHILADELPHIA directed its Commission on Human Relations to investigate Catholic Social Services (CSS) to determine whether CSS's foster care practices violated the city's antidiscrimination laws. The Catholic Church has ministered to Philadelphia's at-risk children since 1798, and CSS has carried on that tradition by serving as one of the agencies the city contracts with to find suitable homes for foster children. Because CSS holds to the Catholic understanding of marriage and family, CSS would not refer foster children to homes headed by same-sex couples.[1] Given Philadelphia's nondiscrimination laws, its Commission on Human Relations determined that CSS's approach violated the law. Subsequently, the city barred CSS from participating further in the foster care system. CSS took the city to court, and the case made its way up to the Supreme Court, which rendered a unanimous decision in favor of CSS in *Fulton v. City of Philadelphia* (2021).[2]

The reasoning of the majority and concurring opinions turned on such substantive constitutional matters as the proper application of previous cases like *Employment Division v. Smith* (1990), the correct level of scrutiny, and whether foster care referrals count as a "public accommodation" under the relevant nondiscrimination laws.[3] Ultimately the Court

---

[1] In over 50 years CSS has never been approached by a same-sex couple for certification. Its policy for such a possibility is to refer such couples to any of the twenty other foster care programs that would accommodate them.
[2] Fulton, et al. v. City of Philadelphia, Pennsylvania, 593 U.S. ___ (2021).
[3] Employment Division, Department of Human Resources of Oregon v. Smith, 494 U.S. 872 (1990).

agreed that CSS's free speech and religious free exercise rights had been violated by Philadelphia's decision to bar them from participating in the foster care placement system. But while the constitutional issues concerning the tension between religious liberty and LGBT rights are interesting in their own right, the fundamental issue lying beneath this controversy is a contest of visions about sex and marriage.

Philadelphia's CSS, like other Catholic agencies across the country, has "a sincerely held belief that a true 'marriage' consists of the union of a man and a woman, not of two men or two women."[4] This religious commitment informs their policy against placing children in homes headed by same-sex couples, and it is the substance behind the religious liberty claim at issue in *Fulton*. The Catholic view of *what marriage is* determines how these Catholic agencies care for foster children. The city of Philadelphia operates with a different understanding of what constitutes a marriage and thus not only what makes for appropriate homes for foster children but also what sort of agencies can partner with the city in connecting those children to those homes. Same-sex marriage has been legally recognized in Pennsylvania since 2014, and Philadelphia's Fair Practices Act prohibits discrimination in employment, housing, and public accommodation.[5] Thus Philadelphia's understanding of marriage not only does not require the same one-man and one-woman understanding held by the Catholic Church for foster care placement but prohibits anyone committed to that understanding from partnering with the city to serve underprivileged youth. For faithful Catholics, and others, sexual complementarity is an essential *aspect* of what a marriage is.[6] For the city of Philadelphia, sexual complementarity is *incidental* to what a

---

[4]Catholic Charities of Springfield IL, and Joliet, IL, *Amici Curiae* in Fulton et al. v. City of Philadelphia, Pennsylvania. Available at www.supremecourt.gov/DocketPDF/19/19-123/144818/20200 603170631374_19-123%20Amici%20Curiae%20Brief.pdf.
[5]Including, crucially, delivery of city services, like foster care placement.
[6]"Sexual complementarity," explored further below, refers to the uniquely corresponding differences of male and female that make procreation possible (among other things). This should not be confused as synonymous with *complementarianism* as it is often contrasted with *egalitarianism*, with all the Christian discussion and debate about gender roles within a marriage (i.e., egalitarianism versus complementarianism).

Marriage, Sex, and the Family 147

marriage is, such that a belief in it being *essential* is instead arbitrary discrimination and thus places Catholics at odds with the common good. This difference about a crucial social institution runs deep, and in this chapter, we venture with some trepidation into this personal and cultural minefield with the goal of describing how Hopeful Realism might engage the issue. In what follows we address the unique features of this issue, describe two competing conceptions of marriage and sex from a natural law and Christian perspective, and then consider what these ideas might look like applied to the current, contested public square.

What makes Marriage Different

In each chapter applying Hopeful Realism, we address controversial issues that divide Christians and non-Christians alike, and yet there is something qualitatively different about marriage, family, and sexuality.[7] We begin with four observations about what sets this topic apart from the others.

First is an obvious point. Sex, marriage, and family are deeply personal matters. While we all may have beliefs, views, and even convictions about economics, religious liberty, and just war, there is something more fundamental about this topic, given that each person has a history that begins with a union (of some sort) between a man and a woman, and in most cases a family (of some sort). Our very formation as children into adulthood is affected of course by economic, political, and cultural forces, but it is even more fundamentally grounded in relationships with those who have been tasked with raising us. Moreover, as adults we all make decisions—and are affected by others' decisions—about personal relationships, family, sex, and those with whom we will journey throughout this life. Both of these claims, about our upbringing and our adult lives, are true for everyone irrespective of relationship status, race, class, sexual orientation, or religion. There is something deeply personal

---

[7] Even the very listing of "marriage, family, and sexuality" will be read differently by different people, as we'll see. We think the three terms are necessarily interrelated though of course not identical. Unless otherwise noted, when we speak of the Christian approach to marriage, we have in mind sex and family as well.

about this topic, and that makes it as difficult to grapple with as it is crucial to do so.

Second, it's important for us as Christians to recognize that we have a rather mixed record in handling these matters doctrinally and especially pastorally. For any important matter of Christian ethics there are standards that should be rooted in Scripture, and there is the practical question of how to apply those standards in daily life and practice. In particular, there is the crucial question of how to love our brothers and sisters who may for whatever reason struggle with the standard.

This is as good a place as any to state that we affirm the traditional Christian sexual ethic, even as we also acknowledge and lament that the church historically has not done very well in loving our fellow image-bearers who are same-sex attracted.[8] We also acknowledge and lament that too often we Christians have emphasized some ways of falling short of the standard and neglected other ways (cohabitation/divorce/pornography) that may be even more prevalent in churches. We recognize these matters beg for a fuller treatment than we are able to give them here.[9]

Third, thinking well about sex, marriage, and family is further complicated by two related yet distinct modes of analysis required by the nature of marriage itself. With one mode of analysis we can consider marriage on an individual level, and we can do so with several lenses: ontology (just what does it mean for me to be married), morality (what makes for a good marriage), religion (how does the church define marriage), and legality (how does the state define my marriage). This is just to recognize that there are marital, sexual, and familial ethics involved on the interpersonal level for all of us, and this is what we probably think of first when we consider these matters.

But there is another mode of analysis as well, and this mode concerns marriage as a social institution. For as long as there have been human beings, the collective group or the political community or the tribe has

---

[8]To be clear, we include ourselves, personally, in this judgment about "the church."
[9]For someone who is doing good work on this, see Beth Felker Jones, *Faithful: A Theology of Sex* (Grand Rapids, MI: Zondervan, 2015).

had a very strong interest in sex, marriage, and family. Those are the means by which new human beings arrive in the world and are raised, if all goes well, to be upstanding members of the community, and who may inherit property when their parents die. Political communities, cultures, nation-states—whatever term you like—all aspire to be more than mere snapshots in history. They aim to endure, and enduring over time means paying close attention to institutions governing the relations between men and women and the children that come about as a result of those relations. There is thus an inescapably public interest in what is for many of us a very personal relationship that is often construed as private. We will do well to keep this dual mode of the subject in mind as we continue.

Fourth, and finally, marriage (and with it, matters of sex and family) is rather distinct from other topics because the nature and definition of this topic is itself bitterly contested. For many who sided with the city of Philadelphia, there is no genuine good-faith disagreement here about what marriage is or how to balance its value with other social priorities. There is the humane and inclusive understanding on the one side, and a backwards-at-best and bigoted-at-worst benighted view on the other.

But there is a significant difficulty even when a genuine divide is recognized, and that's not about whether traditionalists should have a seat at the table but what the divide is about in the first place. While there are controversies about economics and religious liberty and war, we have a pretty solid sense of what those subjects are. There is a range of views about how best to understand and react to the Russian invasion of Ukraine in 2022. There is very little debate as to whether there was an armed conflict taking place. Authors of the amicus curiae briefs ("friend of the court" briefs filed by nonlitigants who have an interest in the case) who argued in favor of Philadelphia in the Fulton case understand quite well what the relevant religious liberty claims are; they just think such claims are outweighed by more important goods at stake for the LGBT community. This is not the case for marriage and sex. When it comes to marriage, beneath all the political, constitutional, policy, and cultural debates is a fundamental divide as to what marriage actually is.

This last observation about the nature of marriage leads us first to describe what we take to be the two competing visions for what marriage is, and then to consider the different options and prudential factors that inform our understanding. We then define the companionship and traditional approaches to marriage and, drawing on our Hopeful Realism framework, consider the goods involved in marriage, the options on the table for securing those goods, and some thoughts about how to choose among those options.

Competing Definitions of Marriage

The current debate about marriage and sexuality is similar to the problem of incommensurable arguments Alasdair MacIntyre describes in the second chapter of his book *After Virtue*.[10] People come at this issue from different premises and thus they mean different things by "marriage" and even "sex."[11] It is not unlike two friends who care deeply about football and get into an argument about how it should be played. Both refer to common terms like football, passes, offsides, tackling, players, coaches, officials, and stadiums, but after some confusion and frustration they come to realize one's favorite team is Manchester United and the other's is the Dallas Cowboys. They haven't been talking about the same "football." These conceptual differences, and the fact that we are often unaware of them, add an additional layer of complexity to an already vexed issue.

Even if we should have modest expectations for how persuasive natural law reasoning about marriage will be for those who begin from a different starting point, we can still expect *something*. Such conversations can still be fruitful in that we can better understand another's approach. We can clarify premises and raise questions about the implications implicit in the chain of reasoning behind a rival approach. It goes without saying we should be open to the same process with our own thinking. Another important aspect of such engagement is to assure those who share one's

---

[10]Alasdair MacIntyre, *After Virtue: A Study in Moral Theory* (Notre Dame, IN: University of Notre Dame Press, 1984). He lists arguments over war, abortion, and socialism/libertarianism.
[11]For most natural lawyers the specific act of male-female sexual intercourse is different in kind from other acts, as opposed to one option among many in the category of "sexual acts."

position that their views are indeed reasonable and that there are legitimate ways to advocate for policies arising from those views in the public square of a pluralistic democracy. That is, one benefit of laying out the traditional position on marriage is to help equip the person who believes in traditional marriage but isn't quite sure he or she can explain why.

This quandary of public advocacy for the (Christian) supporter of traditional marriage is quite common, as is the stance of the progressive believer or (more often) secular citizen who doesn't just disagree with the traditional view of marriage but finds it, and the reasons offered for it, incomprehensible and often offensive. This is not surprising given that there hasn't been a need for a modern cultural and political apologetic for the traditional conception of marriage until the last couple of decades. Marriage's sexual complementarity was so universally held that there was no perceived need to develop and then teach the arguments for its defense. It is no wonder that such arguments can now strike many as strange or benighted. For more than fifty years an alternative conception of marriage has been taking root in Western culture, slowly displacing the grounds for marriage as it has been traditionally understood.[12] It is to the chasm between these two approaches to the meaning of marriage, sex, and public policy that we now turn.

The Companionship View: Marriage, Sex, and Public Policy

What is marriage? Before we can talk about policy positions about something or an equal right to some social good, we need a working definition of what that thing or good *is*. We present here two competing and idealized conceptions of marriage, sex, and the appropriate public policy that might follow those conceptions on offer today, one of which we will call "the companionship view" of marriage and the other the "traditional view." The companionship view sees marriage as an *institution primarily dedicated to recognizing and protecting the longer-term intimate decisions*

---

[12]This gradual rise of an alternative understanding of marriage over the longer term resulted in the more recent realization that traditional marriage needed an apologetic to respond to this shift.

and arrangements made by adults. On this view, at the personal and relational level marriage is usually an emotional, romantic, and sexual relationship that may or may not include children. Marriage provides legal and social recognition to the bond one can create with what John Corvino calls "your number one person."[13] What distinguishes this relationship from others is not necessarily a difference in kind, but in *intensity*. It is the most intimate version of friendship, not necessarily a different kind of relationship altogether.[14]

The core of this approach is the view that marriage is (almost) entirely the creation of those who enter into it. It *may* include what has been understood to be some of the core elements of marriage—sexual exclusivity, sexual complementarity, and permanence—but it need not include those things, or the relationship may be characterized by a more relaxed version of those things. We see this flexibility in the terms and concepts coined to keep up with new and evolving practices. Sexual complementarity in the United States is, post-Obergefell, officially no longer part of the norm for marriage legally and culturally. The understanding that marriage is something that *two* people enter into is also in flux, with "throuples" profiled in popular news outlets[15] and academic books from the most prestigious university presses making the case for plural marriage.[16] A lawyer has proposed in the Washington Post that we adopt the concept of a "wedlease" as a response to high divorce rates and in recognition that the standard of lifelong commitment is simply too demanding.[17] As for sexual fidelity, that is also negotiable: Dan Savage

---

[13] See John Corvino and Maggie Gallagher, *Debating Same-Sex Marriage* (New York: Oxford University Press, 2012).

[14] Which is not to say that the traditional version of marriage precludes friendship, just that it is not reducible to it.

[15] See Molly Young, "He & He & He," *New York Magazine*, July 27, 2012, https://nymag.com/news/features/sex/2012/benny-morecock-throuple/. Benny Morecock is in a "throuple" with two partners. Their family business is a gay-porn company in Long Island City. The Cleavers they're not—and yet their home life is portrayed as positively wholesome.

[16] See the book under review at Micah Watson, "In Defense of Polygamy," *The Gospel Coalition*, January 27, 2016, www.thegospelcoalition.org/reviews/in-defense-of-polygamy/.

[17] Paul Rampell, "Opinion | A High Divorce Rate Means It's Time to Try 'Wedleases,'" *Washington Post*, May 18, 2023, www.washingtonpost.com/opinions/a-high-divorce-rate-means-its-time-to-try-wedleases/2013/08/04/f2221c1c-f89e-11e2-b018-5b8251f0c56e_story.html.

has offered, for example, *monogamish* as a neologism for the loosening of this characteristic of marriage.[18]

What we emphasize here isn't so much our moral judgment of these preferences for intimate arrangements but the notion of fluid autonomy that makes them possible as instantiations of "marriage." The companionship view of marriage means that *marriage is what we make it, with consent being the primary nonnegotiable ingredient*. Number of partners, sex of partners, duration of the marriage, openness to children, and even the act of sex itself can be, but need not be, part of what it means to be married.

Strange as it may sound, this indefinite and flexible account of marriage does not necessarily include the physical act of sex. The traditional view of marriage holds that consummation is an intrinsic part of what it means to be married—a view that at one point was reflected in the law such that inability to consummate the marriage was grounds for an annulment.[19] But the companionship view of sex is quite distinct from a natural law approach. Just as this understanding of marriage is more fluid than the traditional understanding, so the companionship approach alienates sex from any inherent meaning. Instead, sex is depicted primarily as a consent-based activity that can be as meaningful or casual or recreational as one wishes it to be. It can be part of a committed and long-term relationship but need not be. Consent remains a crucial factor, but—given potential health risks associated with "risky" sex—a concern for health is also a factor.[20] Sexual activity then is what you make it. It can be incredibly meaningful on an interpersonal level. Or it can be something more recreational like skateboarding or canoeing: all that really matters is that everyone involved has agreed to play and is using the appropriate safety equipment. In practice, of course, most people practicing a companionship understanding of marriage do differentiate

---

[18] Mark Oppenheimer, "Married, With Infidelities," *The New York Times*, June 30, 2011, sec. Magazine, www.nytimes.com/2011/07/03/magazine/infidelity-will-keep-us-together.html.
[19] John Witte, *From Sacrament to Contract: Marriage, Religion, and Law in the Western Tradition*, 2nd ed. (Louisville, KY: Westminster John Knox, 2012), 172.
[20] There is an irony here, at least for the natural lawyer, insofar as the goods involved with marriage taken out of the proper context are in tension with the good of bodily health, which we include in the category of physical goods.

between their marital relationships and other relationships that they'd characterize as friendships. Our point is that such a distinction is more or less incidental to the companionship model rather than a principled component of it. A way to test this is by asking whether there is any reason from the companionship position to think that a married couple that abstains from sex and sees their relationship as a platonic friendship is *not* married. We suspect many will say something to the effect of, "That's not for me, but who am I to say they aren't really married?"

Given the variable nature of marriage, and the more relaxed understanding of what sex is and what it's for, it remains to consider under the companionship view what role the government has in regulating these important areas of our lives, if any role at all. Same-sex marriage advocates like Jonathan Rauch, Stephen Macedo, and John Corvino want the government to be involved in marriage law because they believe the goods of marriage can and should be available to gays and lesbians. Moreover, they hold that these goods consist not only in privileges and recognition but duties and obligations. If one sees the definitional heart of marriage as an emotional and (usually) sexual bond between consenting adults, then it makes sense that public policy relying on arbitrary criteria (like sexual complementarity) to recognize some unions and not others violates our sense of equality and fairness. One role, then, of public policy according to the companionship view of marriage is to *expand the circle of people who can be designated as married such that they can enjoy all the rights and privileges therein*, whether it be inheritance matters, tax breaks, hospital visitation, military housing, or custody of children. We see this outcome played out in Pennsylvania's 2014 change in the definition of marriage. Another governmental role is to protect those involved in nontraditional relationships from "dignitary harm" from those who disagree by stigmatizing those who act on the traditional understanding of marriage as intolerant or irrational.[21] This is the role

---

[21]See Michael R. Ulrich, and Julia R. Raifman, "How Religious Refusal Laws Are Harming Sexual Minorities," *Health Affairs Forefront*, June 11, 2018, https://doi.org/10.1377/forefront.20180607.856152.

that the city of Philadelphia attempted to play in barring CSS from participating in the city's foster care program. There is no doubt that many public policy advocates for the companionship view act from a deeply held sense of justice and equality. Indeed, many advocates of the companionate view see the movement to expand the definition of marriage as the next phase in the civil rights movement.[22]

This foregoing description of the companionship view is an amalgam, and of course there are different accents and substantive positions among those who adhere to it. But the core commonality is a view of marriage that *emphasizes the consensual relationship that two (or more) adult people enter into and upholds that as the essential requirement for marital status.*

We suspect if we delve deeply into why intuitions may differ regarding this approach to marriage and sex, we'll run into something like MacIntyre's incommensurable and rival foundational beliefs. Fans of the companionship view of marriage will likely see human autonomy as a foundational commitment that involves the goods of freedom as manifested in consent: rights, privileges, and responsibilities; the dignity of public and publicly enforced recognition; and the intrinsic value of companionship. A fundamental commitment to autonomy, characterized by arrangements that can promote related goods, renders a vision of marriage in which participants can choose what they make of it. Indeed, they can require others to respect the content of those choices and employ the government to protect and promote those choices. It is no surprise that the traditional view of marriage is quite different.

The Traditional View: Marriage, Sex, and Public Policy

As described in earlier chapters, Hopeful Realism suggests we can learn about what is good for human beings from both general and special revelation. That is to say, natural law reasoning *and* Scripture can and should inform our understanding, even as we must take care to distinguish which

---

[22]Advocates of this view will differ with regard to how non- or slow adapters should be treated, whether akin to White supremacists who resisted the civil rights movement in the 1960s or to conscientious religious objectors like the Amish or Orthodox Jews.

scriptural norms apply to God's chosen people of the church and what creational norms apply to humanity writ large. The next sections first describe a natural law account of the goods of sex, marriage, and family and then follow that up with some creational insights from Scripture.

While natural lawyers recognize that human choice, reflection, and volition are essential elements of human well-being, they reject the idea of human autonomy as the sole foundation of human nature and flourishing. There are some things that are *givens* about the world and our nature, and living well means not defining these things on our own but adapting our behavior and understanding so as to fit with what has been given.

Hence natural lawyers think that there is a given normative structure to marriage. This doesn't mean that natural lawyers do not recognize that marriage as a cultural practice has changed throughout the centuries, nor do they reject the importance of consent as an aspect of entering a marriage. But the normative structure of marriage means that we can critique various marriage practices and call some changes progress because there is a blueprint of sorts that we think is *natural* and *objective* and *knowable*. The objection that marriage has often looked different from what natural lawyers take it to be is no more fatal to a natural law approach than the observation that human rights have not always been recognized or protected vitiates the claim that human rights exist independently of any particular government that may be abusing them.

The traditional view of marriage is that marriage consists of a relationship between a man and a woman that is ordered toward two intrinsic purposes, and three characteristics that help realize those purposes.[23] There is a *unitive* purpose in marriage, the good that is instantiated in the multi-level union between a man and a woman, and there is a *procreative* purpose, which is fulfilled when a new human being is brought into the world by the one-flesh union of man and woman, and

---

[23]No label is perfect, but we think *traditional* captures our meaning fairly well. That said, we want to be clear that what we mean by *traditional* is what follows in this passage, not culturally relative gender arrangements that have arisen and faded in various times and places. That is to say, nothing in this account commits us to restrictions on women's political rights or educational opportunities that in other contexts have been described as "traditional."

marriage thus unites the man and woman as husband and wife to care for and raise the child as father and mother.[24] The three characteristics are *complementarity* (one man, one woman), *exclusivity* (fidelity to one's spouse), and *permanence* (for life). Together these two purposes and three characteristics comprise marriage as a uniquely relational good that also incorporates the other goods we described in chapter two (physical, volitional, and rational).

The unitive purpose. The union of a man and woman in marriage is itself a good directly related to the kind of beings that we are. That is, in contrast to those who would say that the goodness of marriage is related to its "consequences" (pleasure, companionship, procreation), the traditional view affirms that the unitive nature of marriage reflects its intrinsic goodness and choice-worthiness. (All human beings as such can to some degree apprehend this about marriage, but Christians see an even deeper truth insofar as marriage reflects a theological understanding of humans as created in the image of the Triune God, who are image-bearers in ways that involve unity-in-diversity analogous to the Godhead, manifest in various relationships but particularly in marriage due to its unique unitive character.) Though the traditional view of marriage shares with the companionship view the notion that friendship and emotional commitment are important, this view of marriage holds that the marital bond is distinct in *kind* from other relationships, not in degree. Friends and siblings can have emotional commitments and share a great deal in common. But that does not mean they are married. Because it is a basic good[25] related to our nature as humans, this understanding of marriage

---

[24]This claim elicits the understandable objection about infertile couples. The short answer is that marriage as an objective good is still ordered toward the good of children even if the behavioral conditions needed for a child to be conceived do not or cannot occur. But we admit this objection needs a more careful philosophical (and pastoral) response than we can offer here.

[25]Some philosophers refer to this type of good as "basic" or "per se nota." This means that the good is intrinsic rather than instrumental; it doesn't need a deeper or more fundamental purpose for us to understand it makes sense to pursue it. Think here of the good of friendship as compared to money. When we explain a given action by saying we're helping a friend, it would be strange for someone to respond, "Well, why would you want to help a friend?" Money, on the other hand, is essentially instrumental. You always want it for some other reason, some other good that it might provide, whether that's material or social. Nobody would want one million

as unitive precludes valuing marriage based solely on its potential for children, the benefits of financial security, positive emotions, increased health benefits, or tax breaks—views that are reductive and instrumentalizing. While it is true that many marriages will lead to those positive outcomes, the positive outcomes result from the good that marriage is. Marriage's goodness does not result from them.

Of course, this may come across as a mere bald assertion. We're not sure that it's any more assertive than the claim that marriage is by definition *not* heterosexual, but that is one of the quirky things about goods that can be described as "basic." If one accepts the notion of basic goods like friendship or physical health, then one cannot prove their worth by reference to some more fundamental good beneath them. This doesn't mean, however, that there is nothing to say on behalf of this claim about the goodness of marriage. It is just that readers have to apprehend for themselves the truth of a "basic" claim, whether on behalf of human agency or the unitive good of marriage between a man and a woman. There is something suggestive, however, in the observation that only a man and woman can unite comprehensively on an emotional, mental, social, spiritual, and physical level.[26] The physical level here is not sufficient, but it is necessary and directly related to the procreative aspect of marriage.

The procreative purpose. Traditional marriage builds its view in part on the uniqueness of sexual intercourse between a man and a woman. That particular act is unlike any other acts that culminate in sexual release performed by whatever combination of partners (same or opposite sex). It is an act so very powerful that, as Ryan Anderson has quipped, nine months later you might have to give a name to the result of that act.[27]

---

dollars if stranded on a desert island. For the classic articulation of this idea, see Plato, *The Republic*, trans. Allan Bloom, 2nd ed. (New York: Basic Books, 1991), 35, 357b. Perhaps the most important contemporary articulation, especially for natural law arguments, is J. Finnis, *Natural Law and Natural Rights* (New York: Oxford University Press, 1980). We find Finnis's arguments helpful, even if we do not agree in every regard.

[26]On this, see Sherif Girgis, Ryan T. Anderson, and Robert P. George, *What Is Marriage? Man and Woman: A Defense* (New York: Encounter Books, 2012).

[27]Ryan T. Anderson, "What is Marriage?," July 22, 2014, 55:56, www.youtube.com/watch?v=YWIhZ5xJJaQ.

The utter uniqueness and life-giving power of that act tells us something about the inimitable nature of the marital relationship. Unlike the companionship view, which can conceptually separate sex from marriage, the traditional view sees one particular sex act—coitus—as different in *kind* from other sexual activities and as an integral component of the marital relationship itself.

There is also another way to describe this biological clue about the special status of this act that sheds light on its centrality in defining marriage. Almost every biological function we human beings have we can do by ourselves. We are capable of locomotion; we can walk here and there. We each can breathe on our own: respiration. You might have had lunch earlier today and can digest that lunch quite on your own. A human being can perform every biological function on her own, except one. She cannot reproduce on her own. For human beings to engage in the biological function of reproduction, we need another person, and another person of the opposite sex. And it is only in the act of sexual intercourse that we can engage in a reproductive act.[28] The uniqueness of that act sets it off from any other sexual act we can engage in, as it literally unites two people into "one flesh," a one flesh that alone performs the biological function of reproduction. This observation isn't meant to prove that marriage is between a man and a woman, but it is suggestive of the reasons why marriage has traditionally been defined the way it has been.

To be clear, this understanding does not preclude infertile couples from being considered to be fully married. The unitive aspect of marriage is sufficient to create a real marriage, and the physical union of the couple is a reproductive act even if it turns out that the conditions necessary to conceive do not hold.[29] We have an intuitive sense of this insofar

---

[28] It is true that in recent decades new technologies have been developed that can also lead to the creation of a new human being, but this does not change our claim. These new technologies, at least for now, still draw from the contributions of a man and a woman in an attempt to replicate natural reproduction. Such techniques can also not be described as a reproductive "act" but as a series of actions.

[29] For reasons we cannot fully explore here, we agree with Sherif Girgis that sexual intercourse is a reproductive act even if the biological conditions do not align, or may never align, so as to result in a baby in every act of intercourse. His *What Is Marriage?* offers what we think is a

as we recognize that while infertile couples are as married as those who can have children, the inability to have children is felt as a genuine loss. There is some end or aspect of marriage that is frustrated or impeded, even as there is a real marriage.[30]

Complementarity.[31] Traditionally marriage has been between a man and a woman because it is only a man and a woman who can unite in a comprehensive union, and only a man and a woman together can create a new life. Three or four people cannot unite in this way comprehensively. Two members of the same sex cannot unite in this way. This characteristic of marriage is very closely tied to the two goods described above.

Yet this characteristic applies not only to the unique union only possible between a man and a woman but also to the procreative potential in that relationship. A man and a woman not only complement each other in their differences in becoming one flesh, but they bring those differences to their *roles* as father and mother. This claim has also become much more controversial in recent times.

Men and women are different, or perhaps more precisely, a man brings something different as a father to how he and his wife raise their sons and daughters.[32] And a mother brings something different as a woman than her husband does as a man. When it comes to raising children, we think there is a mix of fathering and mothering more than simply a generic practice of "parenting." There is something irreducibly valuable in children being raised by the two people who uniquely brought

---

useful analogy. He likens the practice of marriage, oriented toward the purpose of procreation, with the practice of baseball, oriented toward the purpose of winning baseball games. Baseball players can still play and enjoy the goods of baseball even if they do not win, and no one suggests that they are not playing baseball. Similarly, a married infertile couple is still fully married even if their generative acts do not result in conception.

[30]This is, of course, another extremely difficult and personally affecting subject. For a Christian treatment of infertility and marriage, we recommend Matthew Lee Anderson, "Why the Church Needs the Infertile Couple," *Christianity Today*, April 21, 2017, www.christianitytoday.com/ct/2017/may/why-church-needs-infertile-couple.html.

[31]As noted above, by complementarity we refer to the sexual complementarity of a man and a woman, not the complementarity as it is understood in the Christian discussion and debate about gender roles within a marriage (i.e., egalitarianism versus complementarianism).

[32]At the risk of stating the obvious, noting that there are *some* role differences between fathers and mothers does not by any means legitimate *all* cultural manifestations of parental difference.

them into existence.[33] Men and women are equal, but equality does not denote *sameness*. Each brings different things to the family unit. To be absolutely clear, this is in no way to impugn the mothering and fathering done by single parents, nor to say in any way that two men or two women cannot love and care for a child. It is to say, however, that while two men may both be good fathers, they will not be a good mother, and while two women may both be good mothers, what they provide will not be *fathering*.[34] Moreover, to also be quite clear, acknowledging such differences does not provide any carte blanche basis for reinforcing all cultural gender standards—something that has been badly abused over the years.

One can observe the differences in men and women just by considering the importance of our embodiment as biological men and women. There is a particularly crucial role that a mother plays in her pregnancy and the gestation and early infancy of any child. This close connection is not only literally embodied and connected in utero, but also evidenced by the special role the mother plays in nurturing and feeding the child after birth. Scores of studies and findings confirm what the vast majority of humanity has known from time immemorial: there is a special bond between a mother and a child that is unique to mothers as embodied females connected to their children.[35] Men do not generally lactate or breastfeed. To recognize this is not to denigrate nor deny the role of fathers; it is only to say that role is different.

---

[33]Granted of course this is not always possible in a broken world, but it can be the ideal at which we aim. This is also not to deny nor diminish the undeniable and gospel-related practice of adoption. Adoption, however, is so valuable in part because it is a loving reaction to something having gone awry such that for whatever reason the natural mother and/or father of the children in question is no longer available.

[34]Some critics respond to this line of reasoning with the criticism that such claims harm the children who are not being raised with their mother or their father. We agree that there are pastoral concerns that must be considered in how these claims are made. Nevertheless, we find it quite problematic that such critics are more concerned about the potential harm that may accrue from a child hearing such claims than the actual harm that is the loss of a father or mother. See Katy Faust, "Dear Justice Kennedy: An Open Letter from the Child of a Loving Gay Parent," *Public Discourse*, February 2, 2015, www.thepublicdiscourse.com/2015/02/14370/.

[35]The distinctive importance of fathers has almost become conventional wisdom by now, though not without its dissenters. For a good summary of the social science evidence, see Richard Reeves, *Of Boys and Men: Why the Modern Male Is Struggling, Why It Matters, and What to Do About It* (Washington, DC: Brookings Institution Press, 2022).

The difference of that role is also reflected in more than just what is needed for the flourishing of babies in their early days. Another quip from Ryan Anderson illustrates the linkage between what we know is best for babies and the social and policy arrangements that foster the flourishing of children. Whenever a baby is born, Anderson notes, we can be quite confident that the mother is nearby.[36] But we have no such reassurance about the father, who may have been missing in action for as long as nine months. This tongue-in-cheek insight makes a very serious point about how our biological embodiment matters. Mothers are by biological necessity tied to the initial well-being of their children; men have no comparably *necessary* attachment. Marriage as a social institution, particularly given the second, wider-framed social mode of analysis mentioned above, is a means of encouraging fathers to commit to help mothers raise the children that may result from the union of a man and a woman. It's a way of encouraging men to take on the role of fatherhood by committing to be by the mother's side when she gives birth and stay by her side as they raise the child together.

Permanence. To truly commit comprehensively means committing not just for the moment, but also for the future. Truly caring for someone, truly committing to them in marriage, means committing to that person for life. This is because we know that knowledge of the future informs our experience of the present. When one promises to love someone completely and comprehensively, there cannot be a predetermined time limit on that promise. And we do not mean by "love" merely emotional affection or enjoyment of another person, as important as those can be. Rather, love for another person is a conscious commitment to that person's good. The remarkable and unique feature of marital love is that conscious commitment to the person's good also redounds to one's own good. When a wife gives herself completely to her husband, and the husband to his wife, the two become one while remaining themselves. Just as one naturally has a commitment to one's own good for life, so in marriage one

---

[36]Ryan T. Anderson, "What is Marriage?," July 22, 2014, 55:56, www.youtube.com/watch?v=YWIhZ5xJJaQ.

commits to the good of the other for life.[37] To "commit" to someone completely in marriage while refusing to commit for life is oxymoronic. The uncertainty of what you may do in the future works its way into the present, and the quality of the relationship now is affected by one's promise to love into the future. This is true both for the sake of the husband-and-wife relationship, and the father-mother-children relationship.

The characteristic of permanence that helps constitute marriage might come across as counter-intuitive given contemporary mores regarding cohabitation and divorce. After all, the no-fault divorce movement arose as a response to what many experienced as a painful, difficult, and overly complex divorce process, not to mention the structural disadvantages for women in the asymmetric divorce and property laws of the past.[38] It is true that permanence as we understand it is an aspiration for what marriage is designed to be, not an exceptionless binding requirement that would trap women (or in rarer cases, men) in abusive or adulterous relationships.

The traditional language of the wedding vow illustrates the vital role of permanence, as does adjusting that language to reflect the direction that marriage mores have taken in the last couple of generations.[39] Here is a traditional version:

> I, Arlene, take you, Alan, to be my wedded husband, to have and to hold from this day forward, for better, for worse, for richer, for poorer, in sickness and in health, to love and to cherish, till death do us part.

There is much to unpack here but consider how this language emphasizes more than just the consensual nature of the vows (the reciprocal "I take you . . ."), and the intimacy of the relationship ("to love and cherish"). There is the commitment to fidelity even when anticipating the unavoidable ups and downs in earthly goods (material *and* relational) throughout life.

---

[37]This is not as "natural" as willing one's own good, of course, which is why marriages require work to succeed. As this description suggests, the trinitarian analog is strongly implicated here.
[38]Brad Wilcox, "The Evolution of Divorce," *National Affairs* (Fall 2009), www.nationalaffairs.com/publications/detail/the-evolution-of-divorce.
[39]While the origins of this traditional language go back to the Sarum rite of the Anglican church before the Book of Common Prayer, it has arguably become part of the generic vernacular in American culture.

There is also the crucial chronological element of the relationship, "from this day forward" signifying the importance of the wedding date for initiating the lived reality of the marriage and bookended by the inevitable reality that seems so impossibly far off in that moment, "till death do us part." That is to say, the wording of the vows captures an intrinsically different dynamic of commitment given the vow is *for life*.

In contrast, now consider a slightly changed version of the vows:

> I, Hugh, take you, Crystal, to be my wedded wife, to have and to hold from this day forward, for better, for worse, for richer, for poorer, in sickness and in health, to love and to cherish, till one or both of us determine that it's not really working out.

The second version communicates something significantly different, does it not? While we don't expect this alternative version of the wedding vows to go viral, we do think it illustrates the qualitative difference between a vow to love someone for life *even if we recognize that not every marriage lasts* and a "promise" that from the start holds something back from the beloved. The characteristic of permanence captures that sense in which we give ourselves entirely to another person in uniting with them in marriage. Anything less than that aspirational commitment diminishes the nature of the one-flesh union and prioritizes something more *transactional* (I commit to you so long as my terms are met) than *transformative* (we come together to create something new and permanent). This bears emphasizing: to engage in a transactional "marriage" is to treat one's husband or wife primarily as a means to an end rather than giving oneself entirely to the spouse and treating them as an end in themselves. While we can know it's wrong to treat people as means rather than ends through reading Scripture, such a moral principle is also knowable through our reason and is grounded on the dignity and relational nature of human beings.

Exclusivity. The last aspect of marriage is exclusivity. The claim is that the marriage relationship is exclusively between one person and one other person. Unlike the companionate view of sex and marriage, the marital act and relationship is unlike any other good or activity. It is different in kind from sporting events, or musical activities, or artistic pursuits. The comprehensive union in marriage (mental, social, physical, and spiritual) is such that it cannot be shared with others without it becoming something other than marriage.[40] A robust conversation between two friends can be deepened still further with the arrival of a third friend, but this is not the case for a husband and wife in their intimate relations. Philosopher Hadley Arkes makes this point for college students of all political and religious persuasions by telling them about two college roommates, Steve and Todd.[41] One week Steve tells Todd that he has a tennis outing with Stella planned but that he cannot make it. Could Todd fill in for him? Sure, Todd says, he'd be happy to do so. Arkes then describes a conversation between the roommates the following week. Steve tells Todd that he and Stella had planned to have sex that Thursday night, but he has a conflict. Would Todd be willing to fill in? The laughter that this illustration elicits from a secular college classroom tells us, the natural lawyer might say, that we implicitly recognize that there's something different about sex. Human nature is such that we can share in some human goods, say music, or intellectual pursuits, or sports, but we cannot share the good that is marriage with others without tarnishing or even destroying that good.

These are the purposes and characteristics that comprise the traditional view of what marriage is. Even if nothing we have written thus far would persuade the companionship advocate (or vice versa), at the very least we hope to have clarified some of the differences between the two conceptions. This account, however, raises the following question for Christians: how does this description square with what Scripture teaches?

Christian Compatibility with Traditional Marriage?

We mentioned earlier that the changes in marital and sexual mores in Western culture have arisen so quickly that those who affirm the

---

[40]There may be a way to imagine playing chess with three to five players, but it would no longer be chess.
[41]Hadley Arkes, "Lecture on Ethics and Public Policy," Lecture, Princeton University, Fall 2003.

traditional view of marriage have often found themselves at a loss to explain what seemed obvious to most remarkably recently. Just as people today would find a campaign to outlaw alcohol ridiculous if not inconceivable, so too would *Obergefell v. Hodges* (2015) appear to the generation that actually did pass the Eighteenth Amendment just a little over one hundred years ago. We are less interested here in telling the story of how the social imaginary[42] around marriage and sex has shifted such that what was unthinkable one hundred years ago is commonsensical now and vice versa.[43] Nor is this the place to go into depth regarding the thorny relationship between marriage as a creational and normative structure and the messy cultural and legal evolution the institution has undergone in Western civilization in the last two thousand years.[44] Rather, we are here interested in reminding ourselves and our readers how much commonality there is between a natural law approach and a biblical approach to sexuality, marriage, and family. This is far from a comprehensive account, but it should make clear just how similar the two are.

The first thing to note is marriage is not in any way a peripheral or side issue in Scripture. From the very first chapter of Genesis we see affirmed the creational goodness of our sexually differentiated humanity:

---

[42]See Charles Taylor, *Modern Social Imaginaries* (Durham, NC: Duke University Press, 2004). There, he defines "social imaginaries" as "the ways people imagine their social existence, how they fit together with others . . . and the deeper normative notions and images that underlie these expectations" (23).

[43]For a book that does tell that story see Carl R. Trueman, *The Rise and Triumph of the Modern Self: Cultural Amnesia, Expressive Individualism, and the Road to Sexual Revolution* (Wheaton, IL: Crossway, 2020).

[44]This is just to acknowledge, even if we cannot do it justice, the work of historians and others who have delved deep into the legal and cultural practices and changes around marriage and sexuality in different times and places. See, for example, Peter Brown's *The Body and Society: Men, Women, and Sexual Renunciation in Early Christianity* (New York: Columbia University Press, 2008). Such books offer invaluable insight and detail into the story of marriage and family in Western history, but do not vitiate the related and important questions that pertain to marriage and family understood from a moral and indeed theologically *given* framework. That is to say, we think it's important to understand the historical context *and* the normative blueprint that led the early church fathers to "set their doctrines of marriage and sexuality in sharp contrast to those of Roman society and law. They single out for harsh criticism the Roman practices of temple harlotry, concubinage, transvestism, homosexuality, incest, polygamy, abortion, infanticide, and child abuse." Witte, *From Sacrament to Contract*, 19-20.

> So God created mankind in his own image,
>> in the image of God he created them;
>> male and female he created them.
>
> God blessed them and said to them, "Be fruitful and increase in number; fill the earth and subdue it. Rule over the fish in the sea and the birds in the sky and over every living creature that moves on the ground." (Genesis 1:27-28)

And the second creation account in Genesis 2 fleshes out this theme by doubling down on the commonality of, and difference between, man and woman. After noting that it was not good for the man to be alone, God responds with the creation of the woman:

> Then the LORD God made a woman from the rib he had taken out of the man, and he brought her to the man. The man said,
>
> "This is now bone of my bones
>> and flesh of my flesh;
>> she shall be called 'woman,'
>> for she was taken out of man."
>
> That is why a man leaves his mother and father and is united to his wife, and they become one flesh. (Genesis 2:22-24)

We see in these passages the remarkable claims about men and women fully sharing God's image, and yet they are distinct from each other. The cultural mandate (noted earlier) includes the instruction to "be fruitful" and increase in number. This entails, not to put too fine a point on it, sex between a man and a woman and the children that will come from that union. That sexual union is even more pronounced in Genesis 2, which adds the generational and familial dynamic of leaving one's raising family and starting a new one by becoming "one flesh." Significantly, this account of equality, sexual difference, procreative marriage, etc., describes creational goods for humans, not just something uniquely redemptive for God's covenant community after the Fall.

Marriage, sex, and family thus have a crucial place in the very beginning of the biblical story, and that priority continues through to the end. For just as there is the introduction of marriage in the beginning of the biblical narrative, so there is a wedding feast to mark the inauguration of the eschaton at the end (Revelation 19). Jesus himself frequently likens the kingdom of heaven to a wedding feast (Matthew 22), and the apostle Paul directly connects instructions about our earthly marriages with the mystery of the heavenly marriage between Christ and his bride the church (Ephesians 5). In addition to these more punctuated references to marriage, there is the consistent theme of God courting Israel throughout the Hebrew Scriptures and the ubiquitous identification of idolatry with sexual unfaithfulness in the prophetic writings. It is also telling that in addition to likening Jesus to a bridegroom, God reveals his triune identity to us with familial language as the Father and the Son in addition to the Holy Spirit. Much more could be said, and has been elsewhere, but the point here is these matters are front-and-center in the biblical narrative, and thus Christians who take Scripture seriously should not characterize marriage and family controversies as minor or distractions from more important things.

So is there a biblical definition of marriage, and if so, what is it? This chapter is not the place for a robust treatment of the question, though it is appropriate to put our cards on the table.[45] Simply put, we follow Jesus' affirmation in Matthew 19 of the creational pattern described in the language from Genesis above:

> Some Pharisees came to him to test him. They asked, "Is it lawful for a man to divorce his wife for any and every reason?"
>
> "Haven't you read," he replied, "that at the beginning the Creator 'made them male and female,' and said, 'For this reason a man will leave his father and mother and be united to his wife, and the two will become one flesh'? So they are no longer two, but one flesh. Therefore what God has joined together, let no one separate."
>
> "Why then," they asked, "did Moses command that a man give his wife a certificate of divorce and send her away?"

---

[45]For an example of a fuller treatment, see Richard Hays, *Moral Vision of the New Testament: A Contemporary Introduction to New Testament Ethics* (New York: Bloomsbury Publishing, 2004), 347-406.

Jesus replied, "Moses permitted you to divorce your wives because your hearts were hard. But it was not this way from the beginning. I tell you that anyone who divorces his wife, except for sexual immorality, and marries another woman commits adultery." (Matthew 19:3-9)

It is true that God allowed at times for legal and cultural accommodations regarding marriage, and we see this in Jesus' implicit correction of the Pharisees' language; they characterize Moses as *commanding* but Jesus says that Moses *permitted* divorce. That there was an accommodation does not vitiate the reality that there is a true teaching, and Jesus appeals to the creation narrative for the source of God's definitive teaching about marriage. He does not take his cues from the latest cultural or philosophical developments but looks back to the source. God's original blueprint does not need to be updated but rather upheld. That blueprint includes the following:

1. Marriage is created by God ("what God has joined together").
2. Marriage is sexually complementary ("male and female," "a man," "his wife").
3. Marriage is for two people, not more ("a man", "his wife," singular; "the two will become one flesh.").
4. Marriage is, except in rare and regrettable cases, for life ("what God has joined together, let no one separate").[46]
5. Marriage is exclusive ("anyone who divorces his wife . . . and marries another woman commits adultery").

The portion that Jesus quotes here in responding to the Pharisees' challenge does not include the procreative purpose of marriage, but that's likely because they weren't challenging that component of marriage (which would have been unthinkable). But Jesus' move to appeal to Genesis helps us answer that question insofar as it gives us a model. When someone asks about a change in one of God's creation ordinances,

---

[46] Malachi 2:13-16 records an even more emphatic judgment of marital unfaithfulness and divorce, while affirming the "be fruitful and multiply" element of marriage.

in this case marriage, Jesus' example suggests we go back to the original design. As such, we can by extension affirm that:

> 6. Marriage has a procreative purpose, from Genesis 1:27-28 ("be fruitful and increase in number.").

Given this understanding of Scripture, we think Christians can find support for what we've called the traditional view through both natural law reasoning and Scripture. We find affirmed in Scripture the unitive and procreative purposes for marriage, as well as its sexual complementarity, exclusivity, and permanence. To be sure, we find even more than that in the apostle Paul's invocation of marriage in Ephesians 5 to describe the mystery of Christ as the bridegroom's relationship to his bride the church. And we also find marriage and family situated as important goods, but not so important as the new family of God.[47] Having described the companionship and traditional views of marriage and the latter's grounding in both nature and Scripture, we're now in a position to consider marriage in the public square.

THE PUBLIC GOOD: FIVE APPROACHES TO SEX, MARRIAGE, AND FAMILY

Our Introduction argued that the Christian can advocate for public policies regarding the environment because both Christians and non-Christians alike can know that a healthy environment is good and they can use their God-given reason to solve problems and promote health. The same is true for marriage. It is *possible* for Christians and non-Christians alike to agree on the end of marriage as defined above, as well as measures that can be taken to promote and protect the institution of marriage in society. But what is the public interest in marriage? This harkens back to the second mode of looking at marriage as a social institution.

One thing that the ongoing tumult and controversy about marriage testifies to is this: marriage matters as a public good. While there are a few activists or thinkers who might abolish marriage as a legal institution

---

[47]This constitutes an important caution against idolatries of marriage, children, and family to which some are prone.

altogether, the fact that we have been fighting about the legal and cultural institution suggests there's something important here worth defining and preserving. On a theological level, this is because God has created us as relational creatures, and marriage is one very significant and indeed unique way of relating. On a societal level, marriage is also a crucial part of the success of any political community. Nearly all significant political philosophers address marriage, family, and sex because political communities aspire to last longer than the current moment. Political communities aim to be more than a snapshot in history but rather an ongoing narrative, and that means attending to how the characters of future chapters will be created, raised, and transformed into the main characters of the story. There is a reason why so many of our national controversies relate to marriage, sex, family, and education. We all sense that what happens here matters a great deal for what happens everywhere else.

In the language of Hopeful Realism, marriage is also important because it is a sort of nexus or connection good insofar as it is primarily a relational good that also makes possible the other three goods (physical, rational, and volitional) described in chapter four. The family is the primary, though not exclusive, provider of physical goods. Through the teaching of parents and other family members, we first learn to choose and think well, developing volitional goods as agents in the world. And while additional institutional and communal layers contribute to learning, the cultivation of education and wisdom also begins at home. These considerations help with the first of the three steps we described in chapter four: identifying the goods (plural in this case) and principles and how they relate to human flourishing. In keeping with our second step, we spell out below several different approaches to securing those goods. Afterwards we apply our political principles and try to discern which of these approaches would best secure the goods of marriage.

How should advocates of the traditional view of marriage engage the public square well on these matters, bearing witness to the truth as we believe God has revealed it while understanding the times and "reading the room" well? The discussion below will consider five distinct approaches to how Christians might engage the public square. Some of these will be incompatible with others, and some will overlap.

National decree option. The first approach is a call to a top-down imposition of the traditional view as legally dominant as a means of shaping the culture—something like a social conservative version of Lyndon B. Johnson's War on Poverty. Advocates of this view might work on a constitutional amendment that would define marriage in the traditional way, perhaps akin to an even more robust version of the Defense of Marriage Act that was passed overwhelmingly by Congress and signed into law by President Clinton in 1996. Another possibility could include confirming like-minded justices to the Supreme Court so as to not only reverse *Obergefell*[48] (much like the pro-life movement eventually succeeded in reversing *Roe v. Wade*) but also treat nontraditional conceptions of marriages as legally impermissible. Other tactics might focus on the state level in addition to the federal, working to impose a top-down vision of the traditional view despite the cultural shift away from it.

Policy nudge option. This approach does not attempt a one-size-fits-all strategy favored by the national decree advocates. Rather, advocates of nudging look for modest to significant incremental changes in policy at any level that can foster healthy practices of and attitudes toward marriage, sex, and family life. On the more modest side this might include lobbying for changes in the federal tax code to facilitate a parent being able to stay home with young children, creative educational reforms to support families choosing schools that best reflect their convictions, or adjusting the adoption process to make adoption more affordable while preserving responsible oversight. More ambitious options might include changing tax laws to reward marriage (rather than just avoid penalizing it), strengthening the "contract" side of marriage to make it more difficult to dissolve absent a serious breach (something more substantive than "irreconcilable differences"), and drawing on social science evidence to

---

[48]Obergefell v. Hodges, 576 U.S. 644 (2015). Of course this is the case in which the Supreme Court precluded states from instantiating any views of marriage that precluded same-sex unions from qualifying as marriages.

support a national ad campaign touting the virtues and benefits of marriage (not unlike anti-smoking campaigns). Advocates for this approach recognize that reversing the Supreme Court's constitutional decisions is unlikely but believe there are *policy* changes that can strengthen marriages and families through other means. They would welcome a cultural sea change in attitudes and practices regarding marriage and family but work on achieving more modest and arguably more plausible advances on a smaller scale.

Hold-the-line option. Believing that the legal and cultural contest between companionship marriage and traditional marriage has been decisively settled, advocates of this approach take a defensive posture. They look to carve out spaces in which traditionally minded citizens of whatever background can continue to put their own convictions into practice, including traditional marriage. This category describes the attorneys who defended the Catholic Church in Philadelphia with which we began this chapter. Those attorneys did not attempt to monopolize the public square such that the city of Philadelphia would only work with traditional adoption agencies and foster children would *only* be placed in traditionally minded families. Rather, they worked to preserve the freedom of Catholic Social Services to serve in accordance with their faith, and the freedom of Philadelphians to choose such agencies. Whether by passing legislation at the federal, state, or local level, or carving out judicial exemptions to laws of general applicability, hold-the-liners look to protect the rights of traditionally minded Christians and others of similar convictions to practice their faith, raise their families, and engage the pluralistic public square without being treated as second-class citizens at best or bigots at worst.

Change the culture option. Another possible approach is to eschew the realm of messy politics and policy altogether and instead focus on cultural renewal at the level of family, church, and intermediate institutions (this last term is a clunky way to describe all sorts of groups that are bigger than the family but are not the state: businesses, fraternal organizations, private educational institutions, nonprofits, clubs, churches, guilds, etc.). This option covers a host of tactics, all of which suppose that cultural change is upstream of political and policy change. What distinguishes this approach from the hold-the-line or nudging advocates is a decisive abstention from the political and the legal (at least for a season) realms. Many of this mindset may feel burned or fatigued by what they see as clumsy or ineffective Christian political movements in the past. They think that instead the true key to cultural renewal on these matters is the church focusing on being the church; families raising well-adjusted children; colleges and businesses going about their work with integrity and witness; and the like.[49]

Privatizing marriage option. Finally, some might think the best thing to happen is for the state to retreat from involvement with marriage and family life altogether. While *some* oversight would be needed as it would be for any household arrangement, and likely custody enforcement for children, the rationale for this approach is to avoid the government putting its official stamp of approval on *any* single model of domestic relations. People can make whatever intimate arrangements they please and sign whatever agreements they choose. The government can enforce those agreements as it does with business and other endeavors but won't favor or disfavor anyone's religious scruples or harm someone's understanding of their dignity.

Evaluating the Approaches

In reflecting on these various approaches, we return to our political principles[50] and draw from our questions as described in chapter four.[51] We

---

[49]James Davison Hunter's argument for "faithful presence," while eschewing politics, resonates with this approach. See James Davison Hunter, *To Change the World: The Irony, Tragedy, and Possibility of Christianity in the Late Modern World* (New York: Oxford University Press, 2010).

[50]The four political principles are (1) the common good and civic friendship; (2) confessional pluralism and religious liberty; (3) restraint and liberty; and (4) democracy and decentralization.

[51](1) First identify what the good (or goods) at issue is in any particular political issue and how that good (or goods) relates to human flourishing; then (2) identify the options for securing that good; think through how the different options secure the good, affect other goods, and comport with our political principles; and finally, (3) identify prudential considerations that inevitably come into play in making these judgments.

think doing so eliminates two options rather straightforwardly. Convinced as we are that marriage and family comprise a core relational good that also acts as a pivotal nexus for the other goods, marriage and family contribute to our shared common good and civic friendship. It is difficult to imagine a flourishing community in which marriage and family relationships are in shambles. Everyone, no matter their own personal marital or familial status, has a stake in a healthy marriage culture. We are also persuaded that marriage is a *public* good and that strictly speaking there is no neutral approach to marriage and family that can be accomplished by the "hands off" approach that the "privatizing marriage" option would adopt.

Because the creational reality of marriage and family transcends any human legal institution's treatment of them, a society's laws and policies should support healthy marriages and flourishing families. While the companionship view sees marriage as an adult-centric arrangement for which children can be an option, as presented above, we think openness to the possibility of children is an essential component to any individual marriage and an inescapable feature of marriage on the social level. We cannot fully articulate this position here. But children by definition do not have the autonomous capacity for choice that adults do, and thus the community (including but not limited to local, state, and federal government) rightly provides not only guardrails for children's safety, but also policies and incentives to promote marriage and family life. Hence, we think the privatization option fails because it will harm not only the relational good inherent in marriage and family, but also the rational, volitional, and physical goods that marriage and family foster.

We also find the "national decree" option wanting, albeit for different reasons. While we agree with advocates of this approach that marriage and family are crucial for the common good and indirectly for civic friendship, our other political principles and prudential considerations mitigate against endorsing a top-down effort to reestablish aspects of the traditional approach[52] that are no longer as accepted as they once

---

[52] A reminder of what we said above in chap. 6, n. 23 about the meaning of *traditional*.

were. While we are not opposed in principle to a national campaign on a given issue X, our commitments to pluralism and volitional goods, the wisdom of limited government given the importance of restraint and liberty, and the importance of decentralized democracy lead us to be wary of such projects.

Moreover, prudence requires that we "read the room" of our culture in determining whether such a campaign would move us closer to the desired end or further from it. Here we follow in the footsteps of Augustine and Aquinas, both of whom suggested that prudence sometimes accepts imperfect social practices as the price of preventing worse outcomes. Both, for example, advised against criminalizing prostitution because they judged the current moral state of the people as so corrupt (with regard to that vice) that such legislation would backfire and *increase* lust and misbehavior. Such a result damages the common good by increasing sexual misbehavior on the one hand and diminishing the authority and efficacy of the governing authorities on the other. Neither Augustine nor Aquinas were squishy on the wickedness of prostitution, and we share their view both on the substance of the matter and on the prudential principle that might be summed up by the quip attributed to Otto von Bismarck that "politics is the art of the possible."

So we don't reject a national top-down decree-type approach to marriage because we think a more-or-less national consensus aligning with marriage and family properly understood would itself be a bad thing. We reject it because it might violate important principles of Hopeful Realism, and because we think such a campaign would, in this moment and in our cultural context, make it harder to advocate for and even live out the truth about marriage, sex, and family. The massive change in norms about sex and marriage did not happen overnight, and so one should not expect that efforts to revitalize a healthier marriage culture will succeed overnight either. Moreover, if traditional views on marriage and family had the sort of widespread support needed to move the needle on a national or constitutional scale, then the current "moment and cultural context" would not be what it is. And this is all assuming such a campaign would be based on consensus-building and persuasion. Any heavy-handed decree-like approach that would bypass ordinary democratic means, like imposing traditional marriage via a Supreme Court decision, would not only be prudentially ill-advised but violate our political principles by repeating the very tactics that we have found questionable at best and illegitimate at worst when employed for the sake of other causes.

What about the second, third, and fourth options: nudging, holding the line, and changing the culture? We think none of these approaches is sufficient by itself, for various reasons, but that each can and should—depending on prudential circumstances—be part of how traditionally minded Christians can work toward a healthier marriage and family culture. All three share a principled commitment to marriage and family contributing to the common good and civic friendship. None of these approaches is relativistic as to the moral standing of traditional marriage as a creational good. All of them can be appropriate depending on particular circumstances. For instance, the "nudging" examples we described above might be plausible for some states or local communities, but not others. Enacting such policies does not illegitimately impose views on others because they can and should be accomplished through democratic means. In a democracy properly understood, citizens *propose* policy and laws; they do not simply *impose* them. Nudging is most likely to be possible, and thus prudentially appropriate, at the state and local level, which accords well with our emphasis on pluralism and decentralization without ruling out the possibility of nudges at the national level (such as a reform of the federal tax code or adjusting refugee and immigration policies to be more family-friendly).

"Holding the line" makes sense when there is not enough support to instantiate what we take to be the strongest position on a policy issue and preserving the freedom for individuals and groups to live out their convictions is still worth doing. This is what happened with the *Fulton* decision, which did not overturn the city of Philadelphia's companionship view of marriage but protected Catholic Social Services such that they could still serve underprivileged youth alongside agencies operating on a different understanding of marriage and family. People of goodwill may differ as to how best to hold the line—whether through general legislation, or legislative or judicially carved out exemptions—and at what governmental level—local, state, federal—such efforts will bear the most fruit. We don't address that question here in depth, except to say that one difference between the nudging option and the holding the line option is we think the latter will be more effective at the federal and state level because in the US system, protections at those levels can act as umbrellas for the smaller communities and legal systems that fall under their jurisdictions (whereas nudging is more likely to be effective at the smaller scales of local politics).

We do not think the "change the culture" approach can work by itself for the same reasons we reject the privatization approach: marriage and family are inherently public and, at least in part, political and legal. It would be a viable option if Christians could somehow cordon ourselves off from the wider culture and concentrate on the "church being the church" or other such well-intentioned thinking. But this is almost as impossible as it is undesirable for Christians. We may think we can withstand cultural pressures without engaging in politics, but we doubt that could succeed even if it was desirable. Because we are convinced that a healthy marriage and family culture is good for *everyone*, those inside the church and out, we should still look to love our neighbors by advocating for laws and policies that further their flourishing. Citizens are responsible for how they wield (or fail to wield) political authority.

At the same time the "change the culture" approach reminds us that law and policy are not sufficient nor is the political the only realm worth our time and effort. The Christian church can (and should) walk and chew gum at the same time, so to speak, and thus nonpolitical efforts to build a healthy marriage culture are a necessary if not sufficient part of the effort. Sponsoring parenting classes in a church's downtown neighborhood, volunteering at crisis pregnancy centers, teaching English and other acclimation skills to newly arrived refugees so they can better provide for their families—these are all invaluable means of furthering the common good and, more importantly, witnessing to the truth of the gospel. Such efforts must complement political, legal, and policy advocacy.

Conclusion

A Hopeful Realism approach offers a framework with which we can both understand what marriage *is* with the help of both general and special revelation and apply our political principles to that understanding. We think this approach rules out both an abandonment of marriage and family policy as well as a top-down imposition of the traditional view through a massive national campaign. We land, therefore, on a principled but broadly prudential approach that will employ different approaches depending on the circumstances. Such an approach is principled because we believe God has revealed true things about marriage, sex, and family in the Word he has given the church and in our natures that we can understand given our reason. It is a prudential approach because applying those truths with wisdom and efficacy means understanding the particular contexts and challenges that not only change from time to time (say, the 1960s to the 2020s) but from place to place (say, Seattle, Washington to Mobile, Alabama). As we have reiterated throughout this book, there is no guarantee for "success" on the political, policy, or cultural level. But we can strive for faithfulness through our efforts whatever the short-term consequences turn out to be.

7

COERCION, VIOLENCE, AND WAR

IT MIGHT SEEM ALMOST TOO EASY to show how Hopeful Realism can help Christians think carefully about war and violence and make practical judgments about any particular conflict. Christians largely developed and have long employed the Just War Tradition (JWT) to do just that, and we will not be reinventing the wheel here. JWT articulates a set of categories and principles that can help discern when a country is justified in going to war and then how to fight that war justly. Starting with Augustine and continuing on through Aquinas, Vitoria, Suarez, Grotius and of late Paul Ramsey, Jean Elshtain, Nigel Biggar, Daryl Charles, and many others, Christians have thought long and hard about the moral contours of war and violence, and have done so almost universally in the company of the natural law.[1] It is not too much of a stretch to say that absent a commitment to the natural law, JWT doesn't really get off the ground—or, at least, it is hard to see how such a tradition might develop in the absence of the natural law. Indeed, as we will describe below, many of its Christian pacifist critics find fault on just this point, namely that JWT relies so much on *nature* and general revelation that it decidedly

---

[1]It is worth noting that JWT is not solely a Christian tradition, and at least until the nineteenth and twentieth centuries, non-Christian thinkers (like, say, Cicero) also relied heavily on the natural law to frame their arguments. Since the 1970s, a number of secular scholars have attempted to re-ground the theory in terms of international law, common practice, or human rights. See Michael Walzer, *Just and Unjust Wars: A Moral Argument with Historical Illustrations*, 5th ed. (New York: Basic Books, 2015); Brian Orend, *The Morality of War* (Buffalo, NY: Broadview Press, 2013); Jeff McMahan, *Killing in War* (New York: Oxford University Press, 2009); Cécile Fabre, *Cosmopolitan War* (New York: Oxford University Press, 2012).

neglects grace and special revelation. That is, for some Christians, distinctively *Christian* attempts to justify war and violence fail primarily because they are not in fact genuinely and distinctively Christian.

We think that claim mistaken, and we offer in this chapter an argument about both how Christians can think about war and violence in general and how Christians can think about war and violence in a particular (and very controversial) case: the US decision to intervene in Iraq in 2003. Using Hopeful Realism's framework, we first sketch out why we think our distinctive view of the natural law does point to the principles of the JWT as a useful way of thinking about war and violence in general. This includes showing that JWT itself reflects a broader set of considerations about the nature and purpose of political orders. Prosecuting war is not quite the same thing as what we might think of as ordinary politics, but they are of a piece, at least in the sense that in both cases political authorities are authorized to secure the common good and a reasonable peace—which sometimes requires the use of coercive force. We then turn to the American decision to invade Iraq in 2003, suggesting that though there were reasonable (though not irrefutable) grounds for invading, the decided unwillingness to secure anything like the common good at the end of the initial invasion rendered the war rather suspect.

War and Violence in General

How should Christians think morally about war and violence? Behind that seemingly simple question lies a tangle of interwoven issues that Christians (and many others) have engaged over the past couple of millennia (and longer). Historically, there have been three broad answers to this question, what we call *realism, pacifism,* and *just war.* (Notably, *realism* as we use it in this chapter denotes the standard amoral pursuit of state interest, rather than the meaning we've described under the descriptor of "Hopeful Realism.") To think about which of these three broad answers makes the most sense for Hopeful Realism, we can put our framework to work and ask, first, what goods are at stake here in the questions around war and violence?

In Karl Marlantes's well-regarded book *What It Is Like to Go to War*, he vividly makes clear what may seem to most blindingly obvious: war is an inescapably physical and visceral enterprise.[2] In an era when too often our own "experience" of war is mediated through screens or other technology, it is helpful to remember that war involves the use of violence to pursue distinctively political (or other sorts of) objectives that always necessarily include death and physical destruction. There are no "clean" wars: death, physical suffering, and tragedy are their constant companions.

It would be tempting, then, to suppose that war is *exclusively* about material or physical goods, that it is just the application of violence to secure territory, acquire material resources, and the like. After all, when someone does win a war (and not all wars have winners and losers) the proof they have won is often that they have established (or retained) control over a piece of physical territory—a city, country, or some other physical objective. Even what is called "cyber-war," where enemies are engaged through computer networks and do "battle" with bytes and bits, only really matters insofar as it has practical effects on people's material lives. Or, to put a finer point on it, cyber-war is war precisely because it allows another entity to gain control of or damage critical infrastructure, logistical trains, and much else. Cyber-war matters because it allows for influence or control of material realities.[3]

So it is not implausible to think that war is primarily (if not exclusively) about physical security. It is, in one reading, how the famous German theorist of war Carl von Clausewitz conceived of it. Clausewitz's famous maxim was that "war is not merely a political act but a real political instrument, a continuation of political intercourse, a carrying out of the same by other means."[4] What he meant was that there is no

---

[2] Karl Marlantes, *What It Is like to Go to War* (New York: Atlantic Monthly Press, 2011). It is perhaps worth noting that one of us did serve as an officer in the US military, though did not see combat.

[3] This is not the only thing it does, of course. The control of information (and disinformation) is an important element of war. But even there, it matters because it contributes to the control of physical territory and people.

[4] Carl von Clausewitz, *On War*, trans. Michael Howard and Peter Paret (New York: Oxford University Press, 2007), 28-29.

fundamental distinction between what we call "war" and politics more generally. War is merely an attempt to pursue political objectives in a particular way, and for Clausewitz that "particular way" is only really just a more obvious version of what politics actually *is*. If war is *simply* a violent contest over physical goods as a way of making ourselves secure, then that would mean that politics is *simply* about a violent contest over physical goods—and vice versa. War, on that account, would just be about physical, material goods.

Accepting that view might oblige us to endorse some form of need for physical security and power and that always puts us in a position of conflict with one another. Human society is in the end just a zero-sum game that is in some sense amoral: the point is to secure yourself (either as an individual or a community) above all else. That view has a long and distinguished pedigree. We find it, in one form or another, in Thucydides's account of the Peloponnesian War, in Machiavelli, and in Thomas Hobbes's *Leviathan*, among many others.[5] The power of this account comes from the way it captures something true about war, namely that it definitively centers on ourselves as physical beings, always interested in our self-preservation and the control of others. For the realist, war—and politics more generally—is always and everywhere defined by the exercise of coercive force in the interest of one's own security and power and with limited attention to moral questions.

Hopeful Realism does not accept that view, as we do not think it captures fully what war is actually about. Indeed, even most realists do not think that war (or politics) is *just* about physical goods. Clausewitz, for example, thought that war also carried with it—or, maybe better, was born out of—a desire for honor and glory, not just security. War is a way of proving one's greatness, not just acquiring territory, resources, or power.[6] Machiavelli, too, is not as much of a strict materialist he is

---

[5]Thucydides, *The Peloponnesian War*, trans. P. J. Rhodes and Martin Hammond (New York: Oxford University Press, 2009); Niccolò Machiavelli, *The Prince*, trans. Harvey C. Mansfield (Chicago: University of Chicago Press, 1998); Thomas Hobbes, *Leviathan: With Selected Variants from the Latin Edition of 1668*, ed. Edwin Curley (Indianapolis, IN: Hackett Publishing, 1994).
[6]Clausewitz, *On War*.

sometimes taken to be. In *The Prince*, he draws on the story of Agathocles to make a rather subtle point about the inadequacy of "merely" acquiring power. Agathocles is a common soldier who schemed and murdered his way to becoming King of Syracuse. Agathocles seems to exercise all the illicit "virtues" Machiavelli commends: he is bold, violent, cunning, and resourceful. But Machiavelli suggests that Agathocles cannot be "celebrated among the most excellent men."[7] Why not? He says it is because of his "savage cruelty and inhumanity," but that's simply implausible as a straightforward answer: Agathocles practices in fact what Machiavelli preaches in the rest of the book. He is, in so many ways, the picture of the successful political operator. The problem is that Agathocles is too open about his crimes and thus he cannot, for all his success, achieve "glory," the state of being *remembered* and *honored* for one's greatness and successes. Machiavelli tells Agathocles's story to help make clear, if in a rather subtle and indirect way, that the point is not *just* to win in politics, but to win in such a way as to acquire glory, to be remembered and thus achieve something like immortality.

The idea that war is *just* about physical goods is actually pretty rare; those who think of themselves as "realists" in our day tend to focus on power and security as necessary means to protecting other things they (and we) care about. Perhaps some Marxists, armed with Lenin's view of imperialism, might be strict realists in this sense, but that illustrates the problem. It is simply incorrect to think that politics and war are just both at root violent conflict where one side attempts to dominate the other. But Clausewitz rightly sees a kind of close relation between how we understand war and how we understand politics. The problem with the strict realist view is that it simply misunderstands politics because it misunderstands human beings. It takes the inevitable conflict and coercion that's interwoven into any political order and mistakes it for the whole. In a world where we are all too aware of how much conflict and coercion play a role, it's easy—and understandable—to make that the sole story. But it's

---

[7] Machiavelli, *Prince*, 34-35.

still a mistake because it inevitably reduces the human person to little more than a power-seeking, self-serving beast—a clever beast, perhaps, but a beast nonetheless, and perhaps all that much worse for the cleverness.

The point here is that politics is not *just* about material goods—even if material goods can matter quite a lot—and neither is war. Realism in this sense is mistaken. But it is still very much the case that war and politics are closely linked. Again, Clausewitz in this sense is correct.

Note something interesting here, though. Part of the rationale that pacifists sometimes offer for thinking that war is out of bounds for the Christian is that it involves a mode of politics anathema to core Christian convictions about what it means to live in a just political community. At least that is one of the arguments advanced by our time's most prominent contemporary Christian pacifist, Stanley Hauerwas. In an essay entitled "Should War Be Eliminated?" Hauerwas rather elliptically suggests that it is not the case that governments remain committed to war on account of security reasons, as most would assume.[8] Rather, they can't abandon it because war—and the use of violence more broadly—is what ultimately defines those nominally secular governments. Christian pacifism, he claims, is non-negotiable precisely in that it so clearly demarcates and distinguishes the church as an alternative and prophetic sort of alternative *polis*. It is an outpost of another kingdom precisely in that it refuses to be defined by the imperative of war and violence.

In this sense, then, Hauerwas and Christian pacifism more generally can often be quite in agreement with Machiavelli in thinking that ordinary politics is indeed about more than just material goods. Richard Hays argues in *The Moral Vision of the New Testament* that the global political order's pursuit of "justice" is largely indistinguishable from a kind of lusty vengeance, and so the Christian cannot participate in that order's wars precisely because we are explicitly called *not* to exact vengeance (Romans 12:19-20). Similarly, John Howard Yoder takes the

---

[8]Stanley Hauerwas, "Should War Be Eliminated? A Thought Experiment," in *The Hauerwas Reader*, ed. John Berkman and Michael Cartwright (Durham, NC: Duke University Press, 2001), 392-425.

"Great Whore" of Babylon in Revelation 13 to be just another facet of the sword-bearing political authority described by Paul in Romans 13.[9] In some (ironic) way, pacifists are sometimes also our most enthusiastic and reliable Machiavellians, at least in their conception of what defines ordinary earthly politics.

Of course, and in much more important ways, pacifists are far from being Machiavellians. The Christian pacifist believes that because of the life, death, and resurrection of Jesus, a quite different sort of politics is possible, not just eschatologically but in the here and now, embodied in the church. The church is, they argue, a new kind of *polis*, though one organized on radically different grounds than ordinary political communities. To be a Christian on this account is to refuse the inherent connection between war and politics, to deny that politics *must* involve coercion and violence. Instead, they insist, we are more properly bound to a community that is defined by the life of Jesus and his teachings, especially those in the Sermon on the Mount (Matthew 5–7). And if that's true, then it's impossible to take up arms or accept war as anything other than an utter betrayal of Christ.

In one sense, this is quite right: the Kingdom of God is indeed not "of this world," where war (and politics more broadly) is always and everywhere wrapped up in the acquisition of glory or self-vindication. So politics in its most fundamental sense is not *inherently* violent, any more than creation itself is inherently violent. And we have already suggested that Scripture asks us to be ready to *wield* political authority as a way of loving our neighbor and securing some sort of justice for them (and us).[10]

It thus seems like we are caught in a dilemma: if war inevitably goes beyond the physical to always and inevitably include a desire for greatness and renown on the one side or vengeance on the other, then it looks as though we should embrace pacifism. Can a Christian claim to follow the

---

[9]Richard Hays, *Moral Vision of the New Testament: A Contemporary Introduction to New Testament Ethics* (New York: Bloomsbury Publishing, 2004); John Howard Yoder, *The Politics of Jesus: Vicit Agnus Noster* (Grand Rapids, MI: Eerdmans, 1994).
[10]See chap. 1.

Sermon on the Mount with its teaching about forgiveness, peaceableness, and so on also be a vengeful or glory-seeking warrior? How then shall we think of war and violence? Are we obligated to think of war as sometimes a kind of "lesser of two evils," meaning that it's evil, but perhaps sometimes less bad than the alternative? Or do we embrace pacifism, even at the cost of any hope to secure the common good?

Neither of these options—pacifism or realism—prove viable for Hopeful Realism's endorsement. To explain why, in this section we will first draw from Scripture and then turn to Augustine. The heart of the pacifist case is that Jesus eschewed violence even in the face of cosmic injustice and calls his followers to imitate him. It's obviously not an insubstantial claim, enough so such that many Christians into the third century embraced it in some fashion or another.[11] But we think it runs into a number of scriptural problems, not least its struggle to reconcile passages where God himself clearly commands and ordains the use of coercion and lethal force. Most struggle to figure out what exactly to do with God's sometimes quite stark martial commands to the Israelites as they settled the land of Canaan, but it would be a mistake to simply ignore them.[12] What's more, as we have already pointed out, immediately after Paul lays out what it means to love one another in Romans 12 (including instructions against taking vengeance, since this is God's purview), he identifies the political authority in Romans 13 as having been ordained by God with the right to use coercion for the sake of fulfilling its purpose. Finally, when Jesus and the very early church meet with Roman soldiers, they commend their faith and encourage them to live rightly *without* any suggestion that their role as a soldier is itself a

---

[11] See Ronald J. Sider, *The Early Church on Killing: A Comprehensive Sourcebook on War, Abortion, and Capital Punishment* (Grand Rapids, MI: Baker Academic, 2012); George Kalantzis, *Caesar and the Lamb: Early Christian Attitudes on War and Military Service* (Eugene, OR: Wipf and Stock, 2012). For a succinct explanation of the context for the early church in this respect, see Oliver O'Donovan and Joan Lockwood O'Donovan, *From Irenaeus to Grotius: A Sourcebook in Christian Political Thought, 100–1625* (Grand Rapids, MI: Eerdmans, 1999), 1-7.

[12] See Paul Copan, *Is God a Moral Monster? Making Sense of the Old Testament God* (Grand Rapids, MI: Baker Books, 2011). It is worth recognizing that advocates of just war also struggle with some of these passages.

problem (see Matthew 8:5-13 and Acts 10). The claim that Scripture or even the life and ministry of Jesus (or the very early church) requires pacifism (Hauerwas sometimes goes so far as to make it *the* distinguishing mark of the church) is simply not persuasive to us *precisely because* it goes against the grain of the holistic witness of Scripture.[13]

Consider an especially evocative vignette as well in Book XIX of *City of God*. Among the many other things that he is doing in *City of God*, Augustine offers a strong and quite effective critique of Rome, especially in its never-ending wars, moral corruption, and prideful idolatry. Book XIX represents the apex of that critique, as he shows Rome's central moral and political concepts profoundly insufficient either to account for the suffering inherent in the human condition or to accurately describe the nature of human political communities. In chapter six, he presses the point with a consideration of a judge in an ordinary criminal proceeding. This official acts as both prosecutor and judge and Augustine relates how he would be expected to torture both the accused and witnesses as a normal and necessary part of his job. In doing so, Augustine recognizes that the judge would sometimes prompt them to lie and thus then at times condemn innocents to punishment, even execution. Even under the best of ordinary circumstances, to be a judge is to be in a calamitous position. Who, Augustine asks, would agree to do this?

His answer is "the wise man." But it's not Rome's wise man, who comforts himself with dreams of a moral and political system in which the tragedies of life in the *saeculum* are smoothed away and where happiness is achieved in this life. Those dreams are simply cold comfort, even hopeless, when confronted with the reality of actually existing, sinful, broken human communities. But neither is it the steely-eyed realist, who might see *little more* than suffering and conflict and wills himself to his duty, almost on account of duty itself. Part of Augustine's subtle genius is his chastened hopefulness in the face of moral and political tragedy.

---

[13]See Nigel Biggar, "Specify and Distinguish! Interpreting the New Testament on Non-Violence,'" *Studies in Christian Ethics* 22, no. 2 (2009): 164-84; "In Defence of War," *New Blackfriars* 96, no. 1062 (2015): 192-205.

Where the realist (and we could add, the Christian pacifist) might see little more than darkness and striving in the judge's dilemma, Augustine sees genuine, if flawed and tragic, attempts to pursue political goods that are real and necessary for the relative flourishing of that community.[14] And, indeed, when he asks why any "wise man" would countenance participating in such terrible acts, his answer is that "society drags him to his duty." He does it because it is necessary, but in this necessity there is no Machiavellian glory. There is only being dragged to one's genuine, if sometimes tragic, duty.[15] Authority can and should be wielded, says Augustine, for the sake of justice—even if imperfect—and the good of those under its care.

As we have described in the first half of the book, political communities exist to secure certain social and political goods, and without authorities exercising judgment over those communities, they fail. No political community would long survive if its authorities refused to actually exercise their authority and do so in ways that are tied up with coercion and force. Or, perhaps more to the point, if they did refuse, other sorts of power would rise up in their place. But authorities always and everywhere wield their power imperfectly, sometimes with terrible consequences.

Some mid-twentieth-century Augustinians fashioned this insight into the basis for a kind of politically pessimistic Christian realism. Of these, Reinhold Niebuhr is probably the most well-known exemplar. They pulled something true out of Augustine and in a context where the theological and cultural *zeitgeist* was unreasonably optimistic, it's not surprising that they framed things in this way. But there's an important distinction to how Augustine's judge thinks about what he is doing: he does not consider what he is doing to be *sinful*. It is terrible, yes, but its terrible-ness is born of ignorance, finitude, and the existence of evil in

---

[14]See Jean Bethke Elshtain, *Augustine and the Limits of Politics* (Notre Dame, IN: University of Notre Dame Press, 1996).
[15]See also the collection of letters Augustine wrote to the vicar Macedonius, who had responsibility for imposing punishments as part of the Roman political system. There, Augustine pleads for mercy for the wrongdoer, even as he acknowledges that unwillingness to punish would undermine the entire social system. See Augustine, *The Political Writings*, ed. Henry Paolucci (Washington DC: Regnery, 1962), 252-74.

the world—not of malice or evil on the part of the judge. (Augustine's views on torture are complicated but for our purposes here, it's enough to say that he didn't think it was inherently evil.[16]) The just judge is doing what he must for his community to function even reasonably well with approximations of peace and justice, and he's doing it within moral boundaries. He is not pursuing the "lesser of two evils."

Of course, he is not fully just and neither is his political community. But within the *saeculum*—the time between the proclamation and consummation of the Kingdom of God—the state can justly apply coercive force and claim (partial) allegiance and support. This is why Augustine is rightly understood to be the father of the Just War Tradition, even if his writings on war are mostly episodic and unsystematic, especially when compared to Aquinas. He grasps that war is first about the physical goods of peace and security. All wars, he rightly notes, are fought with peace in mind; even if it's an unjust peace, it is still a kind of peace. But war is not *just* about peace and security any more than the exercise of political authority in general is *just* about peace and security. There are, instead, a whole host of common goods—rational, relational, and volitional—necessary even to our partial flourishing for which, as described above, political authorities have some responsibility.[17] Politics is never just an exercise in rational deliberation about the nature of justice, but neither is it just the passionate conflict of wills, each looking to secure her own good at the expense of others' good. It is (or it can be) a common effort to secure goods necessary for human flourishing within the inevitable limits imposed by human sinfulness and finitude.

And this is why both the realist and pacifist are mistaken. The realist *and* pacifist, ironically enough, are simply too pessimistic about war and ordinary politics, supposing them (at times) to only be a competition of greedy wills. We are fallen creatures, yes. But as we have been at pains to

---

[16]Just to be clear, we believe that torture is wrong. But the context of book XIX of *City of God* suggests that Augustine does not see torture and warfare as different in kind.
[17]See chap. 4.

emphasize, we are not *just* fallen and so our politics, and even war, can have ends that go beyond conquest and glory. Neither should we suppose, contra to pacifism, that the God in Christ Jesus who calls us to love our enemy as he loves can be divided from the God who authorizes public authorities to wield the sword in defense of good.[18] A decision to go to war is like any other sort of political decision, to be judged by the degree to which it genuinely aims at a reasonable peace and something like the common good, both for our own country and for those whom we might be fighting.[19]

So, unsurprisingly, the Just War Tradition is how Hopeful Realism thinks about war and violence. Pacifism and realism do indeed illuminate elements of our ordinary political life and how very terrible the necessities of coercion really are. But neither takes seriously how within that terrible-ness, we might still look to secure a reasonable peace, what Augustine calls a "concord of wills" that is not fully justice but neither is it simply a victor's vengeance. War is terrible and ought only be entered into for the gravest reasons. But it is also sometimes necessary for the sake of real goods, and JWT illuminates just how Hopeful Realism would approach these terrible judgments.

Hopeful Realism and Iraq

To say that the US decision to invade Iraq in March 2003 was controversial is understating things by a country mile—and it has not become

---

[18]For an argument that love of enemy is not incompatible with war, see Nigel Biggar, *In Defence of War* (New York: Oxford University Press, 2013).

[19]And that's perhaps where what we think of as ordinary politics and war come apart a bit: in both war and ordinary politics, we expect those in authority to have in the front of their mind the flourishing of their own communities, to include the full range of goods we describe in chap. 4. While it is still the case in ordinary politics that the flourishing of other political communities cannot be entirely discounted—recall our critique of mercantilism in chap. 5—in times of war, that question takes on a particular valence. Engaging in war justly requires acting (within the bounds of justice) for the good of one's community and that requires, as a matter of course, visiting death and destruction on those seeking to do your community harm. It also requires prosecuting that war in such a way that it ends such that your enemy's community also may flourish and that your two communities can reconcile and live peaceably. That is, though political authorities obviously do not have the same sort of responsibility for other communities as they do for their own, they still have some sort of responsibility, especially insofar as they prove the victor and end up exercising some power over a vanquished enemy.

less so over the intervening two decades.[20] Indeed, given the post-invasion insurgency, significant casualties, and the subsequent rise of ISIS after the US pullout, it was relatively hard to find an enthusiastic defender of the invasion when various outlets published their twenty-year retrospectives in March 2023.[21] Nonetheless, there is a serious case still to be made that the decision to invade was the right one, and so considering the question can illustrate how Hopeful Realism's framework is meant to work in the particulars. Again, the idea here is not to suggest that our judgments on Iraq (or any other particular issue) represent some kind of infallible judgment or even what a hopeful realist *must* conclude. We are merely modeling how we think Hopeful Realism can approach and illuminate these inevitably difficult judgments.

There is not, as it turns out, one single version of the "just war" argument. It is, really in the best sense, an intellectual and moral *tradition* where generations of scholars and practitioners have wrestled with two broad questions: Under what conditions is it just to go to war (*jus ad bellum*)? And what does it look like to fight a war justly (*jus in bello*)?[22] The first requires proper political authorities to articulate just cause and right intent, reasons that would indeed justify being willing to go to war—defense against unjust aggression is the most obvious and clear example. But as we have tried to emphasize, war is such a terrible thing that the tradition also claims that a country ought to be willing to go to war only if really necessary and if it has a reasonable expectation that the cost would be worth the plausible outcome.[23] The second pushes the

---

[20]Though to be fair, there was substantial public support in fall of 2002 and winter of 2003, which is part of the reason Congress authorized military force prior to the 2002 midterms.

[21]For the exception, see David French, "In Defense of the Iraq War," *National Review*, March 20, 2019, www.nationalreview.com/corner/iraq-war-just-cause-saddam-hussein-threat-stability/.

[22]Of late, a number of scholars have argued for offering a third question dealing with the victor's obligations after the conflict, or *just post bellum*. Since it has not generally been a part of the tradition, we do not treat it here as a distinct question, though its moral import will matter significantly. For a strong argument in favor of including it as a distinct question, see Eric D. Patterson, *Ending Wars Well: Order, Justice, and Conciliation in Contemporary Post-Conflict* (New Haven, CT: Yale University Press, 2012).

[23]The formal categories here are proportionality (that the action being taken is proportionate to the injury being redressed), reasonable hope of success, and that war is a last reasonable resort.

combatants to fight the war such that they discriminate in their actions (avoiding as they can noncombatant death and injury) and that they use force proportionate to the end being pursued. At times, in both scholarly and public discussions, these categories can come across as a kind of checklist, which can encourage countries to rationalize their way through the criteria as a way of justifying what they already want to do anyway. A better way of understanding the categories is as a helpful guide to moral and political deliberations—cues, if you will, to the sorts of considerations that ought to be on the table when thinking about a possible war.

These considerations map well on to the framework we developed in chapter four, where we ask how the different options do with respect to securing the primary goods at stake and then how they do with respect to securing other goods that might be affected, all within the orbit of the political principles we articulated in chapter three. To put a point on this, what we are after in this section is to think through how Hopeful Realism's framework can help us choose among the plausible options available with respect to Iraq in 2002–2003.

So what were the options for the United States vis-a-vis Iraq in 2003?[24] Recall the situation in the fall of 2002. About a decade prior, the United States led an international coalition to kick Iraqi troops out of Kuwait and then the United Nations imposed a series of sanctions to force Saddam Hussein to come clean about any Weapons of Mass Destruction (WMD) programs. Hussein had a rather long history of developing and using WMDs and there was reason to think he had reconstituted at least some of those programs.[25] The United States had been attacked on 9/11, and its National Security Strategy clearly prioritized what it deemed to

---

[24]It is worth noting here that our evaluation of options aims to have a kind of *prospective* and not retrospective framing. What we mean is that the last twenty years have revealed a great deal about Iraq, American policies, etc. Hindsight is not actually 20/20, but it does impart important lessons. But in thinking through the question of whether the United States was right to invade, we should pay most of our attention to what was understood at the time.

[25]Hussein had used chemical weapons as part of the Iran-Iraq war in the 1980s and had a surprisingly advanced nuclear weapons program as well.

be rogue regimes with possible access to WMDs.[26] The United States, it seems, had three options:

1. End the sanctions (which were beginning to fail anyway) and more or less make its peace with Hussein's soon-to-be-nuclear Iraq.
2. Try to sustain the status quo by maintaining significant economic and military sanctions and press Iraq to permit expansive inspections of suspected WMD program sites.
3. Use military force to topple Hussein's regime.

One of the challenges in making the sorts of judgments necessary for choosing between these three options, even at a remove of two decades, is that many disagree widely on just what the situation in Iraq truly was at the time and what sort of threat the country actually posed to its neighbors and the United States. Making moral judgments inevitably involves making empirical judgments, and in this case there are passionate, deeply held, and widely opposed understandings of just what the situation on the ground was and what American policymakers in particular knew about it. To keep things relatively straightforward, we rely here on Melvyn Leffler's recent *Confronting Saddam Hussein: George W. Bush and the Invasion of Iraq*.[27]

Leffler's book is especially helpful in thinking about the degree to which the Bush Administration in particular was reasonable in thinking that Hussein's Iraq posed a genuine security threat to the United States. He points out that 9/11 had made clear what had been implicitly true for a long while, that the growth of communications and travel networks meant that distance was much less of a barrier than had once been the case for those seeking to do the country harm. What's more, it seemed reasonable to a wide swath of public officials in the United States and elsewhere that an unleashed Hussein, flush with a revived oil-driven

---

[26] See https://georgewbush-whitehouse.archives.gov/nsc/nss/2002/.
[27] Melvyn P. Leffler, *Confronting Saddam Hussein: George W. Bush and the Invasion of Iraq* (New York: Oxford University Press, 2023). For similar sorts of considerations, see Paul D. Miller, *Just War and Ordered Liberty* (New York: Cambridge University Press, 2021). The war's critics are, of course, much more numerous.

economy, would indeed pose a threat to the United States and the region. If the decision hinges first on whether an option does well in securing a reasonable peace in the United States and elsewhere, then it seems like option one is a nonstarter. And aside from a few fringe officials, that option never really seemed to be on the table.[28]

Thus the initial question comes down to whether the status quo (or something like it) was sufficient or if an invasion was necessary to protect American security. Leffler's judgment is that what the administration called "coercive diplomacy," demanding expanded inspections backed by the threat of force, would actually have been sufficient to keep Hussein in check. And it turns out that was quite likely true, given that Iraq's WMD programs were mostly nonexistent and little threat to the United States. But the United States did not know that in 2002 as it was making its judgment: American officials genuinely, if fallibly, believed that Iraq had an active program and that if it was successful in developing, say, a chemical or nuclear weapon, the United States would be at serious risk.[29] It is challenging, to say the least, to disentangle what the US government *should* have known about Iraqi weapons (Leffler suggests that President Bush at least was not committed to an invasion until very late in the process), but one can accept the threat assessment as genuine and recognize that the decision to go to war was at least reasonable in this respect.

What was not reasonable, and here Leffler is highly critical, was the administration's studied refusal to plan for the securing of Iraq after the invasion and then its shambolic attempts to make up for that lack of planning after a quick success in the invasion. This was not World War II, when the United Stated entered in not quite sure what victory would look like (or even, really, if they would win). With Iraq, the administration

---

[28]This is not to say that there weren't legitimate concerns about the effects of sanctions on ordinary Iraqis. The sanctions had significantly damaged the Iraqi economy and led to shortages of medicine and basic goods.

[29]Other countries at least publicly agreed with the United States' worries about Iraq's WMD programs, even if they did not then judge that they were good grounds for military action on the proposed US timeline.

knew the United States would win and would win relatively quickly (though the speed of the victory was somewhat surprising). As we noted above, going to war is justified as a way of securing the goods necessary, first, for peace and security and then for the other aspects of our (and others') flourishing. When it comes to other countries, victory imposes on the victors the responsibility to extend that to them as well. This means, in the Just War Tradition, that one must fight in such a way that a reasonable peace is possible, and it certainly means in this case that the United States was responsible for securing the country and taking reasonable steps to make a decent life possible for its citizens. The United States was not obligated to turn Iraq into Switzerland, but the Administration was obligated to try to promote some measure of peace and good order. They failed to do that, and if that failure had simply been the outcome of clever or better resourced enemies or bad luck, then we might make some moral accommodations for mistakes. But the failure came from an unwillingness to do the work required or even initially to commit to it as an obligation, to disastrous consequences that in truth continue to reverberate in Iraq, Syria, and the United States today.

So when we ask the question of whether the United States should have maintained the status quo in 2002–2003 or invaded, we can acknowledge that it was reasonable to think of Hussein's Iraq as a threat that needed neutralizing with military force, but that the studied unwillingness to secure the peace in Iraq after the invasion rendered the decision to invade in that sense unjust.[30]

Conclusion

It is, of course, quite possible to come to a different set of conclusions with respect to Iraq, and our short sketch above is hardly meant to deliver an irrefutable verdict. But it should give a taste of how Hopeful Realism can think through these kinds of issues. War, as we have been careful to emphasize, inevitably involves us in any number of terrible

---

[30]This matches Paul Miller's argument in *Just War*.

judgments, and the temptation is always and everywhere to find some sort of moral shortcut. Some, like political realists, simply resign themselves to committing immoral acts in the name of some greater good. Others, like pacifists, look to keep their hands "clean" by simply refusing responsibility altogether.

Both of these alternatives to JWT fail, in our judgment, not because they misunderstand war. They both capture a portion of its terrors. They fail because they misconceive *politics*, making it mainly (or completely) the arena of violence, deceit, and the like. It does contain these things, but as we have been at pains to argue here, it is also the arena where together we can secure, in some fashion, the creational goods necessary for our flourishing.

But in a world marked by sin and finitude, that securing is always and everywhere at best partial and demands difficult, even terrible, judgments and actions. Nowhere does this come across more vividly than in the question of war, where our human judgments are inevitably tied up with death and destruction, often even when we decide *not* to go to war. We should always be reluctant to go to war and even in a just war, joy at victory must also keep company with grief at what has been lost. The natural law compels us to seek the good of all while the darkness of the world necessitates the tragic means of war to effect that in part. Or, so we think Hopeful Realism recommends.

8

RELIGIOUS LIBERTY

Setting Up the Issues

At first glance, religious liberty seems fairly straightforward. The liberty to freely practice one's religious convictions is obviously an important good. Who, other than an open totalitarian, is *against* the idea of religious liberty on its face? The freedom of conscience—especially when it comes to matters involving humans' relationships with God—is a fairly uncontroversial good. When courts or legislatures protect this good, most of us applaud, and rightly so.

An example illustrates the point: Abdul Maalik Muhammad (previously known as Gregory Holt) was incarcerated by the Arkansas Department of Corrections. Prison policy banned inmates from growing beards (though trimmed mustaches were permitted), citing clear prisoner identification and preventing hidden contraband as reasons. As a practicing Muslim, however, Mr. Holt requested permission to grow a very short, half-inch-long beard in conformity with his religious beliefs. The prison denied his request—effectively preventing Mr. Holt from fulfilling what he understood to be his religious obligations. He challenged the prison's decision in court, noting that the prison granted exceptions to those with documented skin conditions and the unlikelihood of hiding anything in a half-inch beard. The Supreme Court ruled unanimously in Mr. Holt's favor, finding that the Arkansas prison had placed a substantial burden on Mr. Holt's religious exercise without a compelling reason for doing so. While acknowledging the importance of the prison's interests in prisoner identification and preventing contraband, the Court was unpersuaded that an absolute ban—applied even to short beards—was necessary to achieve these goals. Moreover, Arkansas' claims were weakened by the fact that some forty-one states' prison systems make allowances for short beards. Following the court ruling, Mr. Holt was permitted to grow his beard—for all appearances, a laudable victory for the good of religious liberty.[1]

However, also consider the case of Tracy Elise—the self-described head priestess of the Phoenix Goddess Temple in Arizona. The Phoenix Goddess Temple was raided by law enforcement, and Ms. Elise was arrested and sentenced to jail time for her role in running a prostitution ring. The courts rejected Ms. Elise's claims that the activities at the Phoenix Goddess Temple were primarily religious in nature and cited relevant statutory prohibitions on sex acts offered in exchange for money (a regular practice at the Temple). Even those who place a very high value on religious liberty may pause over Ms. Elise's claims and think that the courts got this one right, leery of expanding "religious liberty" to the point of protecting prostitution and human trafficking.[2]

Most understand that religious liberty is an important good, but just how we ought to secure it and discern its limits isn't always clear. To what extent, for example, should religious beliefs serve to exempt practitioners from laws or regulations burdening their religious practices? Can a Seventh Day Adventist be denied unemployment benefits after refusing available employment that would require her to work on Saturday—the Sabbath of her faith?[3] Should Old Order Amish parents be required to send older teenage children to high school in accordance with anti-truancy laws, even when they believe that their faith requires them to educate older children at home through familial and communal labor?[4] Should Native Americans who ingest peyote (a hallucinogenic cactus) as part of a religious ritual be prevented from receiving unemployment benefits when they are fired for failing a drug test?[5] While court cases

---
[1]Holt v. Hobbs, 574 U.S. 352 (2015).
[2]State of Arizona v. Elise, 2018 Ariz. App. No. 1 CA-CR 16-0373.
[3]Sherbert v. Verner, 374 U.S. 398 (1963).
[4]Wisconsin v. Yoder, 406 U.S. 205 (1972).
[5]Employment Division, Department of Human Resources of Oregon v. Smith, 494 U.S. 872 (1990).

associated with the first two of these cases (*Sherbert* and *Yoder*) crafted a pathway to protecting religion through judicially enforced exemptions from existing laws, the *Smith* decision (the peyote case) pursued a very different approach—rejecting those sorts of exemptions because they are "courting anarchy" and undermining the rule of law.[6]

More recently, corollary puzzles have arisen with respect to the relation of religious liberty and antidiscrimination law. How far should state power extend into religious practice in its efforts to limit or eradicate discrimination? Do laws prohibiting disability discrimination limit a church school's authority to retain or fire at will its teachers that are designated as "ministers"?[7] Does an inclusive public accommodation law require a baker to decorate a cake for a same-sex wedding over his objection that this would violate his religious conscience?[8] In these situations, the question of exempting religiously motivated citizens or actions comes to the foreground—but without an easy solution. Even if we think that exemptions should sometimes (or even generally) be granted, boundary issues abound: When should they be granted and on what grounds? What state interests are sufficiently compelling that they might justify burdening religion by preventing or limiting its free exercise?

Thinking about the state's interests prompts a host of additional questions, since sometimes the state may itself have commitments or take actions that have religious implications. To what extent may religious majorities, for example, practice their religion in public contexts before they imply state support or infringe upon the freedom of religious (or nonreligious) minorities? Does a law requiring nonessential businesses to close on Sundays wrongly enforce a particular religious vision on non-Sabbatarian citizens?[9] Does the public display of the Ten Commandments in a courtroom or in a public park as a foundational moral code pose

---

[6]The majority opinion of the *Smith* decision does not oppose exemptions as such but holds that the proper actor to make those exemptions is the legislature.
[7]Hosanna-Tabor Evangelical Lutheran Church and School v. Equal Employment Opportunity Commission, 565 U.S. 171 (2012).
[8]Masterpiece Cakeshop v. Colorado Civil Rights Commission, 584 U.S. ___ (2018).
[9]Braunfield v. Brown, 366 U.S. 599 (1961); McGowan v. Maryland, 366 U.S. 420 (1961).

similar problems?[10] What about a privately donated cross displayed on public land?[11] Or prayers at public events held in civic, educational, or athletic contexts, the absence of which might imply a thinning or minimizing of the significance of the event?[12] In each of these contexts and more, the religious practices, symbols, and language that matter to millions as sources of meaning run the risk of getting tied up with the exercise of the state's coercive power.

Nowhere, perhaps, have the questions about state power and religious liberty come to the fore more acutely of late than with state funding and how it is distributed. Should a religious organization that provides an important societal good (like transportation to education, education itself, or safe playground spaces) be equally eligible for public funding alongside secular providers, or does this wrongly implicate the state's endorsement of the organization's religious mission?[13] If you believe that a state should generally stay away from supporting religious organizations (even if this may place them at a relative disadvantage), what about private citizens who wish to direct public benefits in religious contexts, such as scholarships that they have won, or school vouchers they've been granted?[14] The answers to these questions are controversial and strongly contested.

In light of this complexity and these competing goods, it is safe to say that the path forward for religious liberty is by no means clear, even for those who endorse it as a key and distinctive good, as most supporters of liberal democracy do.[15] What's more, the basic commitment to religious liberty is itself no longer a given. While at one time disestablishment and freedom of conscience were broadly accepted norms, the rise of post-liberalism in its

---

[10]Van Orden v. Perry, 545 U.S. 677 (2005); McCreary County, Kentucky et al. v. American Civil Liberties Union of Kentucky et al., 545 U.S. 844 (2005).
[11]The American Legion v. American Humanist Association, 588 U.S. ___ (2019).
[12]Lee v. Weisman, 505 U.S. 577 (1992); Santa Fe Independent School District v. Doe, 530 U.S. 290 (2000); Town of Greece, NY v. Galloway et al., 572 U.S. 565 (2014).
[13]Everson v. Board of Education of the Township of Ewing, 330 U.S. 1 (1947); Lemon v. Kurtzman, 403 U.S. 602 (1971); Meek v. Pittenger, 421 U.S. 349 (1975); Trinity Lutheran Church of Columbia, Inc. v. Comer, 582 U.S. ___ (2017).
[14]Locke, Governor of Washington, et al. v. Davey, 540 U.S. 712 (2003); Zelman, Superintendent of Public Education of Ohio et al. v. Simmons-Harris, et al., 536 U.S. 639 (2002).
[15]Of course, most does not mean all. See Brian Leiter, *Why Tolerate Religion?* (Princeton, NJ: Princeton University Press, 2014).

various forms has cast that into doubt. A growing skepticism of basic liberal norms has arisen on both the political right and the political left. On the right this has included skepticism of markets, internationalism, multiculturalism, and state neutrality on moral and religious issues—including an openness to various forms of authoritarian controls.[16] On the political left, many worry that pursuing liberal goods may perpetuate unjust power structures in the status quo—structures that should be destroyed.[17] On both sides, political actors suspicious of individualism and increasingly open to consequentialism have treated group identity and power—rather than moral goods—as the primary political currency.

Applied to religion, post-liberals on the right are more suspicious of religious neutrality, more open to explicitly religious political actors and institutions (including establishment), and more comfortable with restrictions on minority religious groups.[18] On the left, post-liberals are more likely to see religion as a smokescreen for discriminatory power structures—concealing racism, sexism, and economic self-interest (among other things)—and thus making protections for religion complicit in injustice. The principle of religious liberty thus warrants attention and a defense. Can Hopeful Realism describe and explain the basic value of religious liberty and help navigate the challenges of applying it? We believe that it can.

What Are the Goods and Principles at Issue and How Might They Be Secured?

We begin by naming the goods involved in religious liberty, grounded in the frameworks articulated in chapter four. Most prominently and directly implicated are relational and volitional goods. *Relational goods* specifically name religious life as itself worthy of pursuit and preservation for human

---

[16]Samuel Gregg, "The Post-Liberal Right: The Good, the Bad, and the Perplexing," *Public Discourse*, March 2, 2020, www.thepublicdiscourse.com/2020/03/60593/.
[17]Richard Delgado and Jean Stefancic, *Critical Race Theory: An Introduction*, 4th ed. (New York: New York University Press, 2023), 26-31.
[18]Adrian Vermeule, "Integration from Within," *American Affairs Journal* II, no. 1 (Spring 2018): 202-13, *American Affairs Journal* (blog), February 20, 2018, https://americanaffairsjournal.org/2018/02/integration-from-within/; Stephen M. Wolfe, *The Case for Christian Nationalism* (Moscow, ID: Canon Press, 2022).

beings, not just individually, but also corporately in families, churches, and other social institutions.[19] Any political framework that does not recognize relational goods—including religion—*as goods* simply runs afoul of any conception of the natural law. Similarly, *volitional goods* aim to preserve the responsible agency of individuals and groups for self-direction. Insofar as religion involves a volitional response from individuals and groups, religious conscience cannot justly be compelled by the force of law. To do so strikes at the heart of human dignity, an idea that the Christian natural law tradition has long held (if imperfectly applied). Especially given our commitment to the principle of *confessional pluralism and religious liberty* (and, to a lesser extent, the principle of *liberty and restraint*), Hopeful Realism provides a clear basis for rejecting the post-liberal ambivalence toward the goodness of religious liberty. Religion is a key natural law good, and any reasonably just political order will take its protection seriously.

Of course, as we have noted, *how* a political order will do that is not always so obvious, in part because protecting religious liberty can implicate a number of other goods as well. These include the *volitional goods* of others who do not share the same religious convictions of the majority (such that they may need protections from intrusions on their own consciences), as well as *physical goods* where regulations meant to protect against physical harms, economic insecurity, and so forth touch on religious beliefs and practices. Additionally, our description of these goods points to *equality* as crucial to understanding their interrelation. Other things being equal, shared participation in the four primary goods highlights the moral and political equality of human beings. It makes little sense to embrace these goods and their resulting political principles—especially

---

[19]This provides some guidance for how we think about what "religion" is. Here, we conceive of religion as a "relational" good—a framing consistent with article XVI of the Virginia Declaration of Rights (1776)—also cited by James Madison in his "Memorial and Remonstrance against Religious Assessments" (1785), which describes religion in vertical relationship terms as "the duty which we owe to our Creator and the manner of discharging it." We won't attempt to provide a comprehensive legal definition of religion here—a challenging undertaking, given the extent to which a substantive definition for free exercise purposes has been seen by some as "establishing" those categories for special protection and illegitimately excluding other religions that might be included under a different definition. But this main case of the vertical relationship between humans and God provides a helpful baseline and starting point.

the principles of the common good and democracy—and think one could at the same time ignore deep human equality.

What might be our options for religious liberty? Suppose we start with these five, all of which have been and continue to be live options in the modern world:

1. Established state church with no free exercise of religion
2. "Weak Establishment" of a state church with protections for free exercise of religion
3. No establishment of a state church with protections for free exercise[20]
4. Established secularism with protections for free exercise[21]
5. Established secularism with no protections for free exercise

We can quickly dismiss options one and five, since both inherently reject the good of religious liberty and violate multiple principles of Hopeful Realism. While the "weak establishment" aspect of the second and fourth options may also seem unlikely (especially in the American context), they are not implausible answers and indeed are reasonably apt descriptions of actually existing liberal democratic polities.[22]

---

[20]We recognize that in some contexts it is possible to subdivide option 3 into two iterations:

(a) Formal neutrality: laws that are written with apparent neutrality toward religion are fine. As long as they are written without reference to religion, laws can permissibly have the effect of impeding free exercise of religion or allowing government support for religious organizations.

(b) Substantive neutrality: the effect of laws (rather than the language in which they are written) is what matters and these effects should neither help nor hinder religion. So laws that have the effect of impeding religious practice or of providing government support to religious organizations warrant heightened legal scrutiny.

Both options a and b provide for no establishment and protection of free exercise, but in very different ways that we can assess. Generally speaking, a "formal neutrality" approach is permissive with Establishment Clause issues (allows school vouchers to go to religious schools, permits disproportionally Christian legislative prayers, etc.) but less amenable to Free Exercise Clause claims (absent discrimination, allows significant burdens to be placed on religious practice). See Douglas Laycock, "Formal, Substantive, and Disaggregated Neutrality Toward Religion," *DePaul Law Review* 39 (Summer 1990): 993-1018.

[21]One might reasonably wonder how options 3 and 4 differ. The primary distinction of option 4 as regards establishment is the clear normative priority of nonreligion on the part of government. The primary distinction of option 3 regarding establishment is that it prohibits only institutional union of church and state, but does not privilege secularism.

[22]Alfred Stepan, "Religion, Democracy, and the 'Twin Tolerations,'" *Journal of Democracy* 11, no. 4 (October 2000): 37-58.

How is one to choose among these three options? Exploring a particular policy area in light of Hopeful Realism may prove illuminating. In what follows, we consider the application of civil rights laws to religious organizations by identifying the goods at issue, describing the options available for securing those goods, and then walking through how Christians might best choose among those options.

A Specific Example: Civil Rights Laws and Religious Organizations

Civil rights laws in the United States provide protections against discrimination of various kinds. Most prominent is the *Civil Rights Act of 1964* (CRA), which prohibits discrimination in public accommodations—including public facilities and public education—and employment on the basis of race, color, religion, sex, national origin, disability, or age. This landmark legislation provided important and sweeping legal grounds for rolling back racial segregation and discrimination (among other ills) in the United States. Congress recognized, however, that religious organizations may have deeply held religious convictions that conflict with the law's application to them. Balancing the goals of the law with a desire to protect the integrity of religious organizations, section 702 of the Civil Rights Act provides an exemption for religious organizations and individuals carrying out religious activities in such institutions.[23] Thus, the Roman Catholic Church can follow its theological convictions in only ordaining men to the priesthood, the CRA's provisions against sex-based employment discrimination notwithstanding. But how far should such protections extend?

Consider the case of *Hosanna-Tabor Evangelical Lutheran Church and School v. EEOC* (2012), in which the Supreme Court unanimously held

---

[23] 14th Congress, "The Civil Rights Act of 1964," U.S. Government Publishing Office, 1964.

SEC. 702. This title shall not apply to an employer with respect to the employment of aliens outside any State, or to a religious corporation, association, or society with respect to the employment of individuals of a particular religion to perform work connected with the carrying on by such corporation, association, or society of its religious activities or to an educational institution with respect to the employment of individuals to perform work connected with the educational activities of such institution.

that an ecclesial school was not bound by the antidiscrimination provisions of the Americans with Disabilities Act and could hire and fire staff based on its own convictions.[24] (A church-based school had fired a teacher during a dispute that arose while she was on medical leave for a narcolepsy diagnosis.) Here, the court favored religious liberty over and against nondiscrimination, though its scope was limited by the fact that the school's teachers were considered "ministers" in that they were specifically "called" by the church and underwent significant religious training.

Much remains undecided in these sorts of issues. For example, should religious colleges and universities be able to hire and fire according to their convictions, even when employees may not be explicitly considered ministers?[25] Moreover, as efforts to expand civil rights laws' protected categories at both federal and state levels gain ground, this will remain a charged legal and political question well into the future, particularly around issues of sexual orientation and gender identity. To put the issue directly, to what extent should religious organizations be exempted from civil rights law that would otherwise constrain their hiring and firing decisions?[26] And can a Hopeful Realism approach to natural law thinking bring clarity to this difficult issue? We believe that it can and does.[27]

---

[24]Hosanna-Tabor Evangelical Lutheran Church and School v. Equal Employment Opportunity Commission, 565 U.S. ___ (2012). The school fired a teacher following a disagreement about her return to the classroom following a medical leave for a narcolepsy disorder. The court unanimously decided that the state could not adjudicate the dispute because it fell within what is called a "ministerial exception," whereby religious organizations' choice of "ministers" stands outside the reach of antidiscrimination statutes on the idea that the state should not have a say in who leads churches, synagogues, mosques, etc. The court was divided, though, on just who should count as a "minister."

[25]See our discussion below of just this sort of case involving Gordon College.

[26]It's worth noting that different sorts of civil rights cases raise different sorts of issues. Consider also the case of Bob Jones University v. United States, 461 U.S. 574 (1982). Bob Jones University (BJU), a private Christian university in Greenville, South Carolina, put this question to the test, culminating in a Supreme Court decision in 1982. BJU had institutional rules prohibiting interracial dating and marriage among its students, rules it attributed to its religious commitments. In an effort to enforce relevant antidiscrimination law, the IRS revoked BJU's tax-exempt status. While the Supreme Court's ruling in *Bob Jones University* did not prohibit BJU from living out its commitments in this area, it upheld the government's decision to withdraw the university's tax-exempt status, favoring the state's antidiscrimination interests over the school's religious liberty claims.

[27]It's worth noting that in approaching this normatively in terms of what *ought* to be the case, what's offered here is more relevant for legislative purposes than judicial purposes. That is, if the

As with the more general issue of religious liberty as outlined above, the goods at issue here feature the *relational goods* of social life (think institutions like churches, educational institutions, and religiously motivated businesses, among others) and religious life (humans relating to God, both individually and communally). Moreover, *rational goods* (to be persuaded in one's own mind about important questions) and *volitional goods* (the freedom to act on these persuasions) are clearly featured here as well. There are also key goods on the side of nondiscrimination laws. These include *volitional goods* on the part of those seeking employment (choosing where to work), the *physical goods* involved in earning sustenance, and the *human equality* implicit in the protection of all goods linked to a nature we all share.

Given these challenges, what are the options available for securing the relevant goods? It seems to us that there are broadly five approaches that might be considered.

1. Let institutions do whatever they want—remove any aspect of civil rights legislation that raises challenges for religious institutions. *Roll back civil rights law.*
2. Grant religious institutions *categorical* exceptions from specific civil rights laws if they demonstrate a good faith religious mission. *All churches, mosques, religious schools, and so on can be exempt from civil rights law.*
3. Grant religious institutions *specific* exceptions from civil rights laws if they demonstrate a good faith religious basis for the particular exception.
4. Grant *any* institutions specific exceptions from civil rights laws if they demonstrate a good faith religious basis for the particular exception.
5. Grant institutions *no exceptions*—apply civil rights laws regardless of any institutional religious objections.

---

judicial task is, as John Marshall once observed, "to say what the law is," the legislator's task is to *make it what it should be*. We are here more interested in and focused upon the latter.

While we could no doubt describe more options, these five allow us to illuminate the details of Hopeful Realism's approach.

How does one choose among these options? As we argued in chapter four, Hopeful Realism asks first "Which of the options is most likely to secure the primary goods at issue in a manner consistent with our political principles?" We've already flagged relational, volitional, and rational goods (with the first two being primary), but which of the four political principles are likely implicated? The most obvious is no doubt "confessional pluralism and religious liberty" but the principle of "restraint and liberty" will certainly matter as well, highlighting the importance of liberty (more generally) for human moral agency, including the liberty protection for families, schools, and churches—*and* the dangers of any alternative.

Focusing on these goods and principles brings some clarity among our five options. Option five (no exceptions) is clearly the worst option. It seeks to secure equality goods, but at the cost of other relational and rational goods, and in ways that directly violate the principles of "confessional pluralism and religious liberty" and "restraint and liberty." Indeed, by siding wholesale against institutional religious considerations, it also runs afoul of the *social* (as opposed to political) aspects of decentralization, plausibly undermining the vitality and health of social life. Likewise, option one (rolling back civil rights law) is not viable for similar (though inverted) reasons: it fails to take seriously the other important goods at issue in these kinds of cases. In particular, it neglects the concern for human equality implicit in the protection of all goods for humans *as humans*, as well as the physical goods at issue in employment, namely the means of sustenance. So while both options one and five would look to secure a particular good, both significantly damage other goods or violate our political principles, failing to protect civil rights (equality) protections on the one hand, and failing to protect religion on the other. We can summarily reject both.

This leaves options two, three, and four (categorical exceptions and several varieties of specific exceptions) as more likely to secure these goods while respecting Hopeful Realism's political principles. Choosing among them proves challenging, as each of the remaining options offers a different approach to balancing competing goods and making judgments about such tradeoffs remains inevitably difficult. Nevertheless, we can chart a path forward. If we focus primarily on the goods directly related to religious liberty, the principle of confessional pluralism points to option two—categorical exceptions for religious institutions. These categorical exceptions for religious institutions provide the strongest available protections for religion without clearly running afoul of our basic political principles. But of course this leaves those religious institutions free to use that liberty in ways we might find troubling—and perhaps damaging to other goods. Even in the case of the *Hosanna Tabor* decision, where it is not altogether clear that the teacher's firing was unrelated to her narcolepsy disorder, any alternative to the ministerial exemption could expose the school and its sponsoring church to troublesome state interference.

We could easily imagine other cases where exempting religious institutions from whole classes of law would be morally unacceptable. Deciding not to apply laws against murder or physical abuse out of a "natural law" concern for protecting religious liberty would run smack into the state's natural law obligation to do otherwise. Of course, antidiscrimination law, as important as it is, isn't *as* central to the state's mission as protecting against murder and abuse. Some ostensibly religious acts are unequivocally unjust under the natural law and exempting religious institutions in those cases would itself obviously violate the natural law. Preventing interracial dating or marriage is a moral wrong—rooted, ultimately, in a denial of our common humanity in the *imago Dei*—but associating with others who share that sort of immoral view is not the same thing as associating with others in order to murder or physical abuse.[28] And so the political and legal response might in turn be different as well. Whereas the state has an obvious mandate to shut down (and imprison) members of a murder-for-hire association, it might have good

---

[28]Just to be clear, our view is that there are no reasonable moral grounds for being opposed to interracial relationships nor for a political system that prohibits them.

associational liberty reasons for doing something less dramatic than criminal sanction in other cases, perhaps by expressing its *disapproval* through, for example, withdrawal of certain tax benefits.[29] It's possible to affirm giving categorical exemptions to antidiscrimination laws, though only insofar as we recognize those exemptions as limited by other laws meant to protect or secure other fundamental social and political goods. But it doesn't come without some potentially serious costs.

Perhaps option three or four (only offering specific exemptions, not categorical ones) might be better. These promise to better protect the integrity and application of civil rights laws more generally, securing important goods associated with civil rights (volitional, physical, equality). However, in order to provide meaningful protections for religious liberty, options three and four would require state scrutiny of particular religious institutions and beliefs. Examining each particular religiously motivated request for an exemption from civil rights law means the government must understand, evaluate, and weigh citizens' religious commitments over against state interests. These are difficult judgments that are pretty clearly outside of governments' primary competencies and at least potentially at odds with a commitment to confessional pluralism. It is a challenge to remain fair with respect to the wide range of religious (and nonreligious) confessions we encounter in our highly pluralist society, and to expect the state—even within the more constrained confines of court opinions—to do so consistently is expecting a lot. It's not altogether *impossible*, but it is difficult.

Moreover, limiting exceptions to *religious organizations* only (what options two and three do) risks precluding the conscientious religious commitments of individuals in nonreligious organizations (what option four would protect) *and* perhaps elevating those religious organizations above their nonreligious counterparts in ways that seem in tension with equality concerns.[30] There may be something of a real dilemma in that

---

[29]This is perhaps one way of understanding the Bob Jones University case cited above.

[30]On the one hand, in terms of the principle of liberty and restraint, associational rights should in most circumstances protect organizations of *any* sort to hire and fire those who agree with the basic commitments of that organization. It is worth noting, though, that associational liberties are not that well protected in the United States. See John D. Inazu, *Liberty's Refuge: The*

categorical exemptions invite abuse, whereas specific exemptions ask the state to make judgments for which it is ill-suited and around which a host of other problems lurk.

The principle of "democracy and decentralization" provides some important wisdom that can help us navigate through this thicket. Our discussion so far highlights the importance of *judgment* in discerning the proper relationship among competing values within certain legal and moral boundaries. The *democratic* aspect of the principle of democracy and decentralization does more than simply make governments accountable via removal (restraining power); it also reflects a means through which responsible human agency (volitional goods) can be applied to politics. As we've already observed, in a world of diverse perspectives and commitments, this regularly requires working out compromises in contexts where people disagree. This suggests that the highly particularized balancing of competing goods should primarily be done through democratic means. Likewise, the decentralization aspect of this

---

Forgotten Freedom of Assembly (New Haven, CT: Yale University Press, 2012). At the same time, in terms of the principle of confessional pluralism and religious liberty, the distinctiveness of religion is significant. The relational goods our natural law framework pursues explicitly acknowledge the *vertical* relationship (humans to God) as significant—in addition to the horizontal relationships of human-to-human. James Madison puts it thus in section 1 of his "Memorial and Remonstrance Against Religious Assessments":

> The Religion then of every man must be left to the conviction and conscience of every man; and it is the right of every man to exercise it as these may dictate. This right is in its nature an unalienable right. It is unalienable, because the opinions of men, depending only on the evidence contemplated by their own minds cannot follow the dictates of other men: It is unalienable also, because what is here a right towards men, is a duty towards the Creator. It is the duty of every man to render to the Creator such homage and such only as he believes to be acceptable to him. This duty is precedent, both in order of time and in degree of obligation, to the claims of Civil Society. Before any man can be considered as a member of Civil Society, he must be considered as a subject of the Governour of the Universe: And if a member of Civil Society, who enters into any subordinate Association, must always do it with a reservation of his duty to the General Authority; much more must every man who becomes a member of any particular Civil Society, do it with a saving of his allegiance to the Universal Sovereign.

While this is a contested understanding, many others have made related arguments regarding the priority of the vertical relationship (religion) and its implications in relation to horizontal relationships. See, for example, Thomas C. Berg, "The Pledge of Allegiance and the Limited State," *Texas Review of Law & Politics* 8 (2003): 41; Kathleen A. Brady, *The Distinctiveness of Religion in American Law: Rethinking Religion Clause Jurisprudence* (New York: Cambridge University Press, 2015); M. W. McConnell, "Believers as Equal Citizens," in *Obligations of Citizenship and Demands of Faith*, ed. N. L. Rosenblum (Princeton, NJ: Princeton University Press, 2000), 90-110.

principle recognizes that the scope of power should be most constrained at higher levels of government, where substantive agreement about shared goods remains thinner and more limited, leaving as much of the substance of thicker decisions to lower levels of government and society to work out in ways that reflect the values—the "shared objects of love"—of that particular subcommunity.

Of course, as we've noted, those "shared objects of love" can lead democratic majorities into some rather unhappy territories—on both sides of the religious liberty and civil rights equation. There is a strong argument that grave evils like legislatively supported racism (think Jim Crow laws, voting restrictions of various kinds, redlining) or laws that clearly target particular religious practices for discriminatory treatment require legal remedy at the highest levels of government to protect against grave moral harms of clear natural law goods.[31] Some boundaries must be drawn to protect against clear, grave harms that violate the natural law and so should be written into the basic law or constitutions and thus enforced at the highest level. This means that constitutional provisions like those found in the First and Fourteenth Amendments (with provisions protecting a baseline of religious free exercise and the equal protection of the laws, respectively) constitute important limits on democratic majorities.

However, because legislation may have an impact on the basis of race (or other civil rights categories)—even without intentionally discriminating against a religion or racial group—more guidance is needed. Clear, grave moral wrongs can and should be addressed at a national level. Moral atrocities like child sacrifice and legally enforced racial segregation demand legal prohibitions! But legislative aims go a good deal further than only addressing clear, grave moral wrongs—they extend to a range of judgments about the common good, such as education, economic development, public works, health, support for cultural

---

[31] A municipal ordinance specifically seeking to keep a church out of a community would be an example of this. See Church of the Lukumi Babalu Aye, Inc., et al. v. City of Hialeah, 508 U.S. 520 (1993). For an argument that both emphasizes robust protections for pluralism and core civil liberties, see John D. Inazu, *Confident Pluralism: Surviving and Thriving Through Deep Difference* (Chicago: University of Chicago Press, 2018).

development, and holidays. Such laws can unintentionally limit or even harm voluntary and relational goods. We think the more a law must juggle competing goods, and the more that law delves into individual and institutional liberty (apart from serious moral wrongs), the better it is that such laws are made at lower levels of government. This is what the principle of decentralization requires. Indeed, Hopeful Realism's inclination is generally toward decentralized decision-making, such that more comprehensive policymaking should be done in smaller subcommunities in ways that reflect their own commitments and values.

In a healthy democracy, choosing how competing values relate in a particular context necessarily means *laws* arise from a particular community's compromise of wills about this or that policy or issue. That is to say, the US Constitution has not already answered all political questions and just needs to be applied in the "proper" way. Rather, communities need to make their own important policy decisions on how to balance competing values. These should be established democratically and legislatively, not primarily judicially (though there are, again, times where judicial intervention is not just appropriate, but necessary to interpret and apply the law). This stands in contrast to the judicial balancing approach that the Supreme Court has at times used in related cases—which depends on a view that the court, rather than the community, should be the default actor to reconcile competing values.[32] We think the community through its elected representatives should be the default actor instead. A commitment to the principle of democracy requires no less.

Applied to our question about religious liberty and civil rights law, all this suggests that for national (centralized) policy, categorical exceptions for religious organizations (option two) would be best. This is the most restrained and least intrusive of the three main options for reconciling religious liberty with civil rights provisions. The alternatives to a

---

[32]To be clear, courts do at times need to reconcile conflicting interpretations of a law or statute, though even here they should be clarifying and applying the laws created by previous legislatures and executed by the executive branch. A Supreme Court determining law and policy by its own lights violates not only our commitment to decentralization but also democracy given the unelected and unaccountable nature of life tenures (at least for federal judges).

significant degree of institutional autonomy regarding employment (in the case of religious institutions) don't work out as well. Anything else has the central government involved in judging how religious organizations decide who to hire. There are several policy alternatives that can mitigate the potential harms of this without direct interference. In some instances, where finer-grained protections and exceptions can be worked out (including for individual nonreligious organizations) these are best addressed at lower levels of government, where different communities can render policy judgments about how to reconcile competing goods. These more local solutions will reflect both community values and can account prudentially for societal circumstances by providing policy responses that balance competing goods—judgments that will differ by time, place, and context. But care must be taken to respect the integrity of religious organizations to operate in a manner consistent with their missions, just as care must be taken to provide protections for natural law goods protected by civil rights laws.

Consider the situation giving rise to *Gordon College v. Margaret DeWeese-Boyd* (2021), where the central question was whether or not the college's religious status protects it from civil rights liability in firing a faculty member.[33] (In this case, the faculty member objected to the institution's stance on issues of human sexuality and gender identity, as framed by its religious commitments.) While the Supreme Court declined to review the Gordon College case, under the Hopeful Realism framework described here, the clearly religious nature of the institution should exempt it from sweeping federal civil rights laws (aimed at goods other than grave moral wrongs) as regards hiring and firing, as per option two.[34] Given the principle of liberty and restraint, voluntary associations should be able to form around shared moral visions.[35] So *national* civil rights laws protecting various groups should only apply in a

---

[33] Margaret DeWeese-Boyd v. Gordon College & others., 487 Mass. 31 (2021).
[34] A complication to this example is that Deweese-Boyd's suit involved both federal (The Equal Employment Opportunity Commission or EEOC) and state-level civil rights laws.
[35] Further, the consistency of Gordon College's moral vision with the natural law as we understand it is not insignificant.

narrow range of cases. But one can nevertheless imagine that state and especially local laws might craft fine-grained ways of balancing religious liberty with civil rights goods. That is, one can imagine the State of Massachusetts or the Town of Wenham legislating a variety of scenarios in which particular religious exemptions might be balanced with civil rights provisions of varying urgency.

We began this section with this main question: *To what extent should religious organizations be exempted from civil rights law that would otherwise constrain their hiring and firing decisions?* As this analysis suggests, Hopeful Realism offers meaningful guidance. The goods involved rule out the extreme options of no exemptions and no civil rights laws as absolutes. The principles of Hopeful Realism helpfully highlight the benefits of *categorical exemptions at the national level and more fine-grained balancing treatments at lower levels of government*. While no doubt imperfect, this provides a principled and prudent approach to a thorny challenge.

Conclusion

Hopeful Realism offers meaningful guidance for Christians thinking about religious liberty. First and foremost, it provides a vital rationale for religious liberty itself. The principle of religious liberty and confessional pluralism points to the moral and political good of refusing to collapse the diversity of religious views in a particular political community. Moreover, Hopeful Realism offers meaningful limits on religious liberty—limits themselves grounded in the natural law. These limits are not just about the clout of the majority, but about true moral claims grounded in the created order. Last, Hopeful Realism provides steps for navigating the nuanced judgments that have to be made in this area—a claim that bears reiteration.

Broadly speaking, the approach we have just explored can easily be extended to other areas of religious liberty law (beyond those involving civil rights laws). Returning to the five general options above, it seems that option three is the best option for a national government.[36] This

---

[36]The options provided at the end of section two were these: (1) Established state church with no free exercise of religion; (2) 'Weak Establishment' of a state church with protections for free

specifies "no establishment of a state church with protections for free exercise," an option consistent with the vision articulated in the US Constitution. "No establishment" protects confessional pluralism and free religious exercise protects conscience and volition within the limits of the natural law. That said, recognizing how questions of establishment regularly intersect with communal values, and the intersection of the public with the political, one can imagine certain aspects of the second and fourth options (weak establishment of religion or secularism in tandem with free exercise protections) operating at lower levels of government.

Lower levels of government remain significant in working out policy here. Much of the actual policymaking in this sector inevitably makes judgments about how to balance competing values, and apart from grave evils (defined by the natural law), that should be done democratically at lower levels of government. Can a town in Maryland allow the American Legion to set up a cross on a public area?[37] It's probably best for this to be worked out on a local rather than national level.[38]

It is important to note that in the decentralized framework suggested here, the national laws or constitution will draw some firm—albeit limited—boundaries around the protected category of religion. Not all serious religious claims can be accommodated. Governments have to place boundaries on behavior, religious claims notwithstanding. In identifying clear, grave harms against natural law goods, these laws constrain the realm of legitimate religious practice. Obviously, a group of Neopagans who wished to sacrifice their children to Moloch would be prevented from doing so by laws recognizing the sanctity of human life and

---

exercise of religion; (3) No establishment of a state church with protections for free exercise; (4) Established secularism with protections for free exercise; (5) Established secularism with no protections for free exercise.

[37]The American Legion v. American Humanist Association, 588 U.S. __ (2019).

[38]Moreover, the distinction between formal neutrality and substantive neutrality articulated above (what laws say on their face versus what actual effects they have on the ground) may also pertain to decentralization. Formal neutrality may work well at centralized levels of government (provided that these are adequately shaped by a commitment to the principles of [1] restraint and liberty *and* [2] decentralization), while the careful examination of the contextual *effects* of laws associated with substantive neutrality may (or may not) be more desirable to subcommunities.

the rights of the children under our constitutional order.[39] Such boundaries on religious practice that reflect the natural law are not a tragic necessity of infringing on real religious beliefs that we wish we could protect but just can't find a way to—an absurd suggestion in cases like child sacrifice. Rather, the political order's recognition and protection of human life conveys the belief that the Moloch-worshipers are in fact *wrong* in some meaningful respect because the natural law clearly counters their disregard for human life, and thus it is not a tragedy to prevent them from following their consciences in this regard.

A historical example of the Supreme Court recognizing this can be found in the Mormon polygamy cases of the late nineteenth century. *Reynolds v. United States* (1879) follows on from the 1862 Morrill Anti-Bigamy Act, which criminalized plural marriage in US territories. The Supreme Court, in rejecting a religious liberty claim against this law, affirmed the judgment of the legislature by citing a natural law limit to religion. Quoting Thomas Jefferson's "Letter to the Danbury Baptist Association," Chief Justice Waite asserted that man "has no natural right in opposition to his social duties."[40] While religion is free as a matter of natural right, the clear social duty of monogamous marriage (as a question of natural law—see chapter six) provides a boundary on the right of legitimate religious exercise. A few years later in *Davis v. Beason* (1890), the court made this even more explicit: "To extend exemption from punishment for such crimes would be to shock the moral judgment

---

[39]There are many related cases involving the limits of parental rights in the case of parents who are Jehovah's Witnesses who wish—due to religious convictions—to forgo lifesaving blood transfusions for their children. As the political theorist Bill Galston quips, no one is in favor of religious liberty for human-sacrificing Aztecs. See W. A. Galston, "Two Concepts of Liberalism," *Ethics* 105, no. 3 (April 1995): 516-34.

[40]Reynolds v. United States, 98 U.S. 145, 164 (1879). The quotation comes from Jefferson's famous letter to the Danbury Baptist Association, where he links natural rights to First Amendment liberties:

> I contemplate with sovereign reverence that act of the whole American people which declared that their legislature should "make no law respecting an establishment of religion or prohibiting the free exercise thereof," thus building a wall of separation between Church and State. Adhering to this expression of the supreme will of the nation in behalf of the rights of conscience, I shall see with sincere satisfaction the progress of those sentiments which tend to restore to man all his natural rights, convinced he has no natural right in opposition to his social duties.

of the community. *To call their advocacy a tenet of religion is to offend the common sense of mankind."*[41] These claims show how natural law boundaries on behavior also place some limits on religious liberty when clear grave harms are involved.[42] Of course, to be consistent with confessional pluralism, these would have to be serious, clear, and limited in scope.

For all of the other myriad judgments about religious liberty that involve weighing competing values, democracy and decentralization leave much to particular subcommunities—which will vary in their assessments. As Augustine observed, the better the community, the better its loves. Are the medical or social harms of peyote sufficiently grave so as to warrant limits on its use—even for religious purposes? This is a question that legislators in a particular community ought to assess, with due regard for the import of religious liberty. At what age might Amish schoolchildren be exempt from mandatory schooling based on the religious convictions of their parents? Again, this is a question requiring careful balancing of competing goods. A meaningful "overlapping consensus" about the common good (including creational moral norms) in a particular democratic context can and should place boundaries on behavior, though these will always be tangent lines *around* the ideal rather than the ideal itself. Since this is a question of the varying objects of shared love in a particular political community, these are necessarily the domain of *laws* arising from a compromise of wills about the moral order. While judicial recourse is essential for certain sorts of rights protections, the kinds of nuanced judgments for balancing competing goods are best guided by legislatures rather than the judiciary, and subject to the principle of decentralization that Hopeful Realism pairs with democracy.

---

[41]Davis v. Beason 133 U.S. 333, 341-42 (1890). Emphasis added. Strikingly, the Supreme Court's clarity on rejecting polygamy stemmed from its commitment to democratic equality and its association of plural marriage with patriarchal power structures.

[42]This shows how natural law reasoning can provide genuine limits on religious liberty, though we cannot address here how this works when the nature of a potentially grave harm is more contested in society than polygamy was in 1890.

CONCLUSION

OVER A DECADE AGO, we organized a conference at Westmont College around the theme of evangelicals and natural law. We asked our participants to explore whether and how evangelicals might take up the natural law tradition, believing that one of the ills bedeviling evangelicalism in the United States and elsewhere was the absence of a common tradition offering moral guidance for political reflection and action. Over the past decade, that conviction has only grown, even if our goals have become a bit more modest.

It has become ever clearer that we evangelicals suffer on account of neglecting the resources of the Christian intellectual tradition such that we lack the concepts, frameworks, and commitments needed to guide political reflection and action. We have Scripture, and as chapter one shows, that can teach us a great deal: truths about creation and human nature, the role (and limits) of government, and much more. But Scripture does not provide a blueprint for how to organize government in its particulars nor does it directly address many of our most challenging contemporary issues. Evangelicals who attempt to be *singularly* biblicist in their political engagement all too often end up neglecting or even functionally rejecting what Scripture actually teaches—including its teaching about natural law. Our lack of a common tradition leaves many rudderless and vulnerable to political capture. While evangelicals have had some noteworthy political successes—*Roe v. Wade* would still be the law of the land absent evangelical political organizing—in other ways our political engagement has been a marked failure. Perhaps most importantly, there is good evidence to suggest that many people have found themselves alienated from the church on account of their frustrations with evangelical politics. The damaged moral witness of the church ranks high among these frustrations. Evangelicals in the United States need help.

We might think, then, that a recovery effort might focus on developing a cohesive, robust tradition of political thought, something akin to Catholic Social Teaching.[1] Over the centuries, the Catholic Church has built up an impressive body of magisterial teaching that to one degree or another should guide Catholics' consciences regarding their social and political commitments. If we had a comparable set of concepts and principles that evangelicals widely endorsed and employed, it's reasonable to suppose that evangelical politics would be more thoughtful, consistent, and perhaps less prone to scandal.[2] Of course, much would depend on the *content* of those concepts and principles, but even just having a common language with which we grapple with the challenges of political engagement would help.

We once thought that our goal should be to contribute to such an effort: constructing or recovering that tradition. However, the past decade we have moved toward a more modest approach, in two ways. First, it's not clear just how much such a tradition can fix. Yes, it is dispiriting to see prominent evangelicals make fools of themselves politically, but when the most prominent Catholic politician in the country, who declaims repeatedly just how central his faith is to his politics, knowingly and persistently contravenes principles central to his faith's social and political teachings, it does temper expectations.[3] It's always better to have good ideas rather than bad ones, but as much as it hurts three political

---

[1] See U.S. Conference of Catholic Bishops, *Compendium of the Social Doctrine of the Church* (Pontifical Council: Washington, DC, 2005).
[2] As we described in the introduction, we think of a "tradition" in the way that Alasdair MacIntyre describes it: a set of beliefs and practices within which we have an extended discussion around those beliefs and practices and how they are to be understood and applied.
[3] We refer here of course to President Biden, whose public endorsement of limitless (and publicly funded) abortion rights puts him squarely at odds with some of the Catholic Church's core social teachings.

theorists to write, politics is not just the interplay of ideas. Lived practice is important, and so a coherent tradition of Christian political thought may be necessary, but it is definitely not sufficient. Second, it is not at all clear that the significant theological differences *within* evangelicalism can in fact be reconciled within a single tradition of political thought. Bringing together Baptists, Presbyterians, Methodists, and all the rest often seems to showcase our distinctions rather than make a common framework or guide to reflection and action more plausible. The absence of an evangelical equivalent to the Catholic Magisterium—a source for authoritative, unifying guidance—means some degree of fragmentation may be inevitable.

One answer would be to simply give up on the idea of "evangelicalism" and to judge that whatever sense it might once have made for common social and political action, its time has passed. Evangelicalism on this count is "fracturing" and in fracturing it is actually just dying.[4] To try to fix what ails evangelicalism is on this telling a fool's errand, and we would be better off leaving well enough alone. For those who see a meaningful theological tradition in their particular segment of evangelicalism, perhaps this warrants deeper engagement, but one confined to a particular denominational lane: political thought for Baptists, Methodists, Anglicans, neo-Calvinists, etc. The trouble with that counsel of despair is that it leaves the millions who still think of themselves *as* evangelicals (and not as part of a denominational tradition) right where they are.[5] And where we are is, as the introduction outlines, insufficiently coherent, consistent, credible, or constructive for the common good. Maybe it's true that evangelicalism itself isn't an entirely coherent category, theologically or socially, but certainly lots of Christians around

---

[4]For a helpful description of this "fracturing" see Michael Graham, "The Six Way Fracturing of Evangelicalism," *Mere Orthodoxy*, June 7, 2021, https://mereorthodoxy.com/six-way-fracturing-evangelicalism.

[5]See, for example, Richard Mouw, "Despite Trumpism, I'm Not Quitting Evangelicalism," *Religion News Service* (blog), December 13, 2016, https://religionnews.com/2016/12/13/richard-mouw-despite-trumpism-im-not-quitting-evangelicalism/. This assessment is particularly true for evangelicals who find their church home in sectors without a well-developed or retained tradition of political theology—true for many nondenominational churches, among others.

the world consciously identify as evangelical and even more do in practice if not in name. It seems churlish, at best, to simply ignore that fact. Moreover, it is irresponsible to neglect a clear problem faced by many sisters and brothers.

More importantly, just because it may be difficult or even impossible to develop a complete tradition of political thought for even the broad swath of evangelicals does not mean that we cannot do something that many may find congenial and helpful. As we argue in chapter two, precisely because Scripture teaches about the natural law, those *evangelical Christians who claim first and foremost to prioritize Scripture's authority, should be the first to make the natural law a centerpiece of their politics*.[6] Evangelicalism's broad unwillingness or inability to do so is an indictment of evangelicals' own commitment to Scripture—and an opportunity.

While it seems unreasonable to expect that we can build out the sort of tradition of Protestant political thought akin to Catholicism's,[7] what we offer here instead is a recovery of the moral framework of natural law politics that begins in Scripture but looks also to nature, *precisely because that is what Scripture reveals*. Because Scripture points to moral knowledge available to all through the witness of creation, evangelicals must attend to this. We do not imagine that our theory, Hopeful Realism, will displace the already existing denominational or more specific theological traditions extant within evangelicalism. Instead, it both offers a common language among them and a resource for each—grounded in the Christian intellectual tradition. Whether you agree with any of our particular judgments, either theoretical or practical, we think there is little here that most evangelicals could not in principle affirm.[8] Hopeful

---

[6] It hopefully goes without saying, but we think what we have to offer here should be of interest to a wide range of Christians, especially since evangelicals are obviously not the only Christians who take Scripture seriously! Indeed, our theory of Hopeful Realism is likely to resonate strongly with our Roman Catholic sisters and brothers, who will recognize much held in common here despite the evangelical distinctives that set this apart from Catholic Social Teaching more broadly.

[7] We could emphasize the "we" here as well. If our little project inspires other evangelical thinkers to work on a cogent tradition of thought, we would certainly welcome that.

[8] One important exception here would be our Anabaptist friends, who would find our understanding of government's proper authority to be incorrect.

Realism represents a genuine opportunity for evangelicals and other Christians to be more faithful and thoughtful in their politics. In the current context, this is a vitally important opportunity that we believe should not be missed.

Whose Mereness? Which Shalom?

Very few Christians, either historically or today, explicitly deny the reality of natural law. It is nearly impossible to read Scripture and deny that God's creation has both physical and moral laws to govern it. Those who largely ignore the natural law or question its utility tend to do so because it can seem difficult to know (or agree upon) what the natural law is and how to apply it. These are especially acute problems where there is a widespread skepticism that we can know meaningful truths about human flourishing, let alone shape policy in ways that reflect this. We disagree—and disagree radically—about what creational morality *is*, and while there are many moral claims believers all still affirm—murder is still frowned upon—what divides Christians sometimes appears greater than what unites us. In that sense, some conclude that natural law might be true in principle but not much (practical) use in the realities of our political life.

In the preceding chapters we have offered a way to address those difficulties, acknowledging that they are real difficulties, facts of our social and political life that we cannot just wish away and that do not admit of easy answers.[9] What distinguishes our theory of the natural law, and gives it both its "hopeful" and "realist" aspects, is its Augustinian attention both to the *reality* of the natural law as well as our eschatological moment within the *saeculum*, the time between the inauguration of God's Kingdom in Christ and its ultimate consummation. The natural law is undeniable and we can indeed know something of it, though it is

---

[9]Policy planners at the Department of Defense will sometimes make reference to "unobtanium" to mock supposed solutions to challenges that depend on some technical advance that is either highly improbable or simply contrary to the known physical laws that govern the universe. Building a political theory on the assumption of broad social consensus—for example, the liberalism of John Rawls—about what are highly contested issues is to traffic in "unobtanium."

obscured to some degree by our own sin and finitude. We have, as Augustine says, merely "twilight knowledge" of the natural law, but *this is not darkness*. It is a kind of real knowledge—even if limited—and it is enough to oblige us as agents acting in God's good creation. This means, as chapter three describes, that natural law politics is not *liberal* in the sense of endorsing individual autonomy as the highest good or being indifferent to conceptions of human flourishing and the common good. But it is also not *illiberal* given how it can support the core institutions of a liberal democratic order: a presumption toward liberty and political restraint; an embrace of democratic and decentralized power; and principled protections for confessional pluralism.

It is worth explaining a bit more what we mean here. We endorse the natural law tradition's teaching that political institutions have an important role to play in making it possible for people to flourish. Indeed, we think it incontrovertible that political institutions do in fact necessarily shape us. And that formation both *reflects* existing visions of human flourishing and forms citizens *into* one understanding of human flourishing and not others. This happens more or less formally and more or less effectively, but in thinking about how to organize a common political life, one cannot escape some sense of what it means to live well as a human being. For some, this suggests a kind of wholesale rejection of liberal political orders because those orders have both philosophical roots and practical outcomes inimical to any decent Christian understanding of human well-being.[10] We think that sort of rejectionism oversells liberal political orders' dependence on a particular set of philosophical commitments and neglects how liberalism as a practical political tradition owes more to Christian moral commitments than either secular liberals or Christians sometimes remember.[11]

---

[10] For the most obvious recent example of this, see Patrick J. Deneen, *Regime Change: Toward a Postliberal Future* (New York: Sentinel, 2023).

[11] See, from rather different perspectives, Oliver O'Donovan, *Common Objects of Love: Moral Reflection and the Shaping of Community; the 2001 Stob Lectures* (Grand Rapids, MI: Eerdmans, 2002); Tom Holland, *Dominion: How the Christian Revolution Remade the World* (New York: Basic Books, 2021); Jürgen Habermas, "On the Relations Between the Secular Liberal State and

No doubt there will be skeptics who suggest that it is rather convenient that the moral law embedded in creation just happens to cash out politically in a set of principles broadly constitutive of the political order we inhabit and tend to rather like. God is not an American, after all. But that's not the claim we make nor is it a fair understanding of how any natural law theory thinks through its distinctively political implications.[12] The natural law gives broad moral principles that we then try to work out both in terms of political principle and practice. And that "working out" is itself not some ahistorical process of logical deduction, as if political theory was akin to a complicated math problem. Rather, doing this necessarily takes into account what we have learned historically about social and political orders in the United States and elsewhere. It's a mistake to think that one can just read the natural law from an abstract and ahistorical "nature" per se, and it's an analogous mistake to suppose that one can read its political implications without reference to history, political science, and the like. We are confident that our political principles flow out of what we think the natural law teaches *and* that they reflect our best understandings of what makes societies work, all things considered, better rather than worse. Would-be authoritarians of all stripes, for instance, are persistently tempted to ignore the lesson that sinful and finite human beings should be wary of centralized political power, if they are genuinely convinced that much good could come from that centralization.[13] Similarly, because human beings are created as agents with the

---

Religion," in *Political Theologies: Public Religions in a Post-Secular World*, ed. H. De Vries and L. Sullivan (New York: Fordham University Press, 2006), 251-60.

[12] And sometimes we may not actually like the conclusions we draw from Scripture and the natural law, which is what we would expect given our own ongoing growth and sanctification.

[13] C. S. Lewis offered this rather astringent comment at the birth of the British welfare state that perhaps still has some punch today:

We have on the one hand a desperate need; hunger, sickness, and the dread of war. We have, on the other, the conception of something that might meet it: omnicompetent global technocracy. The question about progress has become the question whether we can discover any way of submitting to the worldwide paternalism of a technocracy without losing all personal privacy and independence. Is there any possibility of getting the super Welfare State's honey and avoiding the sting?

C. S. Lewis, "Is Progress Possible?," in *God in the Dock: Essays on Theology and Ethics* (Grand Rapids, MI: Eerdmans, 1994), 346-53.

capacity to choose and act, we would be foolish to have the state govern in an overbearing manner as if that were not true. We have a great deal of experience of states that treat their citizens as objects to be molded rather than subjects with dignity and agency—and those tend to be the places where people climb walls and cross rivers to flee. They were not and are not places worthy of emulation.

Political principles, though, are not yet guides to action, to making judgments about particular issues or candidates or causes. For that, we have in chapter four offered a framework centered around a series of questions that will help individuals and groups figure out how to secure the goods necessary for individuals and communities to flourish in keeping with the natural law and our political principles. This framework, to be sure, does not operate like some machine, spitting out incontrovertible answers to political dilemmas, but it can help us think through those dilemmas and come up with defensible, solid answers. Chapters five through eight then try to model what that looks like, not so much in the service of giving the "correct" Hopeful Realism answer but showing how Hopeful Realism can help Christians think about political challenges in fruitful and faithful ways.[14] Diligent attention to the moral framework of Hopeful Realism and careful deliberation and application of it to politics could make a meaningful difference for evangelicalism.

What's Next? A Lens, a Meeting Room, a Bridge, and a Spur

Evangelical politics in the United States (and elsewhere) is a mess, and the modest expectation for this book is that Hopeful Realism can help make it a bit less of a mess, in four different ways. First, it can help Christians of all stripes, but evangelicals in particular, do a better job of connecting their most basic and scriptural commitments to their political

---

[14]Of course we do think our answers are correct, otherwise we would not have arrived at them, nor would false or bad answers contribute much to fruitful or faithful Christian political thinking. But we want to stress here the process as prior to the result. The results matter, but we think their mattering follows from the integrity of the process and the principles.

judgments. As we affirm in chapter 1, Scripture is the "norming norm" that should frame and shape all we do and think. Christians who set aside (or misconstrue) what Scripture *does* teach morally and politically deny themselves the benefit of the chief means through which God reveals himself and, in Christ, reveals us to ourselves. In the Incarnation we see what we will become as true and, ultimately, redeemed human beings, and we would be fools to ignore what wisdom Christ has to offer, not least about what it means for us to flourish. As Calvin once put it, Scripture is a lens—something that one *looks through at other things*. The goal of Hopeful Realism is to look at creational morality through the lens of Scripture's guidance.

But Christians who try to extend that wisdom beyond what it teaches make a similar, if opposite, error. The Bible is not a political handbook or a work of political theory, at least not in ways that are meant to govern our wider society within the *saeculum*. Indeed, in its very teaching about natural law (implicit and explicit), Scripture affirms what sort of thing it is. Or, to put it another way, in teaching about the natural law, Scripture encourages us to pay attention to what we can learn about ourselves through observation and reasoning—guided and corrected by Scripture as a lens. Hopeful Realism affirms both Scripture and the natural law and in so doing equips us to think and act faithfully and reasonably.

Second, we think Hopeful Realism can serve as a kind of meeting room where the various streams within evangelicalism can come together and find a better and more fruitful way to talk with one another about political morality. As we mentioned above, the three of us started thinking about evangelical political thought in earnest well over a decade ago, with outsized ambitions about helping develop a tradition that could serve the broad swath of evangelicals. That is probably unrealistic, given the theological differences among evangelicals as well as our current fractured state. But Hopeful Realism can provide a structured space within which the evangelicals of varying stripes (and perhaps other Christians as well) can engage and deliberate with one another. In this sense, then, Hopeful Realism can be "common" to evangelicals broadly without pretending to be the only (or even always dominant) game in town. This dialogue is not just for its own sake: we think *this can lead to greater faithfulness, coherence, consistency, and clarity when it comes to the moral judgments that guide our political engagement.*

Third, Hopeful Realism can provide a way for evangelicals to deliberate reasonably with fellow citizens who do not share their basic commitments and too often find much of what passes for evangelical politics off-putting or even alarming. Too often, Christians have made recourse to natural law arguments in the hope that they could be persuasive on highly contentious political issues when more obviously religiously based arguments would not get a hearing. That has not worked out as well as hoped, and we do not offer Hopeful Realism as some kind of rhetorical "silver bullet" that will somehow make Christian claims about human flourishing and its political implications a rhetorical or electoral juggernaut. Different lenses provide different views on the political landscape. We do not offer our argument here in order to underwrite a political movement as such. As we noted in the introduction, we actually think the current moment is a real opportunity for evangelicals to reconsider how they think and act politically precisely because their influence is in significant decline. To the degree that Christians can explain their policy preferences in the way Hopeful Realism commends—dealing with the common good in a manner compatible with liberal democracy—we think it can help lower our country's political temperature. In that sense, then, Hopeful Realism can be a kind of *bridge* between disparate communities who all too often seem to just shout at one another. To be clear, we expect this book to elicit vigorous disagreement and any attempt to advance a distinctively Christian understanding of the political order is quite likely to be met with cries of "theocracy!" and such. But the theory is called Hopeful Realism for a reason. In a society where citizens disagree about some of their most basic moral commitments, *the ability to explain why we prefer one policy over another in terms that are at least intelligible to others can lessen mistrust even in the midst of continued disagreement.*

Fourth, Hopeful Realism can be a spur to improving not just our political deliberation and judgment but also the practical actions that flow from that judgment. One of the perennial complaints about natural law theories is that they operate at such a high level of abstraction that they are not especially good at directing particular actions. Chapters three and four (and their application in the second half of the book) represent an attempt to meet that challenge in our current context. It is dismaying, to say the least, to see too many of our fellow Christians exhibit some of the worst vices of democratic politics: contempt of one's opponents, the use of deceptive and outright false claims, and the disdain for the common good in favor of self-interest, to name a few. Of course, we Christians are not alone in this, but that should be cold comfort for a people called to follow him "in [whom] there is no darkness" (1 John 1:5). We should be better, and Hopeful Realism can be a means to that end, giving Christians the tools necessary to make good judgments and the confidence to pursue them rightly.

In all four ways, we mean for Hopeful Realism to encourage our fellow Christians who want to think about how to live faithfully in a culture where that feels rather challenging. We are ourselves remarkably fortunate to live where and when we do. We have been blessed with a degree of freedom and prosperity that is, truth be told, practically unmatched in the history of the world. But we also sometimes sense, as do many Christians and others alike, that the ground has shifted under our feet, leaving us unsure about how to stand or where to go. Some respond by just capitulating to the movement (or movements) of the moment, but we Christians should know all too well the mistake of trying to serve "two masters." Others respond by yearning for some sort of return to the simpler days of yesteryear. But that too often is just an exercise in nostalgia, ignoring or downplaying how living faithfully is *always* a challenge. Augustine did not spend over a decade writing *A City of God* to rebut some flailing pagan critiques. He was much more interested in helping his fellow Christians understand themselves as *first* citizens of the heavenly Kingdom and *then* as neighbors to their fellow earthly citizens. We are not Augustine, of course, but we think it is possible to live faithfully, even in the world of politics, and we hope that this book can be a part of a broader effort to help evangelicals bring the best of their insights from Scripture and the Christian natural law tradition to bear for a community and society that desperately need them.

BIBLIOGRAPHY

Acemoglu, Daron, and James A. Robinson. *Why Nations Fail: The Origins of Power, Prosperity, and Poverty*. New York: Crown Business, 2012.

AEI-Brookings Working Group, "Rebalancing: Children First." February 8, 2022. www.brookings.edu/articles/rebalancing-children-first/.

Ambrose of Milan. "Sermon Against Auxentius." In *From Irenaeus to Grotius: A Sourcebook in Christian Political Thought*, edited by Oliver O'Donovan and Joan Lockwood O'Donovan. Grand Rapids, MI: Eerdmans, 1999: 70-75.

Anderson, Matthew Lee. "Why the Church Needs the Infertile Couple." *Christianity Today*, April 21, 2017. www.christianitytoday.com/ct/2017/may/why-church-needs-infertile-couple.html.

Arkes, Hadley. "Lecture on Ethics and Public Policy." Lecture, Princeton University, Fall 2003.

Augustine. *City of God*. Reprint edition. Translated by Henry Bettenson. New York: Penguin Classics, 2004.

———. *Confessions*. Translated by O. Chadwick. New York: Oxford University Press, 1991.

———. *Eighty-Three Different Questions*. Translated by David L. Mosher. Washington, DC: The Catholic University of America Press, 1982.

———. *On Christian Teaching*. Translated by R. P. H. Green. New York: Oxford University Press, 1999.

———. *On Free Choice of the Will*. Translated by Thomas Williams. Indianapolis, IN: Hackett Publishing, 1993.

———. *The Political Writings*. Edited by Henry Paolucci. Washington, DC: Regnery, 1962.

Bailey, Sarah Pulliam. "The Trump effect? A stunning number of evangelicals will now accept politicians' 'immoral' acts." *Washington Post*, October 9, 2016. www.washingtonpost.com/news/acts-of-faith/wp/2016/10/19/the-trump-effect-evangelicals-have-become-much-more-accepting-of-politicians-immoral-acts/.

Balmer, Randall. *Bad Faith: Race and the Rise of the Religious Right*. Grand Rapids, MI: Eerdmans, 2021.

Barry, Ellen, and Martin Selsoe Sorensen. "In Denmark, Harsh New Laws for Immigrant 'Ghettos.'" *The New York Times*, July 1, 2018, sec. World. www.nytimes.com/2018/07/01/world/europe/denmark-immigrant-ghettos.html.

Bebbington, David W. *Evangelicalism in Modern Britain: A History from the 1730s to the 1980s*. New York: Routledge, 2003.

Bell, Daniel M. *The Economy of Desire: Christianity and Capitalism in a Postmodern World*. Grand Rapids, MI: Baker Academic, 2012.

Berg, Thomas C. "The Pledge of Allegiance and the Limited State." *Texas Review of Law & Politics* 8 (2003): 41.

Biggar, Nigel. *In Defence of War*. New York: Oxford University Press, 2013.

———. "In Defence of War." *New Blackfriars* 96, no. 1062 (2015): 192-205.

———. "Specify and Distinguish! Interpreting the New Testament on Non-Violence." *Studies in Christian Ethics* 22, no. 2 (2009): 164-84.

Bob Jones University v. United States, 461 U.S. 574 (1982).

Brady, Kathleen A. *The Distinctiveness of Religion in American Law: Rethinking Religion Clause Jurisprudence*. New York: Cambridge University Press, 2015.

Braunfield v. Brown, 366 U.S. 599 (1961).

Brighouse, Harry, and Adam Swift. *Family Values: The Ethics of Parent-Child Relationships*. Princeton, NJ: Princeton University Press, 2014.

Brown, Peter. *Augustine of Hippo: A Biography*. Oakland, CA: University of California Press, 2013.

———. *The Body and Society: Men, Women, and Sexual Renunciation in Early Christianity*. New York: Columbia University Press, 2008.

Budziszewski, J. *Evangelicals in the Public Square: Four Formative Voices on Political Thought and Action*. Grand Rapids, MI: Baker Academic, 2006.

———. *The Resurrection of Nature: Political Theory and the Human Character*. Ithaca, NY: Cornell University Press, 1986.

———. *Written on the Heart: The Case for Natural Law*. Downers Grove, IL: InterVarsity Press, 1997.

Cahill, Lisa Sowle. "Catholic Social Teaching." In *The Cambridge Companion to Christian Political Theology*, edited by Craig Hovey and Elizabeth Phillips, 67-87. New York: Cambridge University Press, 2015.

Calvin, John. *Commentary on the Book of Genesis*. Vol. 1. Translated by John King. Grand Rapids, MI: Baker Books, 1948.

———. *Institutes of the Christian Religion*. Translated by Henry Beveridge. Grand Rapids, MI: Eerdmans, 1993.

Case, Anne, and Angus Deaton. *Deaths of Despair and the Future of Capitalism*. Princeton, NJ: Princeton University Press, 2020.

Catholic Charities of Springfield IL, and Joliet, IL, *Amici Curiae* in Fulton et al. v. City of Philadelphia, Pennsylvania.

Bibliography

Cavanaugh, W. T. *Being Consumed: Economics and Christian Desire.* Grand Rapids, MI: Eerdmans, 2008.

Charles, J. Daryl. *Retrieving the Natural Law: A Return to Moral First Things.* Grand Rapids, MI: Eerdmans, 2008.

Church of the Lukumi Babalu Aye, Inc., et al. v. City of Hialeah, 508 U.S. 520 (1993).

Clausewitz, Carl von. *On War.* Translated by Michael Howard and Peter Paret. New York: Oxford University Press, 2007.

Cochran, Clarke. "Life on the Border: A Catholic Perspective." In *Church, State, and Public Justice: Five Views,* edited by Paul Kemeny, 39-80. Downers Grove, IL: InterVarsity Press, 2007.

Copan, Paul. *Is God a Moral Monster? Making Sense of the Old Testament God.* Grand Rapids, MI: Baker Books, 2011.

Corvino, John, and Maggie Gallagher. *Debating Same-Sex Marriage.* New York: Oxford University Press, 2012.

Covington, Jesse. "Augustine's Aspirational Imperfectionism: What We Should Hope for from Politics." *Public Justice Review* VII, no. 4 (2018).

———. "The Grammar of Virtue: St. Augustine and Natural Law." In *Natural Law and Evangelical Political Thought,* edited by Jesse Covington, Bryan T. McGraw, and Micah Joel Watson, 167-94. Lanham, MD: Lexington Books, 2013.

Covington, Jesse, Bryan T. McGraw, and Micah Joel Watson. "Introduction." In *Natural Law and Evangelical Political Thought,* edited by Jesse Covington, Bryan T. McGraw, and Micah Joel Watson, ix-xvi. Lanham, MD: Lexington Books, 2013.

Covington, Jesse, Bryan McGraw, and Micah Watson. "Hopeful Realism: Renewing Evangelical Political Morality." *Public Discourse* (2022).

Crouch, Andy. *Culture Making: Recovering Our Creative Calling.* Expanded ed. Downers Grove, IL: InterVarsity Press, 2013.

Davis v. Beason, 133 U.S. 333 (1890).

Delgado, Richard, and Jean Stefancic. *Critical Race Theory: An Introduction.* 4th ed. New York: New York University Press, 2023.

Deneen, Patrick J. *Regime Change: Toward a Postliberal Future.* New York: Sentinel, 2023.

Doe v. Bolton, 410 U.S. 179 (1973).

DuMez, Kristin Kobes. *Jesus and John Wayne: How White Evangelicals Corrupted a Faith and Fractured a Nation.* New York: Liveright, 2021.

Dworkin, Ronald, Thomas Nagel, Robert Nozick, John Rawls, Judith Jarvis Thomson, and T. M. Scanlon. "Assisted Suicide: The Philosophers' Brief." *The New York Review of Books,* March 27, 1997. www.nybooks.com/articles/archives/1997/mar/27/assisted-suicide-the-philosophers-brief/.

Ellingsen, Mark. "Augustinian Origins of the Reformation Reconsidered." *Scottish Journal of Theology* 64, no. 1 (2011): 13-28.

Elshtain, Jean Bethke. *Augustine and the Limits of Politics.* Notre Dame, IN: University of Notre Dame Press, 1996.

Employment Division, Department of Human Resources of Oregon v. Smith, 494 U.S. 872 (1990).

Ethics and Religious Liberty Commission. "5 Facts about the history of the SBC and the pro-life cause." January 17, 2020. https://erlc.com/resource-library/articles/5-facts-about-the-history-of-the-sbc-and-the-pro-life-cause/.

Everson v. Board of Education of the Township of Ewing, 330 U.S. 1 (1947).

Fabre, Cécile. *Cosmopolitan War*. New York: Oxford University Press, 2012.

Faust, Katy. "Dear Justice Kennedy: An Open Letter from the Child of a Loving Gay Parent." *Public Discourse*, February 2, 2015. www.thepublicdiscourse.com/2015/02/14370/.

Finnis, J. *Natural Law and Natural Rights*. New York: Oxford University Press, 1980.

Foster, Gaines M. *Ghosts of the Confederacy: Defeat, the Lost Cause, and the Emergence of the New South, 1865–1913*. New York: Oxford University Press, 1987.

Frank, Jerome. *Law and the Modern Mind*. New Brunswick, NJ: Transaction Publishers, 2009. Originally published in 1930 by Brentano's.

French, David. "In Defense of the Iraq War." *National Review*, March 20, 2019. www.nationalreview.com/corner/iraq-war-just-cause-saddam-hussein-threat-stability/.

Fulton, et al. v. City of Philadelphia, Pennsylvania, 593 U.S. ___ (2021).

Galston, W. A. "Two Concepts of Liberalism." *Ethics* 105, no. 3 (April 1995): 516-34.

Girgis, Sherif, Ryan T. Anderson, and Robert P. George. *What Is Marriage? Man and Woman: A Defense*. New York: Encounter Books, 2012.

Grabill, S. J. *Rediscovering the Natural Law in Reformed Theological Ethics*. Grand Rapids, MI: Eerdmans, 2006.

Graham, Michael. "The Six Way Fracturing of Evangelicalism." *Mere Orthodoxy*, June 7, 2021. https://mereorthodoxy.com/six-way-fracturing-evangelicalism.

Gregg, Samuel. "The Post-Liberal Right: The Good, the Bad, and the Perplexing." *Public Discourse*, March 2, 2020. www.thepublicdiscourse.com/2020/03/60593/.

Gregory, Eric. *Politics and the Order of Love: An Augustinian Ethic of Democratic Citizenship*. Chicago: University of Chicago Press, 2008.

Gunton, C. *Christ and Creation*. Grand Rapids, MI: Eerdmans, 1992.

Habermas, Jürgen. "On the Relations Between the Secular Liberal State and Religion." In *Political Theologies: Public Religions in a Post-Secular World*, edited by H. De Vries and L. Sullivan, 251-60. New York: Fordham University Press, 2006.

Hamilton, Alexander, John Jay, and James Madison. *The Federalist*. 2nd ed. Edited by George W. Carey and James McClellan. Indianapolis, IN: Liberty Fund, 2001.

Han, S. J. "An Investigation into Calvin's Use of Augustine." *Acta Theologica* 28 (2008): 70-83.

Hauerwas, Stanley. "Should War Be Eliminated? A Thought Experiment." In *The Hauerwas Reader*, edited by John Berkman and Michael Cartwright, 392-425. Durham, NC: Duke University Press, 2001.

Hays, Richard. *Moral Vision of the New Testament: A Contemporary Introduction to New Testament Ethics*. New York: Bloomsbury Publishing, 2004.

Hirschfeld, Mary L. *Aquinas and the Market: Toward a Humane Economy*. Cambridge, MA: Harvard University Press, 2018.

Hittinger, Russell. *The First Grace: Rediscovering the Natural Law in a Post-Christian World*. Wilmington, DE: ISI Books, 2007.

Hobbes, Thomas. *Leviathan: With Selected Variants from the Latin Edition of 1668*. Edited by Edwin Curley. Indianapolis, IN: Hackett Publishing, 1994.

Holland, Tom. *Dominion: How the Christian Revolution Remade the World*. New York: Basic Books, 2021.

Holt v. Hobbs, 574 U.S. 352 (2015).

Hosanna-Tabor Evangelical Lutheran Church and School v. Equal Employment Opportunity Commission, 565 U.S. 171 (2012).

Hunter, James Davison. *American Evangelicalism: Conservative Religion and the Quandary of Modernity*. New Brunswick, NJ: Rutgers University Press, 1983.

———. *To Change the World: The Irony, Tragedy, and Possibility of Christianity in the Late Modern World*. New York: Oxford University Press, 2010.

Inazu, John D. *Confident Pluralism: Surviving and Thriving Through Deep Difference*. Chicago: University of Chicago Press, 2018.

———. *Liberty's Refuge: The Forgotten Freedom of Assembly*. New Haven, CT: Yale University Press, 2012.

Jacobs, Alan. *Original Sin: A Cultural History*. New York: HarperOne, 2008.

John Paul II (pope). "Centesimus Annus." Delivered May 1, 1991, www.vatican.va/content/john-paul-ii/en/encyclicals/documents/hf_jp-ii_enc_01051991_centesimus-annus.html.

Jones, Beth Felker. *Faithful: A Theology of Sex*. Grand Rapids, MI: Zondervan, 2015.

Kalantzis, George. *Caesar and the Lamb: Early Christian Attitudes on War and Military Service*. Eugene, OR: Wipf and Stock, 2012.

Kearney, Melissa S. *The Two-Parent Privilege: How the Decline in Marriage Has Increased Inequality and Lowered Social Mobility, and What We Can Do About It*. London: Swift Press, 2023.

Keiper, Caitrin. "Do Elephants Have Souls?" *The New Atlantis* (Winter/Spring 2013). www.thenewatlantis.com/publications/do-elephants-have-souls.

Koyzis, David T. *Political Visions & Illusions: A Survey & Christian Critique of Contemporary Ideologies*. 2nd ed. Downers Grove, IL: InterVarsity Press, 2019.

Kuyper, A. *Lectures on Calvinism*. Grand Rapids, MI: Eerdmans, 2000.

Lamb, Michael. *A Commonwealth of Hope: Augustine's Political Thought*. Princeton, NJ: Princeton University Press, 2022.

Larson, Edward J. *A Magnificent Catastrophe: The Tumultuous Election of 1800, America's First Presidential Campaign*. New York: Simon and Schuster, 2007.

Lasswell, Harold D. *Politics: Who Gets What, When, How*. Potomac, MD: Pickle Partners Publishing, 2018. Originally published in 1936 by McGraw-Hill.

Laycock, Doug. "Formal, Substantive, and Disaggregated Neutrality Toward Religion." *DePaul Law Review* 39 (Summer 1990): 993-1018.

Lee v. Weisman, 505 U.S. 577 (1992).

Leffler, Melvyn P. *Confronting Saddam Hussein: George W. Bush and the Invasion of Iraq.* New York: Oxford University Press, 2023.

Leiter, Brian. *Why Tolerate Religion?* Princeton, NJ: Princeton University Press, 2014.

Lemon v. Kurtzman, 403 U.S. 602 (1971).

Levin, Yuval. *A Time to Build: From Family and Community to Congress and the Campus, How Recommitting to Our Institutions Can Revive the American Dream.* New York: Basic Books, 2020.

Lewis, C. S. "Cross Examination." In *God in the Dock: Essays on Theology and Ethics*, 285-98. Grand Rapids, MI: Eerdmans, 1994.

———. "Is Progress Possible?" In *God in the Dock: Essays on Theology and Ethics*, 346-53. Grand Rapids, MI: Eerdmans, 1994.

Locke, Governor of Washington, et al. v. Davey, 540 U.S. 712 (2003).

Luther, Martin. "On Secular Authority." In *Luther and Calvin on Secular Authority*, 1-46. Edited by Harro Höpfl. New York: Cambridge University Press, 1991.

Machiavelli, Niccolò. *The Prince.* Translated by Harvey C. Mansfield. Chicago: University of Chicago Press, 1998.

MacIntyre, Alasdair. *After Virtue: A Study in Moral Theory.* Notre Dame, IN: University of Notre Dame Press, 1984.

———. *Whose Justice? Which Rationality?* Notre Dame, IN: University of Notre Dame Press, 1988.

MacMullen, Ian. *Faith in Schools? Autonomy, Citizenship, and Religious Education in the Liberal State.* Princeton, NJ: Princeton University Press, 2007.

Margaret DeWeese-Boyd v. Gordon College & others., 487 Mass. 31 (2021).

Margolis, Michele F. *From Politics to the Pews: How Partisanship and the Political Environment Shape Religious Identity.* Chicago: University of Chicago Press, 2018.

Markus, Robert Austin. *Saeculum: History and Society in the Theology of Saint Augustine.* New York: Cambridge University Press, 1970.

Marlantes, Karl. *What It Is like to Go to War.* New York: Atlantic Monthly Press, 2011.

Marsden, George. *Understanding Fundamentalism and Evangelicalism.* Grand Rapids, MI: Eerdmans, 1991.

Marx, Karl. *Selected Writings.* Edited by Lawrence H. Simon. Indianapolis: Hackett Publishing, 1994.

Masterpiece Cakeshop v. Colorado Civil Rights Commission, 584 U.S. ___ (2018).

Mathewes, Charles T. *A Theology of Public Life.* New York: Cambridge University Press, 2007.

McCarraher, Eugene. *The Enchantments of Mammon: How Capitalism Became the Religion of Modernity.* New York: Oxford University Press, 2021.

McCarthy, R., D. Oppewal, W. Peterson, and G. Spykman. *Society, State, and Schools: A Case for Structural and Confessional Pluralism*. Grand Rapids, MI: Eerdmans, 1981.

McConnell, M. W. "Believers as Equal Citizens." In *Obligations of Citizenship and Demands of Faith*, edited by N. L. Rosenblum, 90-110. Princeton, NJ: Princeton University Press, 2000.

McCreary County, Kentucky et al. v. American Civil Liberties Union of Kentucky et al., 545 U.S. 844 (2005).

McGowan v. Maryland, 366 U.S. 420 (1961).

McGraw, Bryan T. "Liberal Multiculturalism and Confessional Religious Education." *Political Studies* 63, no. 5 (2014): 1087-1102.

McKenzie, Robert Tracy. *We the Fallen People: The Founders and the Future of American Democracy*. Downers Grove, IL: InterVarsity Press, 2021.

McMahan, Jeff. *Killing in War*. New York: Oxford University Press, 2009.

Meek v. Pittenger, 421 U.S. 349 (1975).

Meilaender, G. *Bioethics: A Primer for Christians*. Grand Rapids, MI: Eerdmans, 1996.

Mill, John Stuart. *On Liberty*. Indianapolis, IN: Hackett Publishing, 1978.

Miller, Paul D. *Just War and Ordered Liberty*. New York: Cambridge University Press, 2021.

Miranda, Lin-Manuel. "Washington on Your Side." *Hamilton: An American Musical*. Atlantic Records, 2015, MP3.

Mouw, Richard. "Despite Trumpism, I'm not quitting evangelicalism." *Religion News Service* (blog), December 13, 2016. https://religionnews.com/2016/12/13/richard-mouw-despite-trumpism-im-not-quitting-evangelicalism/.

Murray, Charles. *Losing Ground: American Social Policy, 1950–1980*. New York: Basic Books, 1984.

Niebuhr, H. Richard. *Christ and Culture*. Expanded ed. San Francisco: HarperSanFrancisco, 2001. Original edition published 1951 by Harper.

Niebuhr, Reinhold. "Augustine's Political Realism." In *The Essential Reinhold Niebuhr: Selected Essays and Addresses*, edited by Robert McAfee Brown, 123-41. New Haven, CT: Yale University Press, 1986.

Obergefell v. Hodges, 576 U.S. 644 (2015).

O'Donovan, Oliver. *Common Objects of Love: Moral Reflection and the Shaping of Community; the 2001 Stob Lectures*. Grand Rapids, MI: Eerdmans, 2002.

———. *Desire of the Nations: Rediscovering the Roots of Political Theology*. New York: Cambridge University Press, 1996.

———. "The Political Thought of City of God 19." In *Bonds of Imperfection: Christian Politics, Past and Present*, by O. O'Donovan and J. L. O'Donovan, 48-72. Grand Rapids, MI: Eerdmans, 2004.

O'Donovan, Oliver, and Joan Lockwood O'Donovan. *From Irenaeus to Grotius: A Sourcebook in Christian Political Thought, 100–1625*. Grand Rapids, MI: Eerdmans, 1999.

Oppenheimer, Mark. "Married, With Infidelities." *The New York Times Magazine*, June 30, 2011, sec. Magazine. www.nytimes.com/2011/07/03/magazine/infidelity-will-keep-us-together.html.

Orend, Brian. *The Morality of War*. Buffalo, NY: Broadview Press, 2013.

Patterson, Eric D. *Ending Wars Well: Order, Justice, and Conciliation in Contemporary Post-Conflict*. New Haven, CT: Yale University Press, 2012.

Plato. *The Republic*. Translated by Allan Bloom. 2nd ed. New York: Basic Books, 1991.

———. Translated by C. M. A. Grube. Indianapolis: Hackett Publishing, 1992.

Pontifical Council for Justice and Peace. *Compendium of the Social Doctrine of the Church*. 1st ed. Washington, DC: United States Conference of Catholic Bishops, 2005.

Rampell, Paul. "Opinion | A High Divorce Rate Means It's Time to Try 'Wedleases.'" *Washington Post*, May 18, 2023. www.washingtonpost.com/opinions/a-high-divorce-rate-means-its-time-to-try-wedleases/2013/08/04/f2221c1c-f89e-11e2-b018-5b8251f0c56e_story.html.

Rawls, John. *Political Liberalism*. New York: Columbia University Press, 1996.

———. *A Theory of Justice*. Cambridge, MA: Harvard University Press, 1999.

Reeves, Richard. *Of Boys and Men: Why the Modern Male Is Struggling, Why It Matters, and What to Do About It*. Washington, DC: Brookings Institution Press, 2022.

Regan, Richard J., trans. *Aquinas on Law, Morality, and Politics*. 2nd ed. Indianapolis, IN: Hackett Publishing Company, 2002.

Reynolds v. United States, 98 U.S. 145 (1879).

Roth v. United States, 354 U.S. 476 (U.S. 1957).

Rushdoony, Rousas John. *The Institutes of Biblical Law*. Vol. 1. Vallecito: Ross House Books, 2020. Originally published in 1973 by Craig Press.

Santa Fe Independent School District v. Doe, 530 U.S. 290 (2000).

Sherbert v. Verner, 374 U.S. 398 (1963).

Sider, Ronald J. *The Early Church on Killing: A Comprehensive Sourcebook on War, Abortion, and Capital Punishment*. Grand Rapids, MI: Baker Academic, 2012.

Smith, C. *Moral, Believing Animals: Human Personhood and Culture*. New York: Oxford University Press, 2003.

Spencer, Nicholas. *Magisteria: The Entangled Histories of Science & Religion*. London: Oneworld Publications, 2023.

Stark, R. *The Rise of Christianity: A Sociologist Reconsiders History*. Princeton, NJ: Princeton University Press, 1996.

State of Arizona v. Elise, 2018 Ariz. App. No. 1 CA-CR 16-0373.

Stepan, Alfred. "Religion, Democracy, and the 'Twin Tolerations.'" *Journal of Democracy* 11, no. 4 (October 2000): 37-58.

Stone, Lyman. "More Choice, Fewer Costs: Four Key Principles to Guide Child Care Policy." Institute for Family Studies, May 20, 2021. https://ifstudies.org/blog/more-choice-fewer-costs-four-key-principles-to-guide-child-care-policy.

Bibliography

Taylor, Charles. *Modern Social Imaginaries.* Durham, NC: Duke University Press, 2004.

Taylor, Justin. "An Interview with Robert P. George on *Roe v. Wade.*" *First Things*, January 22, 2010. www.firstthings.com/blogs/firstthoughts/2010/01/an-interview-with-robert-p-george-on-roe-v-wade.

The American Legion v. American Humanist Association, 588 U.S. __ (2019).

Thomson, Judith Jarvis. "A Defense of Abortion." *Philosophy and Public Affairs* 47 (1971): 3-22.

Thucydides. *The Peloponnesian War.* Translated by P. J. Rhodes and Martin Hammond. New York: Oxford University Press, 2009.

Town of Greece, NY v. Galloway et al., 572 U.S. 565 (2014).

Trinity Lutheran Church of Columbia, Inc. v. Comer, 582 U.S. __ (2017).

Trueman, Carl R. *The Rise and Triumph of the Modern Self: Cultural Amnesia, Expressive Individualism, and the Road to Sexual Revolution.* Wheaton, IL: Crossway, 2020.

Twenge, Jean M. "Have Smartphones Destroyed a Generation?" *The Atlantic*, September 2017. www.theatlantic.com/magazine/archive/2017/09/has-the-smartphone-destroyed-a-generation/534198/.

Ulrich, Michael R., and Julia R. Raifman. "How Religious Refusal Laws Are Harming Sexual Minorities." *Health Affairs Forefront*, June 11, 2018. https://doi.org/10.1377/forefront.20180607.856152.

Van Orden v. Perry, 545 U.S. 677 (2005).

VanDrunen, David. *Natural Law and the Two Kingdoms: A Study in the Development of Reformed Social Thought.* Grand Rapids, MI: Eerdmans, 2010.

Vermeule, Adrian. "Integration from Within." *American Affairs Journal* II, no. 1 (Spring 2018): 202–13. *American Affairs Journal* (blog), February 20, 2018. https://americanaffairsjournal.org/2018/02/integration-from-within/.

Voegelin, Eric. *The New Science of Politics: An Introduction.* Chicago: University of Chicago Press, 1987.

Von Heyking, John. *Augustine and Politics as Longing in the World.* Columbia, MO: University of Missouri Press, 2001.

Walton, John H. *The Lost World of Adam and Eve: Genesis 2–3 and the Human Origins Debate.* Downers Grove, IL: InterVarsity Press, 2015.

Walzer, Michael. *Just and Unjust Wars: A Moral Argument with Historical Illustrations.* 5th ed. New York: Basic Books, 2015.

Watson, Micah. "Another Meditation on the Third Commandment." *Perspectives on Political Science* 46, no. 1 (2017): 43-50.

———. "In Defense of Polygamy." *The Gospel Coalition*, January 27, 2016. www.thegospelcoalition.org/reviews/in-defense-of-polygamy/.

Wax, Trevin. "Baptist Press Initial Reporting on Roe v. Wade." *The Gospel Coalition*, May 6, 2010. www.thegospelcoalition.org/blogs/trevin-wax/baptist-press-initial-reporting-on-roe-v-wade/.

Wehner, Peter. "The Deepening Crisis in Evangelical Christianity." *The Atlantic*, July 5, 2019. www.theatlantic.com/ideas/archive/2019/07/evangelical-christians-face-deepening-crisis/593353/.

Wilcox, W. Bradford. "The Evolution of Divorce." *National Affairs* (Fall 2009). www.nationalaffairs.com/publications/detail/the-evolution-of-divorce.

Wilken, Robert Louis. *Liberty in the Things of God*. New Haven, CT: Yale University Press, 2019.

Willard, Dallas. *The Disappearance of Moral Knowledge*. Edited and completed by Steven L. Porter, Aaron Preston, and Gregg A. Ten Elshof. New York: Routledge, 2018.

———. *Knowing Christ Today: Why We Can Trust Spiritual Knowledge*. Grand Rapids, MI: Zondervan, 2009.

Williams, Daniel K. *Defenders of the Unborn: The Pro-Life Movement before Roe v. Wade*. New York: Oxford University Press, 2016.

Wisconsin v. Yoder, 406 U.S. 205 (1972).

Witte, John. *From Sacrament to Contract: Marriage, Religion, and Law in the Western Tradition*. 2nd ed. Louisville, KY: Westminster John Knox, 2012.

Wolfe, Stephen M. *The Case for Christian Nationalism*. Moscow, ID: Canon Press, 2022.

Wolters, A. M. *Creation Regained: Biblical Basics for a Reformational Worldview*. Grand Rapids, MI: Eerdmans, 1985.

Wolterstorff, Nicholas. *Justice: Rights and Wrongs*. Princeton, NJ: Princeton University Press, 2008.

———. "Theological Foundations for an Evangelical Political Philosophy." In *Toward an Evangelical Public Policy: Political Strategies for the Health of the Nation*, edited by Ronald J. Sider and Diane Knippers, 140-62. Grand Rapids, MI: Baker Books, 2005.

Yeginsu, Ceylan. "U.K. Appoints a Minister for Loneliness." *The New York Times*, January 17, 2018, sec. World. www.nytimes.com/2018/01/17/world/europe/uk-britain-loneliness.html.

Yoder, John Howard. *The Politics of Jesus: Vicit Agnus Noster*. Grand Rapids, MI: Eerdmans, 1994.

Young, Molly. "He & He & He." *New York Magazine*, July 27, 2012. https://nymag.com/news/features/sex/2012/benny-morecock-throuple/.

Zelman, Superintendent of Public Education of Ohio et al. v. Simmons-Harris et al., 536 U.S. 639 (2002).

GENERAL INDEX

9/11, 193-94
abortion, 124, 133, 172
    regulations, 1, 103, 117, 172
    stances on, 3-5, 77, 94-95, 220
abuse, 209
    child, 48, 137, 212, 216-17
    domestic, 18, 163
Adam
    calling of, 34-38, 59, 98, 106, 113
    relationality of, 34-38, 109, 167
    sin of, 35-38, 102-6
adoption, 161, 172-73
adultery, 56-57, 163, 168-69
advocacy, 16, 170-74, 178
agency
    exercise of, 98-101, 106, 111-12, 224-25
    good of, 70, 89, 91, 131-33, 208,
    responsibility of, 85-89, 158, 171, 203, 211
amendments, constitutional, 172, 212-13, 216
    First Amendment, 86, 212, 217
anarchism, 41, 200
Anderson, Ryan, 158, 162
antidiscrimination laws, 145-47, 200, 205-6, 209-10
anti-intellectualism, 8
Apostles' Creed, 12, 15
Aquinas, 15
    just war and, 180, 190
    natural law and, 60-61, 96, 101-4
    private property and, 131
    Summa Theologica, 61, 101, 104, 131
antithesis, 50-54, 62, 67, 74-76, 83
Aristotle
    economics and, 124-26, 129-30
    Nicomachean Ethics, 108
    Politics, 96, 129-30
    virtue and, 108

assault, 93, 96
associations, 111, 125, 136, 214
Augustine
    antithesis, 52-54, 62, 66-67, 75
    City of God, 52-53, 59, 62-66, 73-75, 78-79, 85-86, 97, 188-90, 229-30
    Confessions, 31, 97
    Donatism, 65, 79
    earthly peace, 65-66, 72-75, 85-86, 125
    eschatology, 63-67, 74, 78-80, 83, 223
    fallenness, 47, 51-52, 62-66, 71, 83, 105-6
    goodness of creation, 59, 62-66
    human flourishing, 63-67, 73-74
    justice, 74-75, 78-79,
    knowledge, 31, 52-54, 62-64, 73-74, 85-86, 224
    political community, 64-65, 72-76, 78-80, 82-86, 218
    political power, 63-64, 83-84, 88
    political thought, 21, 70-72, 78-79
    prudence, 176
    relationality, 61, 64, 110
    Scripture, 31, 51-53, 105
    two cities, 52-53, 62-67, 72-75, 78-79, 97, 188, 190, 230-31
    virtue, 52, 74, 83, 94, 108
    war, 180, 187-91
authoritarianism, 23, 202, 225-26
authority
    centralization of, 88, 115, 128-32, 138, 144, 215, 225
    of church, 30, 221
    decentralization of, 21, 70, 82-89, 142-43, 174-77, 208, 211-13, 216, 218, 224
    flawed use of, 83-84, 189-90, 197, 213
    of government, 39, 40-45, 128, 176-78, 181, 185-89, 192, 210

of Scripture, 9, 12-14, 17-18, 21, 29-30, 42, 47, 50-53, 58, 133, 188, 219, 222-23, 227
autonomy
   bodily, 94-95, 101
   individual, 108, 224
   institutional, 214
   moral, 102-4, 155-56, 159, 175
baptism, 14, 50, 57
beauty, 59, 93, 98
Bebbington, David, 12, 52
Biden, Joe, 127, 134, 141-42, 220
Bob Jones University v. United States, 206, 209-10
body. *See* embodiment
Bush, George W., 194-96
Caesar, 33, 38-42
Cain and Abel, 36, 56
calling, 9-10, 16, 24
Calvin, John, 21
   authorities and, 43-44
   church tradition and, 21, 31
   Institutes, 31, 43, 54
   knowledge and, 36, 227
   natural law and, 53-54
Catholic Social Services (CSS), 145-46, 155, 173, 177-78
Catholic Social Teaching (CST), 15, 24, 49, 58, 79, 87, 220-22
catholicity, 48, 50, 53, 55, 73, 114
charity, 12, 128-29, 132-33, 178-79, 201
childcare
   subsidized, 135, 137, 139-44, 172
child welfare, 142, 145-46, 173, 177, 216-17
church
   historical, 18, 128-29, 132, 187
   universal, 10, 23
church-state relationship, 49, 78-80, 89, 132, 185-86, 216
   establishment, 23, 32, 201-4, 216, 228
   funding, 201
   separation, 23, 69-70, 185, 200-201, 204, 210, 217, 228
Cicero, 64-65, 78-79, 82-83, 180
citizenship, 9, 33, 44, 72, 230
civil rights
   Civil Rights Act of 1964 (CRA), 205
   laws, 205-10, 212-15
   movement, 155, 205-7, 212
Clausewitz, Carl von, 182-85
coercion, 22-23, 44, 46, 50, 68, 74, 82, 132, 180, 181-84, 186-87, 189-90, 194, 196, 201
commonwealth, 64, 66-67, 72, 74-76, 78, 80, 82-83, 85-88, 149, 171, 185-86, 188-89

community
   conflict in, 38, 183-85, 188, 190
   diversity in, 48, 70, 80, 82, 86-89, 92, 104, 114, 147, 157, 175, 211, 215, 228
   importance of, 35, 37-38, 202, 208, 216, 218
   membership in, 23, 87, 109, 111, 174
   separation from, 35, 110, 167
community, types of
   believing, 7, 23, 49, 109, 125, 167, 174, 185-86
   local, 130, 136, 141-42
compromise, 77, 86-87, 213, 218, 228
conscience, 48, 80, 104, 198, 200-201, 210, 216, 220
   conscientious objection, 155, 200, 207
consensus, 13, 85-87, 176-77, 212, 218, 222, 228
consent
   in government, 44-45, 68-69
   in sex and marriage, 153-56, 162-63
conservatives, 3-4, 127, 131, 172
consequentialism, 202
constitutionalism, 7, 84
context, 108, 120, 179
corruption, 119, 129, 133, 188
Council for Christian Colleges and Universities (CCCU), 15-16
covenant, 37, 58
created order
   goodness of, 11, 16, 35, 54-55, 58-64, 66, 70, 72, 85, 87-88, 92
   intelligibility of, 59, 61, 73, 101, 112, 123, 138, 215
creation accounts, 33-34, 166-67, 169
creation care, 15-20, 24
creation/cultural mandate, 10, 34-35, 37-38, 81, 98-100, 106, 113, 167, 169
Davis v. Beason, 217-18
decision-making, 70, 76, 95, 103-4, 106, 112-20, 123, 131-32, 134-36, 142-44, 147, 155-56, 162-63, 175, 191, 194, 197, 207-13, 213
Defense of Marriage Act, 172
definitions, 34, 94-95
democracy, right of, 21, 85-86, 88-89, 174, 211, 224
denomination, 2, 9, 12-13, 15-16, 221-22, 227
   Amish, 199-200, 218
   Anglican, 221
   Catholic, 1, 145-47, 173, 205, 220, 222
   Methodist, 2, 221
   Reformed, 15, 32, 79, 87, 221
   Presbyterian, 2, 221
   Seventh Day Adventist, 199
   Southern Baptist, 2-4, 15

General Index

Dobbs v. Jackson, 6, 8
disabilities, 133, 200, 205-6, 209
disagreement, 77, 85, 90, 93-94, 104, 178, 211
    Christian, 2, 5-6, 13-14, 32, 123, 147, 149-51, 172, 203, 223, 227
discourse, 25, 92, 106, 150, 227
disobedience, 35-37, 103, 107
divorce, 76, 148, 152, 163, 168-69
duty, 189, 217
    See also responsibility
economics
    definition of, 124-25, 128-32, 147-49
    injustice in, 8, 128
    public intervention in, 93
education, 48, 93
    Christian, 2, 15, 115-16, 131, 137, 206-7, 214
    school, 82, 125, 135-40
    school choice, 140, 172, 199-201, 218
    virtue and, 106-9, 171
embodiment, 73, 96-99, 161-62
employment, 93, 205-8, 214-15
Employment Division, Department of Human Resources of Oregon v. Smith, 145, 199-200, 218
environment, the, 15-20, 24, 170
equality, 3, 48, 161, 167, 203-04, 207-8, 210
eschatology, 10, 19, 21, 37-38, 51-52, 63-65, 67, 78, 80, 83, 89, 168, 186, 190, 223, 227
eternity, 62-65, 74
evangelicalism, 1, 4-5, 8-9, 14, 47, 49-50, 52
    definition of, 11-13, 69
    characteristics of, 219-22, 226-28
Eve, 34-37, 98-99, 102-4, 167
evil, 59, 63, 100, 118, 189
exploitation, 57, 111, 130
faithfulness, 9, 84
Fall, the, 10-11, 21, 33, 51-52, 62, 64, 66, 70-71, 83, 99, 102-3, 107, 130, 167, 190-91
family
    formation, 147, 149, 156, 157, 160, 162, 169-71
    interaction with state, 72, 81, 93, 109, 111, 124-25, 134-43, 160, 171, 174-75
fatherhood, 157, 160-62
Federal Child Tax Credit (CTC), 134, 139
fidelity
    to Christ, 57
    to commitments, 7, 11-12, 14, 20, 109, 123, 144, 157, 162-64, 220, 226
foster care, 145-46, 155, 173
framework, shared, 7, 73, 75, 77, 85, 87 90, 99, 212, 214

freedom
    of religious free exercise, 146, 198-204, 212, 216
    of speech, 86, 146
friendship, 21, 68, 71-72, 74, 77, 88, 93, 126, 152, 154, 157-58, 165, 174-75, 177
Fulton v. City of Philadelphia, 145-46, 149, 154-55, 173, 177-78
garden, the, 34-37, 98, 102-4, 106
garden-city, the, 35-36, 51, 106, 109
    See also new Jerusalem
gender identity, 206, 214
Girgis, Sherif, 159-60
God
    nature of, 10, 33, 57-58, 62-64, 110, 225
    relationship with, 34-38, 40-41, 64, 93, 102-4, 198, 207, 227
good and evil, 76, 102-3
goods, conflicting, 75, 115-16, 120, 128, 130, 133, 139, 142, 149-50, 153-55, 170, 190, 193, 203, 207-14, 216-18
goods, interactions of, 94, 97, 112, 115-18, 120, 126, 136, 153-54, 157, 170, 174-75, 193, 203, 207-9, 214
goods, protection of, 20, 99-100, 104, 115, 138, 173, 190, 203, 207-8
goods, securing, 115-16, 120, 189, 193, 196-97, 199, 207-10, 226
goods, types of, 20, 22, 47, 60-61, 63, 66, 70, 72-74, 80, 85, 87, 93-95, 106, 125, 136-37, 151, 153-54, 163, 189, 199, 203
    basic, 74, 76, 99, 125-26, 134, 139, 157-58, 207
    common, 10, 20-21, 44, 49, 70, 71, 74-76, 85-86, 88, 101, 115-16, 126, 128, 129-30, 131, 135, 139, 143, 147, 165, 174-75, 177-78, 181, 187, 190, 204, 207, 212, 218, 221, 224, 229
    creational, 19-20, 32, 61, 65-67, 73-75, 77, 81-82, 85, 94, 126, 166-67, 177, 197
    instrumental, 157-58
    moral, 48, 66, 74
    rational, 22, 101-3, 111, 115, 125-26, 134, 136, 207-8
    redemptive, 32, 33, 167
    relational, 22, 109, 111, 116, 125-26, 130, 134, 136, 143, 157, 170-71, 174, 202-3, 207-8
    political, 20, 81, 118, 138, 173, 189
    physical, 22, 96-97, 99-100, 104, 125, 134, 136, 171, 182-83, 185-86, 190, 203, 207
    volitional, 22, 61, 73, 81, 88, 102, 106-7, 109, 111, 115, 125-26, 130, 134, 136, 143, 171, 202-3, 207-8, 211

Gordon College v. Margaret DeWeese-Boyd, 214-15
government
    accountability of, 6, 70, 83-84, 89
    levels of, 87, 89, 172-73, 177-78, 212-16
    limitation of, 7, 69-70, 81-83, 89, 94, 105, 144, 176
    involvement in, 9, 70, 89, 177-78
    obligation to, 42-45, 80, 113, 144, 181, 186-87, 189-90, 191-92
    opposition to, 38, 43-44, 69, 71
    power of, 44, 80, 127-30, 138, 226
    reason for, 20, 76, 144, 185, 189
grace, 107, 181
habits, 107, 109
happiness, 63, 96, 188
Hauerwas, Stanley, 185, 188
Hays, Richard, 185
Hebrew Scriptures, 34, 37-38, 40, 168
    See also Old Testament
Holt v. Hobbs, 198-99
hope, 10-12, 62, 70, 188
Hosanna-Tabor Evangelical Lutheran Church and School v. Equal Employment Opportunity Commission, 200, 205-6, 209
human dignity, 37, 48, 77, 86, 139, 164, 203, 226
human flourishing, 20, 22, 24-25, 33, 37, 46, 48, 51, 63, 66-67, 70-71, 73-74, 76-77, 80, 87-88, 92-96, 97, 100, 102-4, 106, 109-10, 112, 114, 120, 123, 126-27, 129-31, 133, 139, 143, 156, 171, 174, 189-90, 196-97, 208, 223-24
    improvement and, 9, 74-75, 106
human nature, 62, 73, 87, 120, 157, 225
    as directional, 17, 48, 98, 103-5, 156
    as finite, 18-19, 24-25, 51, 62, 83, 92, 117, 224
    as image-bearing, 34, 37-38, 41-42, 98, 101, 110, 130, 157, 167, 209
    as physical, 96-97, 183
    as rational, 17-20, 24, 51, 62, 103-5, 111, 113, 125, 156, 185, 187, 223-26, 228-29
    as relational, 61, 92, 109-10, 164, 167, 171, 203
    as sexually differentiated, 166-67
    as sinful, 9-10, 97, 104-6, 117, 189-90
    as spiritual, 97
human rights violations, 48, 100-101, 130, 156
humility, 9, 63-64, 70, 83, 89, 92
Hunter, James Davison, 12, 174
idolatry, 19, 56, 97, 168, 170, 188
imago Dei, 34, 37-38, 41-42, 98, 101, 110, 130, 157, 167, 209
Incarnation, the, 96, 227
infertility, 157, 159-60

institutions, 72, 81-82, 83-84, 85, 94, 109, 114, 117, 125, 128, 136-37, 140, 147, 149, 151, 170, 174, 203, 207-9, 214, 224
integralism, 49, 68-69, 80
invasion of Iraq, 181, 191-96
Irenaeus, 98
Islam, 198-99
Israel, 38-40, 56, 113, 168, 187
Jesus
    and authorities, 38-43, 191
    as Christ, 9, 12, 14, 50-51, 37, 227
    and cross, 12, 31, 37-38, 50-51, 97, 186
    early followers of, 38, 42, 132, 187-88
    and justice, 57-58, 129, 187-88, 191
    and law, 113
    and love, 109, 191
    and marriage, 168-70,
    resurrection of, 12, 96-97, 186
judgment, 5, 8, 22, 90-94, 112-15, 123, 188-90, 215-18, 221-22, 226-29
Judgment Day, 78, 81
just exchange, 57
just force, 44, 194, 196
justice, 3-4, 9, 43, 49, 57, 60, 63, 71, 73, 74-76, 77-78, 127, 129, 133, 154-55, 180, 185-86, 188-91, 202, 209
    biblical, 54, 133
Just War Tradition (JWT), 147, 180-94, 196-97
Kingdom of God, 10, 63, 109, 168, 185-86, 190, 223, 229
knowledge, 59, 223
    common, 10, 24
    limited, 7, 10, 18-19, 24-25, 59, 62-63, 76, 83, 85, 90, 104-7, 117, 190, 197, 224-25
    objective, 156, 179
law, types of
    eternal, 53, 101, 104
    moral, 55-57, 87, 92, 103, 223, 225
    physical, 223
Leffler, Melvyn P., 194-96
left, political, 127, 139, 202
legislature, U.S., 198, 206-7, 212, 217-18
Lewis, C. S., 22, 94, 109, 225
LGBT issues, 6, 78, 145-46, 148-49, 152, 154, 160
liberal democracy, 6-7, 9-11, 21, 23, 26, 68-71, 74, 83-84, 88-89, 90, 92, 123, 151, 204, 224, 228
libertarianism, 127, 129, 131-34, 138-39, 144, 150
liberties, individual, 7, 20, 81, 84, 89, 104-5, 115, 131, 138, 142-43, 151-52, 173-74, 176-78, 198, 203-4, 208, 224
libido dominandi, 21, 63-64, 80, 83-84, 88, 182-84

General Index

love of
  God, 16, 52, 64, 72-73, 109-10, 229-30
  neighbor, 9-10, 16, 20, 71, 76-77, 80, 107, 109-10, 148, 178, 186-87, 191, 230
  self, 52, 63-65, 72-73, 77, 183, 190, 202, 229-31
love, ordered, 52, 65-67, 79, 81, 88
loves, conflicting, 65-66, 73, 76, 77-78, 81, 85, 88, 129, 133-34
Luther, Martin, 21, 43-44, 53
Machiavelli, Niccolò, 183-86, 189
MacIntyre, Alasdair, 13, 25, 150, 155, 220
Madison, James, 84, 203, 211
majority rule, 44-45, 88
male and female, 34-35, 37, 146, 149, 156-59, 163-64, 166-68
market economy, 129-30, 132-33, 137
marriage, 22, 124, 135-36, 139-40
  advocacy approaches for, 172-79
  biblical depiction of, 167-68, 170
  definition of, 146-66, 169, 172-79, 217
  gender roles in, 15, 146, 160
  goods of, 154-58, 165
  norms of, 156-59, 165-66, 176
  nontraditional types of, 217
  purposes of, 156-60, 165, 170
  relationship to state, 154, 172-79
  traditional view of, 151-53, 155-66, 170-71, 173, 176-77
marriage, characteristics of
  autonomy, 153-54, 156
  companionship, 150-55, 157, 159, 165, 170, 173
  complementarity, 146, 151-52, 154, 157, 160-62, 169
  monogamy, 152-53, 157, 164-65, 169, 217
  permanence, 152-53, 157, 162-63, 169
  unity, 74, 80, 156-59, 163-64, 167-68
marriage, types of
  heterosexual, 146, 151, 158, 160
  same-sex, 145-46, 154, 161, 173, 200
Marx, Karl, 132, 184
Masterpiece Cakeshop v. Colorado Civil Rights Commission, 8, 200
means and ends, 18, 24, 48, 66, 72-73, 74, 77, 79, 83, 85-86, 88, 102, 117-18, 164
  pursuit of common, 99, 189, 202
mercantilism, 127, 191
Mill, John Stuart, 99, 115
modesty
  as scale, 138, 141-43, 172-73
  as virtue, 92, 106
motherhood, 157, 160-62

murder, 36-37, 56-57, 93, 100, 119-20, 209, 223
naming, 34, 59, 106
nationalism, 5, 38, 71-72
  Christian, 23, 49
Native Americans, 199, 218
natural law
  definition of, 17, 24-25, 101, 223
  and Protestants / evangelicals, 15, 50-67, 102
  revival of, 53, 219-20, 222
  and Roman Catholicism, 15, 49, 222fn
Nero, 45, 57
neutrality, religious, 202-4, 216
new Jerusalem, 35-36, 51, 106, 109
New Testament
  and marriage, 168-70
  and natural law, 54-58
  and politics, 38-46
norms
  creational, 54, 60-62, 68, 101, 156, 167, 218, 223, 225
  moral, 18, 36, 48, 58-62, 68, 218
  liberal democratic, 10, 23, 92
  scriptural, 30-32, 156, 227
  shifting, 6, 25, 152, 156, 166, 169, 175-76, 201-2
obedience, 11, 13, 44-45, 54, 78-79
Obergefell v. Hodges, 152, 166, 172
Old Testament
  and government, 40, 44
  and justice, 129, 133
  and law, 54, 57, 69, 113, 187
  and New Testament, 31
oppression, 38-43, 98-100
pacifism, 44, 180-81, 185-88, 190-91, 197
pandemic, 128, 134
parenting, 160-62, 217
  biology of, 161-62
  honoring of, 56-57
  importance of, 99, 108, 111, 114-15, 136-37, 139-40
  rights, 217-18
  working, 141-43
partisanship, 5-6
Paul (the apostle), 1, 21, 33
  authorities and, 42-46, 112, 186-87
  knowledge and, 19, 55-57
  marriage and, 168, 170
  physicality and, 96-97
peace, 66, 70, 72-77, 85-88, 97, 118, 125, 181, 187, 190, 195-96
perfectionism, 78-80, 82-83, 117
pessimism, 10, 71, 74, 78, 92, 106, 109-10, 189-90, 221

Pharisees, 21, 33, 38-41, 168-69
Plato
  basic goods and, 157-58
  family and, 136-39,
  physical well-being and, 96-97,
  Republic, The, 96-97, 136-37, 157-58
pluralism, 7, 10, 45-46, 65, 75-81, 85-88, 90, 115, 120, 126, 138, 151, 173, 176-77, 210, 218
  confessional, 20-21, 70, 79, 89, 116, 138, 142, 174, 203, 208-10, 215-16, 224
policy solutions
  community and, 77, 177-78, 213-16, 228
  determination of, 85-87, 116-19, 124, 139-43, 170-74, 205-9, 223
  frameworks for, 90-92, 135, 151
  role of, 154-55, 175,
political leadership, 1-2, 4-5, 42-45, 68, 105, 128, 144
pornography, 133, 148
post-liberalism, 6, 68-69, 201-3
poverty, 125, 132, 135
present age, 10, 19, 21, 51-52, 63-67, 80, 186, 190, 223, 227
  See also eschatology
prison, 198-99
procreation, 61, 147-49, 156-61, 167, 169, 175
progressives, 6, 127
pro-life movement, 1, 3-4, 172
proof-texting, 29, 112-13, 227
prosperity, 129-31
prostitution, 133, 176, 199
Protestant Reformation, 12, 31, 47, 53-54, 58, 82, 87
prudence, 83, 89, 94-95, 117, 120, 123, 136, 143, 174-79
public square, 9, 20, 30, 32, 147, 151, 170-73
public and private, 129-30, 131-33, 147, 149
punishment, 43, 46, 103, 109, 112, 188-89
racism, 2, 5, 8, 77, 87, 116, 155, 202, 205-6, 209, 212
Rawls, John, 69, 75, 87, 223
realism, 60
  in war, 181-83, 188, 190, 197
reason, 18-19, 48, 55, 60, 62, 91, 101-2
redemption, 11, 36-38, 54, 62, 77, 93, 109, 132, 227
redemptive-historical realities, 62, 67, 78
refugees, 178-79
relationship between believers and nonbelievers, 15, 19-20, 32, 50-58, 62, 66-68, 71, 74-76, 83, 93, 105, 128-29, 147, 151, 170-71, 176-78, 203, 228
  See also antithesis
relationship between humans, 102, 147-51, 154-59, 203, 211

relativism, 6, 177
religious liberty, 199-218
  advocacy for, 5-6, 78-81, 146-49
  approaches to, 104, 207-15
  discrimination regarding, 199, 202, 203, 206, 212, 214
  exemptions to, 199-200, 203, 205-11, 213-18
  principle of, 21-22, 70, 138, 174,
  state and, 89, 200, 202-3, 213-18
responsibility, 17, 58, 60, 97, 116, 118
resources, 18, 76, 125, 136, 142-43
restraint
  liberty and, 81-84
  need for, 70-71, 89, 224
  principle of, 21, 115, 138, 143, 174, 176, 203, 208-11, 214
revelation, 17-19, 49-58, 92, 112-14, 123, 155-56, 180, 222, 227
Reynolds v. United States, 217
right ordering, 16, 52, 58, 65-66, 72-73, 94, 107-8
right, political, 127, 139, 202
Roe v. Wade, 1, 3-5, 6, 8, 172, 219-20
Roman Empire, 38-45, 63-64, 71-72, 83, 128, 187-88
Roth v. United States, 86
rule of law, 84, 200
Sabbath, 32, 199-200
salvation, 9, 12-14, 51, 54, 94
sanctions, 193-95
sanctity of life, 3, 48, 61, 216-17
science, 15-16, 59, 81
Scripture
  centrality of, 12-14, 17, 21, 30, 48, 51-52, 219, 222, 227
  interpretation of, 17-18, 30, 113, 130, 148, 219
security, 94, 158, 182-85, 190-91, 194-96, 203
segregation, 2, 206, 209, 212
separation of powers, 84
Sermon on the Mount, 19, 186-87
serpent, the, 36-37, 99, 102-3
sex, 146-60, 165-66
sexism, 5, 8, 202
sexual complementarity, 26, 146-47, 151-54, 156-62, 169-70
sexual intercourse, 150, 153-54, 157-60, 167
sexuality, 87, 147-50, 166, 206, 214
Sherbert v. Verner, 199-200
sin
  and evangelicalism, 7, 47, 54
  and goods, 64, 97, 197
  and knowledge, 18, 50-56, 62-63, 102-6, 188-90, 223-25
  original, 10, 63, 83, 104-5

and power, 70, 74, 81, 88-91
and relationship, 35-38, 51-52, 58, 188
skepticism, 106, 202, 223, 225
slavery
  economic role of, 130, 133
  response to, 1-2, 4-5, 48, 114
Smith, Adam, 127-29
socialism, 128-29, 132
Socrates, 96-97, 136-37
soul, 53, 63, 73, 97
spheres of development, 81-82
spiritual transformation, 9, 12-14, 57, 74, 108
standards
  community, 86-87, 161, 213, 216
  moral, 1-4, 48, 60, 94, 148
  normative, 30, 57, 86, 106
starvation, 96, 127
state, types of
  confessional, 6, 23, 80
  secular, 80, 115, 185, 204, 216
State of Arizona v. Elise, 199
statism, 127-31, 134
stealing, 18, 32, 132
subsidiarity, 81-82, 87
suffering, 48, 64, 85, 96-98, 182, 188
suicide, 96, 100-101, 103, 109-10
Supreme Court cases
  recent decisions in, 145-6
  religion and, 145-6, 198-200, 205, 213-14, 217
  reversals of, 8, 172
  role of, 177, 213-14
taxation, 127
  legitimacy of, 31-32,
  obligation to pay, 17, 38-43, 45-46,
  subsidies in, 93, 134-35, 138, 154, 158, 172, 177, 210
Ten Commandments, 18, 56-57, 103, 132, 200-201
theocracy, 32, 204, 216, 228
  See also church-state relationship
theonomy, 41-42, 49, 68-69
Tocqueville, Alexis de, 111-12
torture, 100, 188-90
totalitarianism, 42-44, 131, 194, 198
trade, 127, 131
tradeoffs, 91, 112, 116-19, 136, 143-44, 209
tradition
  definition of, 11- 15, 220
  church, 21-24, 31, 47, 92, 166, 180, 187, 222
  classical, 31, 53, 61, 63, 74, 108-9

Trinity, the, 10, 35, 110, 157, 163, 168
  Father, 19, 75
  Holy Spirit, 30, 104
  Son, 38
  See also God
Trump, Donald, 4-5, 127
uncertainty, 10, 83, 89, 163, 221
unemployment, 139, 199-200, 206-9
vengeance, 36, 44, 185-87, 191
vice, 25, 94, 134, 176, 229
violence, 56, 79, 96, 180-91
virtue
  characteristics of, 52, 94
  cultivation of, 73-74, 106-9, 111, 115-16, 130, 171
  importance of, 4-5
  types of, 11, 70, 83, 89, 184
volition
  importance of, 48, 101, 103, 175
  sin and, 105-7,
  See also agency
voting, 45, 84, 90, 93, 212
  elections, 1, 4, 81, 90, 93
war
  approaches to, 118-19, 149-50, 180-95
  glory in, 183-84, 186-87, 189, 191
  physicality of, 182-86
  politics and, 74, 93, 183-87, 197
  reasons for, 192-94
wealth, 75, 125-29, 131-33, 143
Weapons of Mass Destruction (WMD), 193-95
wedding vows, 162-64
welfare system, 130, 135-41, 225
well-being
  economic, 93, 127-31, 139-42
  physical, 97-98
  relational, 111
  See also human flourishing
Willard, Dallas, 60
Wisconsin v. Yoder, 199-200, 218
witness
  Christian political, 5-7, 9-10, 29, 171, 174, 179, 220
  scriptural, 17, 21, 30, 46, 54-58, 188, 222
  See also revelation
World War II, 8, 24, 195
worship practices
  Christian, 14, 32, 109-10
  non-Christian, 64, 198-200, 216-17
Yoder, John Howard, 185-86

SCRIPTURE INDEX

OLD TESTAMENT

Genesis
1, *34, 35, 41*
1–4, *33*
1:27-28, *167, 170*
2, *34, 35, 59, 167*
2–3, *34*
2:22-24, *167*
3:1-6, *103*
3:5, *99*
3:15, *36*
4, *56*
6, *56*
9, *56*
11:1-9, *37*
12, *56*
17, *57*
18, *56*

Exodus
20, *57*

Deuteronomy
30:19, *37, 38*

1 Samuel
7:12, *35*

Psalms
19, *18, 55*
19:1-4, *55*
24:1, *40*
82:3, *57*

Proverbs
20:10, *57*

Isaiah
10:12-19, *56*

Micah
4:4, *132*
6:8, *17*

Malachi
2:13-16, *169*

NEW TESTAMENT

Matthew
5, *57*
5–7, *186*
5:14-16, *19*
5:16, *75*
8:5-13, *188*
17:24-26, *40*
19, *168*
19:3-9, *169*
22, *33, 45, 168*
22:15-21, *38*
22:15-22, *33*
22:21, *39*
25:31-46, *129*
28:19-20, *57*

Luke
24:27, *31, 37*

Acts
2:38-412, *57*
5:4, *132*
5:29, *42*
10, *188*

Romans
1, *18*
1:18-23, *55*
1:20, *19*
2, *56*
2:14-15, *56*
7:15-20, *107*
8:22, *34*
12, *44, 187*
12:19-20, *185*
13, *33, 42, 44, 57, 112, 186, 187*
13:1-7, *33, 42*

1 Corinthians
13, *58*
13:12, *104*
15:17, *96*

Ephesians
4:14, *1*
5, *168, 170*

2 Timothy
3:16-17, *18*

Titus
3:1, *45*

1 Peter
2:12, *75*
2:13-17, *45*

1 John
1:5, *229*

Revelation
13, *186*
19, *168*